Helping children read

Peggy Brogan

READING EDITOR / HOLT, RINEHART AND WINSTON

Lorene K. Fox

QUEENS COLLEGE, NEW YORK

Helping

Children

Read *A Practical Approach*

to Individualized Reading

Holt, Rinehart and Winston, Inc.

NEW YORK — CHICAGO — SAN FRANCISCO — TORONTO — LONDON

preface

In this book, the authors have worked to organize, in uncomplicated, readable form, important insights and practical information in line with what is known about the dynamics of the learning process, as well as ongoing research in individualized reading and related fields. They believe that the unique usefulness of the book, therefore—especially to prospective and experienced teachers—lies in the following features:

- *Individualized reading* is conceived of not as something new in the experience of the profession, nor as a single system of teaching reading to be followed by all teachers. Rather the term refers to the variety of practices through which resourceful, sensitive teachers, working with and taking their clues from individual children, are helping each of them appropriately to move ahead in reading.

- Reading is treated here in its broadest context—having to do not only with children's reading of books, but with their written communication generally.

- The reading skills are conceived of as being inherent in children's individual behavior as they read and write, not as a system of specified steps in the teaching of reading through which teachers are expected to "take" children systematically.

- Reading or written communication is viewed in the total classroom context, highlighting the fact that the teacher's role in planning and setting up the classroom for learning to read is, in effect, quite the same as in setting up the classroom for learning in general.

- A wide variety of materials and accounts throughout the chapters shows teachers at work in actual situations, resourcefully setting up their classrooms and giving other help to enable all children increasingly to take the initiative in their own learning.

• The focus throughout the book is on practical help for teachers facing the ever-present problem of challenging and meeting the needs of individual children, whose interests, abilities, and ways of learning vary widely within a single classroom.

• The book leads the readers—students, teachers, and others— to re-examine many of the old and commonly accepted beliefs and practices related to teaching children to read, while at the same time it helps them to discover for themselves sounder ways in which, as sensitive adults, they can work with their own children.

• The authors draw not only from experiences of teachers, school librarians, and administrators, but also from the thinking and writing of college students themselves, as they participated in classroom situations in which teaching and learning were individualized.

Indeed, the authors wish to thank the many children, teachers, administrators, parents, college students, and professors, throughout the country and throughout the years, who have made this book possible. Special appreciation at this time goes to all those who have contributed to these pages by critically reading and reacting to parts of the manuscript, providing materials, dictating notes, and permitting the authors to write up or to use their own reports (without use of actual or full names), of selected experiences they have had with children or teachers.

The following are among the many to whom particular thanks are due: Jean Betzner, Marion Billhardt, Eunice Bishop, Edith Bowen, Whit Brogan, Robert Clausen, Nora Farnham, Charles D. and Mary Fox, Dorothy Gray, Rita W. Hemachandra, Avah Hughes, Eleanor Jaeger, Richard Larschan, Jean LePere, Viola McSears, Doris Marmorek, Lucile Meenihan, Roberta (Bobbe) Morris, Elisabeth Muller, Audrey Oshansky, Marilyn L. Rapport, Mildred Roberts, Polly Scheidt, Edith K. Segal, June Segerman, Doris Spinadel, Louie F. Squires, Inga M. Stanton, Miriam B. Wald, Ruth F. Williams, Caroline Wilson, Florence Urdang Zinker.

Needless to say, it is the authors, and not these generous, helpful friends, who must take responsibility for the philosophy and argument of the book.

New York City　　　　　　　　　　　　　　　PEGGY BROGAN
April 1961　　　　　　　　　　　　　　　　　LORENE K. FOX

contents

PART TWO

HELPING CHILDREN READ . . . THROUGH INDIVIDUALIZING WAYS OF TEACHING AND LEARNING 89

Helping children read

Introduction

All children need to read. They learn this need simply by living in our society. Children who are ready to read and able to read learn this feeling of needing to read long before they come to school. But so indeed do the children whose language experiences are less related to books. In our modern culture, to excuse a child from reading—to let him sit through first and second grade without any kind of reading, telling him that it is all right since he isn't ready to read, and expecting him to feel good about it—is like excusing him from being human. Not that children should be pressured into reading lessons or workbook exercises designed for their particular age or grade levels, as every chapter in this book is meant to show. But, as responsible adults, we have to respect and *do something about* this need which children inherit and willingly claim as their own. Respecting each child's need to read means, in an

1

important sense, looking through the eyes of the individual children who are actually doing the learning to read. This means that a teacher cannot, looking backward, swear allegiance to any established system of teaching reading, however successful it has proved to be. The teacher's allegiance must be *forward*—forward toward the meeting of reading needs which will come alive in the children she will teach today, tomorrow—toward each individual child and *his* ways of learning to read.

Those teachers who have eyes and ears open to the reading needs of individual children—needs which do not seem to be respected in the more generalized systems of teaching reading—are always coming up with concrete possibilities and solutions which no textbook ever described. The shared need of a particular child and his teacher to do something new, something that will work in *this* situation, invites such creativity in teaching and learning. Old information, old ideas, are seen in new light. New ways are created—new ways for seeing and hearing the children as they communicate their need to read. It is this concept of creating new teaching and learning potential which is concretely presented in this book.

With each successive chapter, help is offered to the person who needs it—to the teacher, the librarian, the other adults who interact every day with children at some important moment in their learning to read. The suggestions come not from tested theory alone but from individually given firsthand accounts of people who themselves have met the challenge of sensitively individualizing some moment of teaching. From those who have tasted the satisfaction of seeking and discovering what to them are new and better ways for respecting children's need to read.

In Part One of the book, these new and better ways have to do primarily with teachers and children and books. They have to do with a variety of ways adults are finding for helping children—individual children—to make maximum use of their time and association and pleasure with books, including also ways that school administrators are finding for helping teachers in this all-important task. Not that reading books constitutes the whole of the reading program for children. Far from it, as succeeding chapters of the book will bear out. But books are the symbol of reading in the schools of our highly schooled culture. They are what school children spend much of their reading time using. Books, in some measure, are the dream and the tools and the purpose for learning to read. "Books are a record of human life," to quote the children's librarian a few chapters hence. "Out of them come keys to human understanding." Part One has to do then primarily with teachers and children and books.

Part Two of the book helps us to see individual children using reading (and writing) within the broader context of responsibly planned, dynamic group living which increasingly sensitive, skilled communication makes possible. The crucial role of the teacher in deliberately structuring materials, space, time, and available help, is stressed in all of the chapters. They bring together the variety of possible practical ways which teachers throughout the country are successfully discovering or devising to this end. The responses of the children doing the selecting and organizing—since no one else can do this *for* them—are also viewed widely and from a number of vantage points, drawing, as the chapters do, from actual examples of children and teachers together reaching out. Within the framework of possible choices which his teacher sets up, we see many a child responding to motivation which he initiates within himself; and which, we are reminded through countless examples, it is within the nature of every child to do when conditions are right. To lend reality to the presentation, materials devised by teachers and children are reproduced in their original form. The chapters of Part Two, then, all emphasize the importance of and practical ways for the teacher to provide continuously for this active reaching out in the use of the skills, so that learning may be kept where it belongs—in the hands of the learner.

part one

HELPING CHILDREN READ

*...through individualizing
the use of books*

1

One teacher tells her story

This happened a long time ago. Our school was small and our classes were large. I was young and our principal was older—and very very wise. She was glad when we teachers tried out new ideas. Even if it was something she herself had never done and neither of us knew how it would turn out, if it seemed to make sense and she could see we had thought it through, not only did she allow it—more than that, she *helped* with it. What turned out to be mistakes we would discuss and learn from together—and no longer consider them mistakes.

Improvising a Library

We had no library in our little school, though we all loved books. We teachers not only brought in our own books but regularly gathered up armloads from the public library, encouraging children and their parents to do the same. Furthermore we ordered books for the school whenever the budget allowed. Even when it didn't we handed our lists in just the same, and from time to time miracles would happen. As the orders were filled and the books arrived, our principal would scatter them among the rooms with the usual fanfare which arrival of long-awaited packages can stir up. We did a bit of exchanging too, adding these to our begged, borrowed, but not yet stolen classroom libraries.

Then somebody—I think it was the principal herself—had a brainstorm. Over the summer she moved out of her office, which was nothing more than a large-windowed, partitioned-off end of our rather wide hall, to a similar but not so well-lighted space which her office was to share with the supply room—and lo and behold, we *did* have a library! Two walls of the tiny place were lined with bookshelves which more than adequately held all the books we had purchased up to that time. Humble though it was it was a start, and things happened fast. With enthusiasm thus kindled, the parents of the school put on a wonderful Hallowe'en Carnival—the usual kind with everything, including home-cooked family suppers, generously donated and just as generously bought back. There were also *un*usual contributions, such as those of a few handy fathers and mothers who built "the most scarey spook alley" ever to be ventured into and later come out of safely by young or old. The Carnival had a dual purpose, of course—to give the youngsters some wholesome fun to keep them off the streets on Hallowe'en night and to raise money for library books. All the families of the neighborhood turned out with high enthusiasm, partly because they had something to bring as well as to buy. The affair was a great success, setting a healthy precedent for years to come, thus netting our little library some several hundred cherished books each year.

In the meantime, we advertised for furniture donations, and because the place was so small we had to call a halt almost immediately. A large round table with legs cut down (from the old college library on the hill), a long low bench that went the limited length of one wall, and a half-dozen old chairs collected from as many attics, were almost more than we had room for. A colorful print of Franz Marc's *The Red Deer,* a lovely water color by one of the children, a framed Navajo sand-painting and several pieces of pottery brought from New Mexico by our principal completed the furnishings. Except of course for the books—all kinds of wonderfully colorful, well-chosen books, hundreds of them! We loved the place, all of us, inadequate though it was in so many ways.

Because one of the doors of their classroom opened into it, the sixth grade and their teacher took over general responsibility for the operation of the library, drawing up a schedule for each of the classes to use it for a one-hour period once or twice a week, and allowing for intermittent use by individuals or small groups of children as needed. This was sheer heaven for my fourth grade children who loved to read anyway—albeit a crowded heaven. We therefore had to improvise a plan to keep hazards down, since our forty-some boys and girls and their teacher more than filled the empty inches, including the floor which they loved to have an excuse to sit on.

Our room was not far from the library, really not too far for me to keep an eye on both places at once if need be. So our plan worked something like this once the scheduled time had arrived: Those of us who already have library books out that we're reading, just sit at our desks and read for the time being. Those who need to choose new books go to the library first, choose your books as soon as you can, and find a place to sit where you think you'll be comfortable for an hour, preferably toward the back of the library so that those coming in later won't have to walk over you in trying to find seats for themselves. Miss Floyd will be there to help you choose if you can't find what you want. As soon as everyone (or almost everyone) has his book and is sitting down the rest of us will come in with our books. Miss Floyd will have the Book Record. When you finish a book take or pass it over to her before choosing another. If you haven't finished your book by the end of the period bring it back to the class with you and keep it until you finish. To take it home at night, sign up on the board for it and check your name off next morning when you bring it back. (Be sure you do bring it back when you come, so you can stay with a book if it's good till you're finished. Then someone else can take it without having to wait.)

Nor did we use the library during only our scheduled periods. For the first few weeks we used it very frequently indeed, whenever we saw that it was empty during our afternoon reading period. As time went on, however, this caused a little hardship on individual children from other classrooms who came in to hunt up reference material or to exchange books on their own. So the extra library periods had to be confined pretty much to our own room—where we were much more comfortable, incidentally, and where individual children volunteered to take their turns as helpers along with me in different sections of the room, just *telling* the words as they were asked them without any comment.

Searching for Sounder Ways of Helping Children Read

I should have said earlier that the common plan for teaching reading in our school, as in other forward-looking schools of our area at that time, was the three-group plan. (This was an improvement over the two-group and certainly over the total-class plan still commonly in vogue.) Most of our reading books had been purchased by the school in sets of twelve or fifteen copies, or at most twenty, and were arranged this way in the supply room to which all teachers had access at any time. It was understood that you were free to use books of the grade below yours at any time, and toward the close of the year one set of those of the grade above for your fastest group. The children were grouped according to ability (teacher's estimate), Group I being made up of the best readers, Group III of the slowest, and Group II of those in between. Again, this was thought at the time to be the most effective method for meeting the wide range of differences which every teacher meets in her class. Some professional books and specialists advocated using names for the groups, letting the children choose the names for their own groups, as a way of camouflaging which group was best or poorest. In our school we were more realistic than that. We knew you couldn't fool the children for long; rather, we tried to soften the distinctions by planning the rest of our program so that every child had opportunity to work successfully with others and would be working on different committees and in different capacities from time to time. I am sure we did everything possible in our school (and I certainly did in my classroom) to counteract the harmful effects on children that in our hearts we knew such grouping could have and, in most of the places we knew, did have. We worked very hard at this, I guess, because even though it was highly recommended throughout the teaching profession (and still is, by many, these almost twenty-five years later!) we continually sensed this ability grouping to be inconsistent with our educational and human values.

Indeed it was the bane of my existence, young teacher that I was. I just plain looked at what it was doing to us and did not like what I saw. Group I was the largest group, for which I was glad, and life was rosy for us all the time—well, almost all the time. We could simply sit in our crowded circle and read around the group, once we had finished reading the story to ourselves, and no one had to prompt anyone. The only difficulty was that as the children read to themselves first, some would finish before the others. Sometimes they would slide on into the next story without pause. This bothered me, young and recently trained teacher that I was, since I knew we were supposed to start each story afresh. But how can you when children read at different rates, which they do even in the highly selected group? I tried cutting out the silent reading first. These children didn't need it as preparation, really. Even when reading something they had not seen before, they rarely stumbled or failed to understand what they were reading. So we just ripped through the stories together and loved them, one reader after another. My conscience bothered me, though, for two reasons:

(1) It did not seem right that the children should do so much oral reading. I had long felt that the overstress on oral reading in my own elementary school days— which I had always enjoyed tremendously, it is true— had tended to lower rather than accelerate my silent reading speed. (Indeed, accentuated by two high school electives in oral expression or Interpretation of the Printed Page, both courses favorites with me, I found my silent reading to be reading-aloud-to-myself, complete with the proper inflections as I had learned them!)

(2) I kept wondering if, as a teacher, I was really giving this group the help that I should. Just sitting listening to them read, one by one, seemed rather an undemanding and unimportant way for the one adult in the situation to be behaving all this time.

With the second group, reading represented a little more conscious struggle, and differences seemed to matter more. Again, several children always finished first. My admonition, "How about reading it again to make sure you know all the words," must have seemed as absurd to them as it did to me. Of *course* they knew all the words, else why would they have finished the story so soon? "Don't go on to the next story. That will spoil it for the lesson tomorrow," seemed even more sense- less. So did asking pointed questions, one at a time, for which they were supposed to read to find the answers, paragraph by paragraph or page by page. If the object was to read during this period, why not *read?* I asked myself. Why hold children back when they could go right on, understandingly and absorbedly, and finish the book and then read another—and still another? True, the basic and supplementary readers specified would not begin to last the year if the children really set about to read them to themselves, continuously and with few interruptions as mature readers try to read. But isn't that just the way they learn to read best, I asked myself, and really get into the reading habit?

How valuable, for example, were these "motivation" periods so widely advocated? I had observed two things about such periods as I tried them: either the children were already opening their books and getting impatient to read—some of them actually sneaking in a bit of reading as we talked—or the discussion became so interesting, with everyone wanting to tell all of his own experiences brought to mind, that it was like cutting short what old Dr. Driggs used to call a "live language lesson," just as it had gotten off to a good start, in order to bring the children back to the purpose of the motivation in the first place which was to get them to want to read—not to talk but to *read*. More than anything else this called to my mind an art class I attended in college, in which, eager to get back to the painting I had had to leave unfinished the day before, I had first to sit and listen to our professor's "few" extemporaneous words of advice before we started (maybe because one of us had innocently asked him a question on the way in), frequently to realize that at least half the period was over before we had a chance to get out our paints! Could it be wrong, as a teacher I now asked myself, to have the children do one thing or the other—exchange experiences, which they would already do any time of day at the drop of a hat, or *read,* which they were usually geared to do anyway by the time they had gotten their readers out and come back to the reading group chairs? Indeed, if I was held up on my way back to the group for any reason, to give some help to a child along the way, say, I would be apt to find most of the youngsters already reading to themselves from somewhere in the book.

Word drill, too, at least for the first two groups, seemed for the most part an unprofitable use of time. Many of the children knew all the words to start with. Others knew all but a few, but usually not the same few. Some really needed help, but the carry-over from the list on the board to the word in the actual sentence seemed weak for those particular children. We tried drilling or at least previewing the words *in context,* which did make more sense or have more meaning. But asking children who already knew the words to go through all this rigmarole, constantly advising them to put down their waving hands until the others had had time to try to figure them out, and certainly not to give help to their struggling classmates beside them, seemed to be teaching just the reverse of intelligent word attack, of wise use of their time, good study habits, consideration for others, or anything else of the democratic co-operative spirit. Certainly it was not conducive to building a thirst for and enjoyment of reading. So, after trying out an infinite variety, I gave up word drills as a part of the group reading period (confining these instead to our spelling period, when the words were already out of context) and gave the children individual help as I found they needed it.

Nor did I find the current theoretical advice of much help here. "Don't tell the child the word. Help him to sound it out," we were told. And that sounds like good sensible advice—until you try it and see what happens. Help him *try* to sound it out, yes. But if he cannot, without taking him too far afield from the idea of what he is supposed to be reading, then *tell* him the word and let him go on about his business. Helen came to the word "sharpen." I covered *en* but she didn't know *sharp*. I started with *sh;* she could get that but was stuck on the *arp*. I tried *ar;* no go. So on the board I wrote *car;* yes, *car,* she could read that. Good! Now, not *car,* but *sh - ar;* what would that much be? No, stuck again. In the meantime, the other children were bursting to tell her or shaking their heads in dismay that she couldn't even get something that easy . . . So, out of respect for her, we came back to the book; belatedly, I let one of the others who was about to pop say the word *sharpen,* and poor Helen and I, now a million miles from the hang of the story—as were any of the children who had not "cheated" and gone on reading to themselves—tried to get ourselves re-oriented to who was going to sharpen what? We all got back to the story then, dutifully helping one another to find the place so we could go on. Something inside, much stronger than anything I had learned in education classes, told me that this was not the way to help children with reading.

Neither was this business of keeping the place when children read at such different rates. I remembered my own childhood, when everyone in the room had the selfsame reader and listened or at least sat quietly while one after another read aloud. We had to keep the place or miss our turn at reading for the day as well as endure some mild ridicule, perhaps. So we worked out our own ingenious and individual ways. Who wants to listen and follow along while somebody reads what you've already read—especially if he stumbles along in a slow halting way? No, you mustn't *tell* him the word, that's not fair to him. No, you mustn't look off into space while he reads. Otherwise the teacher will call on you for sure and you won't know the place. What then? What is the best way to live through this grinding reading lesson? Well, you might try to see how many times you can read the paragraph while your poor droning classmate (maybe your best friend) is reading it once. But that gets to be pointless and it does seem to be a little unkind to the friend who can only read so slowly. Finally you note the last phrase in the paragraph under way, put your finger underneath it, speak it out strongly under your breath, have your ear cocked for it in case the teacher calls on you at the close of the paragraph, then let your mind move along to the afterschool play, to what you'll say to your mother so she'll let you go to your new friend's house, or to what your father might be bringing you home from his trip to Lehi. Ear still cocked? Sure enough, on those very words the teacher says, "That'll do, Beulah. All right, Arthur, you may read next." And in a harsher voice, "So you don't have the place again, Arthur! Mary, you read." And *you're* safe for another paragraph, repeating the precaution. Guess it won't be your turn till after everyone in the second row has had a chance—but you can't be sure.

So . . . again the question of wise use of time in this group, listening to one another read, sometimes fast, sometimes slowly and jerkily. Was it helping the youngster who could read a mile a minute to make him follow along at half the rate—or even two-thirds of the rate, or say 90 percent? And what was it doing to the self-respect of the faulty reader to have his classmates sink down in their seats, maybe with an audible groan or two, as he began to read? These things I asked myself as a young teacher, observing closely as I worked with this roomful of children I loved.

And if all the above bears hard on Group II, what of my hard-working, self-discipling, uncomplaining little Group III! Theirs is not an easy fate. If sheer effort counted most, they would be the tip-top group. They deserve so much more than they get in return for what they expend of themselves. Little wonder I bend over backwards to find ways in which they can truly succeed with their fellows.

Thinking through the Pressures of Ability Grouping

As I have said, the children in Group I enjoyed reading, and I did whatever I could to build the status of those who might otherwise feel they were any less valuable, in my eyes or those of the class, because they were in Groups II or III instead of I. And because we were a happy, hard-working, hard-playing class, doing interesting things together in a bold, venturous, closely knit sort of way, everyone in the room was needed and appreciated for what he was. I purposely made little of the reading groups as such, certainly not threatening or goading anyone with the possibility of a change one way or another, though occasional changes were made, of course, as the situation seemed to warrant. Still, I don't think I was fooled for one minute. Of course, there was feeling; there was bound to be, minimize it though I tried.

Indeed, the day school began in the fall, my second with this group (I had asked to go on with them for a second year together and my request was granted through a trade with a fellow teacher), Mrs. M. came to school with her daughter

Verna. We greeted each other warmly as usual, more warmly, in fact, with the prospects of being associated for another year. A lovely facet of having a group of children for a second year, I discovered, is that you come to know their parents so well. Mrs. M. and I chatted about our respective summers in high mood. She told me proudly how throughout their whole vacation, Verna had spent two hours a day at her reading. "And that's what I wanted to ask, Miss Floyd. *Could* Verna be in Group I this year? She's wanted it so badly and all her friends are in Group I, you know. And though she wouldn't let you know it for the world, she was really quite unhappy about being in Group II last year."

Here it came, quite as I had expected that it would even earlier. Of a surety parents care. They care because their children care. And the children care more because it means so much to their parents. Parents compare notes with their neighbors. Wives talk with their husbands. Can't you go talk to the teacher, the husband asks. Surely if it's that important . . .

Surely, if it is that important then what do I say as a teacher? Verna is not the best reader in Group II by any means. If I move Verna up, what of the three or four who read much better than she does, and who, if the matter comes to the fore, can show that they do? What *do* you say? There isn't much difference between the two groups, I could tell her; Verna will be just as happy in Group II, once she gets back with those children. And she can be with her friends in so many of our other activities. But she *won't* be just as happy and you know it; nor will her mother. Maria would like to move into Group I too, I know. Indeed so would all the children were they to be consulted about it. Let's start Verna in II and then see how we come out. She'll probably improve enough that we can make the change before long. You do not mean that, really. She will improve—but so will the others. Diana's mother and Reva's mother and adorable Perry's mother, too, would be pleased no end to have their children put in Group I. So would all the mothers, though, unlike Mrs. M., they have not requested it—

at least not yet. My hunch is that it means more to them than to their happy, rollicking, competent children. But this I have to deal with. Put them all in Group I—everybody—is the only answer I can come up with that will really satisfy them, or me.

Observing Children's Independent Reading

I do not mean to say that we did not have library periods before we got our little school library. Of course we did, this group and the others before it. It had been our practice in the school to have reading groups twice a day, once in the morning and again in the afternoon, with a separate reader for each. Every now and then we had indulged ourselves in a library period of an afternoon instead of reading groups. We had periodic book reports and discussions too. But with the library close at hand now, chock-full of attractive books, we slid into the habit of using it more frequently. During all this time I was observing very closely. Where was the most good healthy reading learning taking place, I asked myself as I watched. Where indeed? If they chose books because they wanted to read them, they somehow read with more gusto. No one had to stop and wait at the end of a story. No one had to stop every few minutes to listen to another read. No one had to keep the place or refrain from telling a word which another child could not get and thus would be holding up the group.

I watched Clark D., my slowest reader of all. With a twinkle in his eye he would grab his library book and start reading, with as much self-respect as anyone else in that room. I usually sat somewhere close at hand so that help would be easy for him to ask. I had to tell him many words, usually only the hard ones, though, and not the ones he would stumble on so often in reading group. Those words he seemed able now through sheer effort to get by himself. I am still not sure how he managed it; maybe the fact that he could choose made the difference—that and the happy realization that he too was reading independently.

arting Individualized Reading with One Group

n one day I tried something else on the basis of what I
n observing. To Group I I ventured, "Instead of bring-
 readers for reading group today, let's try something
w about bringing your library books and we'll use
tead." Everyone's eyes opened wide. "Boy, that's a good
ey all agreed, and back to the chairs they came.

how can we do it when we each have a different book?"
sked.

read our different book, what do you think?" some-
red.

roposal was that we start out just like in a library
st read, uninterruptedly to yourself, asking for words
d, but otherwise just like in a library period. We
 have a vacant chair, next to mine, where each in
come over and read to me only, beginning wherever
d to be reading in his book at the time. If he wanted
or if I wanted to ask anything about the book, the
hapter or story, or the pictures, that too was done
tty voice—just between him and me. In the mean-
 anyone need help on a word (which was seldom;
I started with this group) all he needed to do was
ook toward me with a finger under the word and
kly tell him. In this way we were able to take turns
hole circle in the regular reading time.

n took some adjusting on the part of the youngsters,
of voice with which they read to *me* and not to the
the giving of themselves to their own continuous
themselves with no compunction about not listening
ow who was reading to me, and so on. Everyone had
to read to me so I could learn something of what and
was reading. More important, each youngster spent
inute of the forty-minute period *reading*—not listening
rs, not following along, not waiting his turn, but reading
loving it!

"That was great. Let's do that again," they said when I cut in to remind them that our time was up.

"Say, we could have reading like that every day," someone proffered.

"We gotta have some time to read our readers, silly, or we'd never get them finished," his pal answered back.

"Well, most of the time we could do it this way—afternoon reading and some of the mornings." We agreed to see how it went.

But of course not before the other two groups had had their turn at the same plan and with equal success, though with somewhat greater adjustment. More children asked for help and we had to work that in in the most efficient way without disturbing the fellow reading to me. He had to learn to go right on reading without letting my whispering a word to this child or that throw him off balance. But the children worked at it and they learned and we all thought it was a wonderful way to do business. I was in a position to give more help to the individual youngster reading to me, knowing we were not holding up the others and having the chance to focus on his particular need and his way of doing things. This made us both feel good. Sometimes with a child who plodded jerkily along I would purposely help him move on through the story by saying, "Suppose you read a page (or a paragraph) and then I will. It looks like an interesting story. I'll try to get it later and read the whole thing." (Which I would often do.) Anyway, I found that as I took my turn reading smoothly and interestingly, it would somehow help him to push along more smoothly as well.

The interest in reading, in discussing books, in taking them home for the evening, in pulling them out of their desks at every spare moment, steadily heightened—and almost without exception. It was only our adventurous, full-to-the-hilt, dynamic program of other activities that kept some little rascals from being incurable bookworms. It seemed to me, and the children agreed, it might be wise to keep a record of these books they read. For my own part, I wanted to marshal evidence as to whether this was a more effective way for teaching children to read.

another, the record would be a way of noting the child's own progress from time to time, as well as his reading interests. Also, it would give him a feeling of accomplishment. I could go on with the advantages.

Living through the Effects of Competition as Motivation

In this regard, however, I did a foolish thing, a very foolish thing indeed. In my enthusiasm, as a surprise to the youngsters, who usually did most of the chart-making themselves, I prepared a handsome reading chart—a color sketch of children reading at the top, then all their names in alphabetical listing, with space under each for recording dates and titles of books read. It was a great big class so it was a great big chart—several pieces of manila tagboard, I remember, and I was to do the recording because the entries had to be made in very small handprinting to fit and be readable.

We found a good conspicuous place for it and proudly we began the record of individual books read in our book-loving fourth grade. One at a time those who had recently finished books, having checked the library list or hunted through shelves for current titles, dictated to me the entries under their names. Then came the change. In the days to follow the whole attitude toward reading books began to shift. I would not have believed it of this my wonderful group. Everybody went for the thin books, the picture books, the ones they could whip through fast. This included the Group I gourmands too. To be sure, there were those who resisted the numbers racket as time went by. But others complained, "But that isn't fair. If you read skinny books, you get a nice long list and if you read bigger books that take a lot of time, your record looks like you weren't reading much at all!" And they were right. O.K.! *O.K.! O.K.!!* To be fair, we agreed that we would count about every fifty pages the equivalent of a book and we figured out some ingenious way for recording this on the chart.

Then pandemonium broke loose. Talk about motivation for

reading—ulterior motivation, that is! The fun of reading a favorite book, of recommending it to friends, of losing yourself in an exciting tale lost all importance as children argued over size of pages, size of print, amount of room taken up by photographs, "baby" books. "But you really didn't read that," I heard one child say accusingly to another. "You're lying! How could you have read it when you just took it out before lunch?" Even in the reading group right under my nose the fever spread. I could see one or two children sitting restlessly reading for a while, then stealthily turning over page after page without really reading. I was heartsick. For the first time I felt I had to *check* on the youngsters. When sweet old Ronnie came over to read to me I asked him casually about an illustration on the page. What was it about? He hemmed and hawed and was not sure. Then I found he knew nothing at all about the story on pages preceding. Calmly, I suggested that maybe he had better start at the beginning so he could get the hang of the story, or else find another book that he really wanted to read. I controlled my irritation. After all, whose fault was this anyway? Another thing was happening. We were *all* growing suspicious. We all had to check on one another. When I took turns reading with Norma Jean to move her along into the story, somebody was sure to complain, "But Miss Floyd, you're helping her! That's not fair!"

"Look," I found myself having to say to them over and over. "It's not the number of books that you read that's important. We read because we're interested in the story. We want to know what happens or what the author has to say, and we read to find this out. A thick book or a thin, what's the difference? What goes on the chart isn't the important thing." They even used this gag on one another. But wasn't it important what went on the chart? their recent behavior was asking me. Well, then, why have the chart? And why indeed? What had I done to this wonderful gang of children that they should be so chippy and so chesty and so afraid of being cheated? The answer was clear. It was nobody's fault but my own. Keep a public record, introduce competition, and see what happens to the best of us!

Everyone wants a good record: and why not? No one wants to suffer by comparison. No one wants to lose his self-respect.

So one day, after discussing the matter frankly and at length, we took down the chart. And none too soon. We weathered the storm all right and got back into shape because children are like that. But for some it really took a long time to get over the habits and attitudes of those few weeks of quite unnecessary rivalry. As the one adult in the situation, no doubt, I should have foreseen all this. Anyway, I learned my lesson and I learned it well. And many classes of children, college students, and teachers in service have since profited from my mistake.

Organizing for Full-fledged Individualized Reading

The reading groups continued, with the individualized way of working much the more popular and much the more profitable. In time we let the library books replace the group readers entirely. This called for some discussion of what was meant by "basal" and "supplementary" readers. Then we mixed the readers in with other books on the shelf and the children took responsibility for reading one or two of each of the basic and the supplementary books at some time during the year—or their equivalents which, for obvious reasons, I could work out with individual youngsters whose needs would be better satisfied in other ways. And certain readers, personally selected and read uninterruptedly the same as any other books, proved to be very interesting reading, a fact that seemed at first to carry some element of surprise.

By this time we had also changed our plan of grouping, for reasons of convenience as well as those previously stated. Group I had been easiest since my help was hardly needed there. Group III had been most difficult since my help was needed continuously, often by several children at a time. It was an obvious improvement to have the groups mixed. And we used various plans for mixing. Most often the grouping was voluntary. "Will about a third of you bring your books and come for reading?"

(Later a second third, and then the last.) Sometimes geography was the basis. "Will the people in the last three seats of these few rows come for reading? I'll sit about here, within reach of all of you. You can share this seat with me as you read aloud." Sometimes it was a more functional division. "How many have finished your letters (or your diaries or your stories or your arithmetic) or are at a good stopping place? That's about right for a reading group, isn't it? Let's see, where's the best place to sit?"

It was interesting, but not surprising, to note how pleased the Group III people were these days to be reading side by side with those from Group I. It gave me a pang of guilt about what had gone on before. Soon, however, the group aspect of it lost significance. With a book of his own choice every child read with interest, some so engrossed that they had to be reminded when reading period was over. Others wearied sooner—maybe because they had to work harder, though this was not always the case. Many times it was the child who asked for most help, who read most slowly, who was still at the stage of moving his lips as he read—who would beg to finish just this chapter before going out to recess. It was children like this who seemed most happily aware of their progress. They could just feel themselves becoming better and better readers. I could too.

After a while it seemed unnecessary to hear every child read aloud every day. Every few days, yes. And for some every couple of days or every day, yes. By and large they could make this decision for themselves. Every once in a while, though, I would say: "Perry, that looks like an interesting book you have. How about reading some of it to me?" I took care to say this to several different children, not only to those who needed most help.

Nor did they always need to do their reading aloud to me. Every now and then Luana and Catherine or Jack and Leo would go off by themselves with a book and take turns reading together.

For a while our morning reading was usually carried on in groups reading individually now. The afternoon period had become the time for whatever kind of reading organization they chose—a library period for most, with two or three of us sitting where we could give help easily, a time for reading with a pal, or even as a self-selected self-operating group with five or six copies of the same book, to which some youngsters occasionally delighted in reverting. Sometimes best friends varied widely in reading competence. Still they would enjoy reading an exciting mystery or perusing a book on prehistoric animals or the Antarctic together since now, no longer separated or labeled by arbitrary reading groups, both were free to profit from such common ventures.

About once a week we had a time for discussing, reviewing, or reading favorite selections from books we had read. I was pleased with the way the children were becoming familiar with authors, illustrators, and even publishers. These were the periods of contagion—though not the only ones—when a youngster, book in hand, could scarcely finish what he had to say about it before someone would ask, "Can I take that book now?" "Nope, Charlie has spoken for it." "After *you*, Charlie?" "And then *me*?" someone else would call out. Very often, there would be such a run on a book, whether or not it had come up for discussion before the class, that those concerned would find themselves having to draw up a schedule.

Sometimes this was hard on another class because they would have a waiting list too. This was something that several classes of us had to work out together, at least until additional copies could be ordered for the school as budget permitted. In the meantime, we teachers, as well as a number of the children, were still supplementing the library with our own books as well as with maximum loans from the public library. Once children get into and enjoy the habit of uninterrupted reading, we had discovered, there's just no stopping them!

2

Individual teachers discover more adequate ways

Not all teachers have the opportunity to feel, with Miss Floyd, the kind of thrill that comes with the discovery and creation of new and better ways for helping children learn to read. So much depends upon the manner in which the need for change is brought to a teacher's awareness. It is one thing for an outside evaluator to say that a teacher's ways are inadequate, that there is need for change. It is quite another for the teacher, secure within her own classroom, to come face to face with evidence that her ways of working with certain children seem questionable, not adequate, when the need to change is communicated to her through the classroom situation itself.

Inadequacy is never easy to claim, but the reality of a classroom situation makes it impossible to overlook inadequate interaction between learner and teacher. When children aren't learning what teachers are trying to help them learn, the children seem to find a thousand and one ways to communicate this fact to themselves and to their teacher. Experienced, sensitive teachers learn to look for and count on this kind of communication from children. They learn to welcome the signals which children send out with regard to inadequate features in their learning situation. And they learn to impersonalize the evaluation of inadequacy where it is appropriate for them to do so. Rather than feeling, "I (the teacher) am inadequate," or "You (the learner) are inadequate," teachers learn to view the situation as something shared by learner and teacher—as something quite expected and very useful in a world where people try to help one another learn what they want and need to know. This is not a skill which teachers come by for the asking. It is learned through conscious effort and experience.

Moving into Individualized Reading with Early First-Graders

Miss Wainwright found her way to individualizing reading in a situation in which the signals of inadequacy were communicated through the children's behavior. Very early in the school year, in fact, just as soon as her fastest group of readers started working in their first preprimer, Miss Wainwright began having trouble with Stevie. Stevie was an alert, interesting, personable youngster—"Just too smart, I guess," was Miss Wainwright's comment. Stevie was pretty much all right during the discussion preceding the reading. He sat in the circle with the others in the group and, apart from wanting more than his share of time to tell of personal experiences, more turns than anyone else to answer the questions Miss Wainwright asked, or speaking without raising his hand whenever he got really interested Stevie would begin the reading lesson as well-behaved as any of the others.

It was really as the children began reading, one after the other, around the circle, that Stevie would begin to act up—shouting out the word when the child who was reading would hesitate, no matter how often he was reminded not to help; getting into little side conversations with his neighbor about the polo shirt he was wearing, the relative size of his and his neighbor's feet, perhaps a recent movie or television program; pushing his knee hard against the little girl on the other side of him, pulling her handkerchief out of her pocket and throwing it into her lap or in any other way seeking to aggravate her—just a little; slumping down in his seat, legs outstretched before him, and maybe letting his book fall with a clump to the floor. When Miss Wainwright would call on him quickly to read a line, as a way of diverting his attention and getting him back on the track again, he would like as not read the whole page without stopping, turn to the next and race through it also in spite of his teacher's insistent, "That's enough, Stevie. All *right,* Stevie!" This would send the children off into gales of laughter. That was the trouble. It was not so much that what Stevie did was bad; it was more that he would keep the rest of the children from tending to business and moving along with the lesson as planned.

Nor would threats to make him go to his seat or read with some other group help very much. Good-natured Stevie would go to his seat, beaming victoriously. He would sit with a slower group, not bothered in the least, but even more bothersome to Miss Wainwright and to the other children because the reading gait of this group was so much less moving. Miss Wainwright would acknowledge all this to herself when, later on, she could analyze the situation and calmly try to think through a solution. "I guess it's my fault, really," she found herself saying. "He's just too fast for that group, I suppose, and is bored—too fast for any group in here. Well, Wainwright, surely you're not sitting here wishing that Steve *couldn't* read, are you? Maybe you'd like it if that industrious little Lois didn't read so well, either! Syphon off the few top children in any reading group and the very bottom ones and life would be fine, eh?" And right then the idea hit.

"Lois and Stevie, since you seem to know the words in our book and don't need so much of my help, how would you like to find a comfortable place somewhere in the room and try reading by yourselves today, just you two taking turns reading to each other? Do you think you could manage that, or not? Well, we can try it and see how it goes. Read through this story and then, if you'd like to, go right on with the next one. I'll be working with the group here, but if you need help, just come over and ask me. All right? Good!"

Of course they would like it, and of course they could manage it, and of course they would find the most comfortable place in the room—far, far away from Miss Wainwright and the group, just to show that they didn't need help. And it worked; the idea *worked*! Whenever Miss Wainwright glanced over in their direction, the two children were reading away with great satisfaction, sometimes stopping to comment on a picture, to count back to see how many pages they had covered, and then back they would get to their reading with renewed vigor. By the time the reading period was over, they had read through four or five stories and were begging to go on. Within the week, Miss Wainwright had to give them another book and a few days later still another. At odd times, she made it a point to read a bit with them, to ask a question perhaps about this picture and that, just to make sure. Their progress was amazing. So was Stevie's behavior, now that he was challenged and did not have to be bound by the slower progress of the group.

And the group was moving along better also, without these two who were always wanting to tell the words and answer the questions and otherwise preempt the responsibilities of the group. Now Miss Wainwright was finding that there were one or two others who seemed about ready to read independently. Soon they asked, in fact, if they could read by themselves, like Stevie and Lois were doing. Before long, Miss Wainwright had that whole group, ten children, reading at different places in two or three different books and at different tempos. Sometimes they read individually, sometimes with a favored pal, usually sitting around close so they could get their teacher's help as they needed it. When some of them asked to be allowed to go

to another quieter place in the room, Miss Wainwright would
let them go, pretty certain by now that when the responsibility
was theirs they could be counted upon.

As time went on, Miss Wainwright came to question more
and more her long-accepted practice of following a detailed
plan with a primer or reader, lesson by lesson, day after day,
with everyone in the group having to wait silently while everyone else in the group read or answered a question or figured
out a word. A preprimer or primer that was meant to last several weeks with a group lasted only a matter of days with children who read it straight through without interruption, after
which they would ask for another book to read, and then
another, and another. Sometimes, usually later on, they might
ask for the same book over again, just to show how much better
they could read the familiar pages by this time.

Miss Wainwright had feelings of guilt now and then at the
thought of playing such havoc with what had long been an
orderly method of teaching reading. She worked out a system
of individual record-keeping, however, while hearing each child
read to her from where he was in his own book, occasionally
chatting with him about what he read, observing closely in
terms of interest and attitude and growing skills, and thus began
to feel more and more reassured.

Miss Wainwright's immediate problem was one of finding
adequate books. Her usual allotment for the entire first grade
she now brought in from the book room, kept them in her own
classroom closet, and put out a few at a time as they were
needed. Her school did not have a library, so she quickly made
out a list of books that she wanted and took them to her principal. She told the principal what was happening, invited him to
drop in and see how the children were eating up the books they
did have, sometimes reading them over and over again for sheer
pleasure, and asked if her requisition couldn't be honored as
quickly as possible in place of the several sets of new readers
promised her for the coming Fall. In the meantime she explored
the public library facilities. Before long, with her own library
card and the cards of several of the children she took with her to

enjoy the experience and help select, she was bringing in an armload of attractive colorful books every few weeks. The difficulty of finding enough very easy books was a serious one, but the children's librarian, once advised of the situation, promised to see that that part of the library purchase would be increased as soon as possible.

Miss Wainwright had always been one to work rather closely with the parents of her children. She dittoed a personal letter to them telling something of what was happening in their reading program, inviting them to come in to talk with her as they had time, and asking for their help in building up a classroom library for helping their children learn to read. In each letter she enclosed a list of "Good Books for the Youngest Readers" which she and the public librarian had drawn up for that purpose.

Books came in fast from several families. Children were proud to share their own personal libraries, and Miss Wainwright too contributed. She talked over her new plan with two of her colleagues, also in primary grades, who began working out similar plans. (Just as soon as any of her children, in any reading group now, were able to read with some degree of independence, she allowed and encouraged them to read on their own or with a friend.) These teachers pooled their ideas and observations as well as their facilities, working closely with the principal and giving help to any other teachers who became interested.

By Spring, a committee was hard at work and plans had been made for setting up a school library for the following year. Another committee had been given responsibility for selecting and buying books with several hundred dollars from the Parent Teachers Association, earlier earmarked for a film projector, but now unanimously voted for use in making a start on a school library. Further, as a result of a long and fruitful meeting of these teachers and the principal with the Board of Education—who, like their counterparts everywhere, wanted the children in their schools to learn to read better—a sizable item was promised in the budget for both classroom and library collections.

Accommodating Young Children's Need for Oral Reading

Miss Reagan's plan, in the latter half of first grade, was somewhat different. Many a visitor to her classroom at reading time was stopped short by what he saw—and more so by what he heard. "Turn your chairs so you'll be comfortable," Miss Reagan had said to the children, "and so you won't be bothered by anyone else." And this they had done. Children were everywhere, facing in all directions, reading—some to themselves quietly, most to themselves noisily—moving their lips or frankly reading aloud, following along with their finger as needed, or with a marker made for the purpose. Chaos, the visitor might label it at first glance. How can they hear themselves think? Just like those curious schools we once learned of, with everyone studying aloud.

But on second look, it proved to be far from chaos. Everyone was at work—every child in the whole room—everyone oblivious to the others around him. Engrossed, that is what they were, in the stories they were reading. "The . . . mother pig . . . called her three children . . . to her . . ." one child was verbalizing laboriously. The boy next to him was reading without sound, just moving his lips quietly and following with his marker, line by line. Several nearby were reading silently and motionlessly, quite unaware of anyone else in the room at the time. Not chaos, no; a well-organized reading time, in fact, with every child knowing and doing just what the carefully planned period called for. They could do this only because they were accustomed to working hard and responsibly in this way.

The visitor's look about the room revealed Miss Reagan herself working with a small group of children in a corner of the room, her quick eye taking in the whole of the class from time to time as she helped the youngsters near her. These few children had books just alike, opened to the same page. They were reading aloud in unison, again following along with a marker and with great apparent interest and pride. Arranging with one of the independent readers to move ahead with this group, Miss Reagan excused herself and came to greet the visitor who seemed hardly to have caused a ripple in this industrious, absorbed roomful of children. The hum and the concentration of their own reading period was such as to make quite unnoticeable the now animated conversation at the door.

"I *encourage* the children to read aloud during this period," Miss Reagan explained with pride, "so I can get some idea of how they are making out. This is a big class, and I like to listen as well as to look. No, it doesn't mean they will read with their lips throughout life—far from it. They're using their lips or their fingers or their markers to help themselves learn to read well. These are only helps; once the children have learned to read well, they won't need them any more. I have found that if children are free to use these helps when they need them, and for as long as they feel that they need them, then they quickly outgrow the need and move on to more mature ways of reading. Many are reading silently already, you'll notice, without even thinking about it.

"The four children I'm working with back there? They're not to the independent stage yet. I work with them in a number of ways, sometimes individually, sometimes as a group. Today we are reading aloud together, as you noted. I find that in this way the children can follow and read too, gradually getting the hang of reading and feeling themselves quite accomplished."

Recognizing the Integrity of Comprehension

Many teachers, when they take time to think about it, are recognizing that there is good sense in their children's dissatisfaction with over-directed, broken-into-bits reading periods. To understand a story a person needs to read it whole. He needs to respond to the mood. He needs to see the action for what it is. An increasing number of teachers are meeting their children's need for thoughtful, uninterrupted reading by setting aside forty-five minutes or an hour a day as a regular reading time. During this period the children, having chosen their books from a wide selection provided for the purpose, just sit in their own seats and read to themselves throughout the hour.

Miss Meeker, whose very crowded classroom still has rows of screwed-down desks, has planned with her children that she will move about the room, sitting with each child in his turn to hear him read to her, occasionally comment on what he is reading, or whatever else seems appropriate in their few minutes together. She makes arrangements for several youngsters in the class, or maybe an older child or two from another room, to sit in convenient places and be responsible with her for helping children with words too hard for them.

"It was my owlish young Jack who first got me thinking in this direction," Miss Meeker confides. "And it wasn't easy. He's a pretty good reader—often has his head in a book at other times. But in reading group he would always act up. One day I lost all patience with him. 'Look, Jack,' I said crossly. 'If you don't enjoy reading this story, for heaven's sake behave yourself and let the other children enjoy it!' 'Well,' he retorted, 'If it's an interesting story, let me at it! And let me stay at it! Don't always be stopping me to answer some silly old question. What do you think the picture is about? Why didn't the rabbit want to eat the lettuce? What did the little girl hope to find in the box? If it's an interesting story, and we're supposed to read and enjoy it, then *let* us read and enjoy it.' And he opened his book, bent his head down low, and didn't say another word during the rest of the period. I didn't say another word either. . . . I was trying to hold back the tears. The children went on reading to themselves till time for outdoor play, which fortunately came very soon. . . .

"Well, Jack doesn't hold a grudge and I don't either. We're good friends, and we've had a number of good talks since then. And I for one have done some tall thinking. I've decided perhaps children do need the chance to get the thread of the story on their own—without the constant interruption of an overly anxious teacher, such as I was. I guess the plot and the continuity of a good book, which children can't properly get in little spoon-fed gulps, can be more important to genuine reading comprehension than all my carefully planned questions and motivating discussions. With other kinds of books, informational and reference books, perhaps, it's a different matter. I can give them help as they need it. But just watching this gang of children reading their books—fiction, travel, biography— I think I can *tell* if they're comprehending. And if I'm in doubt, or they are, then the two of us, or three or four or however many are involved, work it through together—without interrupting Jack and his ilk when they do *not* need it. Yes. . . . I really owe that boy a debt of gratitude—although he's not one to collect. Look at him over there now. Did you ever see more rapt absorption?"

Miss Meeker does not attempt to get around to hear all of the children read every day. She feels that two or three times a week is enough for most; and they feel the same. But every child is reading for the full hour every day, and understanding and enjoying what he reads, a situation made possible only by the fact that Miss Meeker has provided a wide enough variety of books so that every child can select from them those which he is interested in reading. She keeps an eye on the class as they read, of course; if a youngster seems to be having difficulty finding a book or getting into the reading of it for any reason, she gives him help. Furthermore, because she is not tied to a particular reading group at a given time, any child feels free to ask for her help if he needs it.

Miss Meeker has also provided a variety of simple dittoed forms, on any of which a child can keep a daily dated record of pages he has read, books he has finished, comments of any kind he may wish to make. No one feels under pressure as Miss Meeker notes this record from time to time and on occasion will discuss it with a child when it is his time to read with her.

Providing for Wider Choices in Reading Time

Other teachers vary this procedure in ways with which they feel most comfortable, sometimes giving children more freedom to sit where they like, to read with a buddy if they prefer, to adjust the length of the reading period one way or another as the need arises.

Mr. Carlson contends that for an individualized reading program to be truly effective, it must be so set up as to provide for *maximum choice* on the part of all children. Believing strongly, as he does, in the principle of self-selection in learning, he feels that it is not enough for individual children to have a choice as to *what* they shall read. Every child should have some choice also as to *when* he shall read; as to *how* he shall read—whether to himself or with others; as to *whom* he shall read with when not to himself; as to *where* he will read— at his desk, at the library table, off in the corner with a friend; as to what he will do during the time that some others of the class have selected to read; as to ways of reacting to books he has read and of sharing these reactions with others; as to the purposes of getting together with friends concerned with reading. All of these choices, Mr. Carlson feels, are basic if youngsters are to make maximum progress.

This puts a good deal of responsibility on the children, to be sure. But it puts far greater responsibility on the teacher, who has to set up the classroom in such a way that all of these choices will not only be possible but will also be profitable for the children. That is his job; he cannot shirk it, says Mr. Carlson. And after considerable exploration and trying out of one plan and then another, Mr. Carlson suggests the following as one he finds practicable in his own classroom, and is helping other teachers to work out in theirs—with whatever modifications their particular situations seem to call for.

Mr. Carlson's sixth-grade class begins the morning with Work Time, as they call it. A block of time of *an hour and a half or two hours,* this period is planned to include three kinds of activities in each of which every child is expected to participate, but in whatever order he may choose.

One of the three kinds of activities provided for, of course, is *reading.* A sizable portion of this long block of time is to be devoted to some kind of reading. There is a large collection of books from which to select, and children can read without interruption in whatever way they prefer. They may read a book to themselves or with a friend. Two or three may want to get copies of the same book and take turns reading together. Several children may be reading in search of a story that will make a good play. A child may read to the teacher. Indeed this may well be the time when the teacher will want to work individually with children or with small groups informally set up. There is physical freedom here also. The children may sit wherever and however they prefer—at tables, on the floor against the wall or the bookcase, on their chairs in the hall— wherever they feel most comfortable and will not be too much in the way of others.

A second of the three parts of Mr. Carlson's Work Time is given over to wider choices, individual and group. While others are reading, some children may be working on a play, painting scenery, making costumes, planning choreography. Others may be working with art media of various kinds, or with science materials, if that is what the job involves. Some may be working on a crossword puzzle to ditto for the class, or constructing a table game or quiz board. Two or three children might come with the beginning of a play or newspaper to work on during this time. Materials are provided by Mr. Carlson or by individual children, but the children are expected to set up and work out their own plans. Always they are free to ask help of the teacher or other children.

Then there is the third type of activity in which all of the children are to engage at some time during this long morning period. This is usually some common assignment or jointly planned project for the total group, having to do with social studies, say, or science or arithmetic or some othe area of the curriculum. It may involve the use of teacher-made work sheets, usually a variety of them from which children can select. It may be some aspect of research, the organizing of notes from references read, perhaps the making of plans for an interview, the recording of findings from a trip, some work on a chapter or story to contribute to one of the books which the class has under way.

To repeat, individuals plan the order in which they engage in the three kinds of Work Time activities described above. The teacher, too, joins in—sometimes offering needed guidance, sometimes participating as any other member of the group— choosing a book and reading while they read, taking a part in the play. Children should know their teacher as a doer, says Mr. Carlson, not just as a listener and evaluator. Nor is the teacher the only one on whom they will call for help during these mornings. Arrangements are made with teachers to allow different children from the junior high school classes to come in and serve as helpers or assistants, sometimes reading with individual children, sometimes taking down their dictated stories, helping to make charts, or doing whatever is needed. Teachers of these older students are glad for them to have this experience. They feel it is valuable not only for those who have difficulty with reading and therefore can profit from giving help to younger children on easier books, with no stigma attached, but for other youngsters, too, who need such opportunity to be relied upon.

It should be noted that the children in Mr. Carlson's room are free to use the library as needed during this morning period. From time to time there are spontaneous and informal discussions about books they have read and want to share with others, sometimes in small groups, sometimes in the total group. They have a card file set up, where children are encouraged now and then—but not required—to insert cards bearing their reactions to books they have read. It may be, as time goes on, that there will appear several cards on the same book, not infrequently with varying, even contradictory, reactions. This may make for an interesting discussion, Mr. Carlson finds, among those who have read the book in question, as well as others who may want to read it, maybe in part because of the controversy. All of the sharing and reporting of books read is of this informal, spontaneous, contagious nature, either in small group or large.

Mr. Carlson, like other teachers developing similar plans, is continually evaluating the adequacy of his program in terms of what is happening to the children, individually and as a group. He feels that this kind of unpressured, informal, responsible working together not only challenges children to thoughtful choice and action—a required condition for maximum growth in reading—it also gives the teacher a chance, on a good friendly basis, to work more closely with his children, to better observe their individual needs and resources, and thus to give them more appropriate encouragement and help.

Extending Children's Awareness of Kinds of Books Available

As a way of encouraging her children to extend the scope of their reading, and to become more aware of different kinds of books and authors, Mrs. Raleigh finds some such informal planning as the following to be workable and worthwhile: She and her fifth grade children one day draw up a list of book categories—history, adventure, autobiography, biography, plays, mysteries, travel, and others that may be pertinent. Each youngster selects a category and for the next few weeks reads everything he can find in that category. Those reading in the same category get together in informal groups from time to time to compare the books they read, discuss what the authors have in mind, find out what is distinctive in their purposes and methods, set up some kind of book exhibit or display, perhaps, prepare and duplicate book lists, and in other ways let the class know what they have been reading and finding out. Mrs. Raleigh tries to keep the project spontaneous and unpressured. "Tomorrow, let's discuss biographies," she may propose, and the children concerned assume the responsibility for helping to make the discussion a profitable one for all.

During one such discussion of plays and playwrights, it comes out somehow that none of the children has ever seen a professional play, although their school is located in a metropolitan area. With great enthusiasm they decide to cancel plans already under way for a class picnic and to make it a theater party instead. After studying the theater list and reviews from the press and television, they agree on *The Diary of Anne Frank* as the play they want to see. They purchase a large block of tickets, of course, and when the great day arrives, spend a most interesting and exciting afternoon. Later, they invite one of the actors out to their school to answer their questions and help them understand more about plays and play production. Needless to say, not only an increase in play reading follows this experience, with different children getting together to read the parts, but also some serious playwriting emerges, with plans as well for eventual production.

Helping Seventh- and Eighth-Graders to Contribute through Reading

Mr. Seidle works with a group of children in the junior high school who have difficulty with reading, who are from one to several years "below grade" in reading. Realizing how sensitively children react, especially at this age, to any kind of unfavorable label or to being set apart from their friends, he explores with the school librarian possible ways of setting up their reading program which are self-respecting and both personally and socially satisfying to the children. In other words, he wants to help these children so that their own reading can improve, rather than limit, their standing with other boys and girls in the school. He and Miss Lee, the librarian, try to help them set purposes for their reading other than that of "trying to improve in a school subject in which they are far behind."

The range of individual differences in this class is sufficiently wide to indicate that the major part of their program will necessarily be individualized. This will mean the reading of a variety of books, of course, and a variety of books all of which are comparatively easy to read. How to get some of these nearly grown-up boys and girls to read and enjoy books written for younger children, rather than resent them, because they are so obviously baby books that even to be seen carrying them about will do damage to their individual dignity, is of continuous concern to Mr. Seidle.

Wise, understanding teacher that he is, and with the continuous and resourceful help of his colleague, Mr. Seidle works out the problem in this way. Having just completed one project to which the group has given wholehearted cooperation, he tells them one day that he has been doing some serious thinking. He wonders if these boys and girls would be willing to give him and Miss Lee some help on a piece of research they have long been wanting to do but, limited by time and insufficient staff help, have been unable to undertake. For years, he tells them (in sincerity because it is true), they have wanted to make a study of the element of horror in children's books—especially in books read by children of elementary school age. Because this class has shown such an interest in books generally, and because most of them have brothers and sisters or neighbors in the elementary schools, he feels that if willing to tackle the job—which is a big as well as an important one—they can do a real service to the school system and to children generally.

The boys and girls are willing. As they begin to see the significance that such a piece of research can have for schools and libraries and parents and children's authors, they are indeed very eager to be of help. Their own school library, the elementary school libraries, and the new public library in the town, as well as their respective staffs, will provide the class with ample resources. So will interested elementary teachers and administrators, parents, and the younger school children themselves. Although it will require several class periods to lay out their plans, Mr. Seidle and Miss Lee make sure that by the end of the very first session, these youngsters are far enough into the project that at least some preliminary investigations can get under way.

The children are full of enthusiasm, ideas, and individual and small-friendly-group plans by the close of the first session together. They go after the books at once, even as the criteria for judging and classifying are still in formation. Indeed, this is a good and a necessary way for exploring the kind of criteria that are appropriate.

"What a hard-working, earnest group of youngsters these

are!", Mr. Seidle observes to Miss Lee as the children leave the room, talking excitedly among themselves. And Miss Lee agrees. "You just have to hand it to children," she declares. "When they see a real job to be tackled, and they have the chance to set up the plans and conditions, they're ready to give it their all."

Individualizing the use of books then, since it cannot be based on a formula, will always be defined in ways unique to a particular teaching-learning situation. Teachers and student teachers reading this chapter may have been able to locate themselves and their children on different pages as they read, paying special note to discussions pertinent to their own situations, considering what are appropriate next steps for them, what is waste motion, what is not, what are techniques needed by them as teachers, needed by their children, and, in many instances, needed by their communities. (In some communities, for example, parents feel reassured only if they can look into a classroom and see children sitting as if in a reading group, whatever the methods used.)

Basic to this identification of one's own specific needs, is a kind of perspective that comes from viewing a variety of orientations and experiences. Since no one person can have all the insights possible, no matter how broad or valid his experiences in the field, this sincere attempt to view problems and possibilities from another's vantage point can deepen and extend one's own resourcefulness and sensibilities. It is in this spirit that the variety of concrete descriptions of individualizing the children's reading of books and the way in which in each case this comes about, have been presented.

Some of these descriptions are firsthand accounts written by teachers at work in their classrooms. Others have been recounted by teachers and written up in the authors' words. Some depict experiences and observations of the authors. Many more such accounts are available, certainly, than space has allowed for here. Even this limited selection, it is hoped, will have highlighted the variety of ways in which thoughtful, sincere teachers are individualizing their reading program. This dynamic way of working with widely differing individuals, because it is based on the principle of self-selection, will lose its meaning if ever it becomes crystallized into a patterned step-by-step routine for teachers or children to follow.

3

Librarians help to meet the realities of selection

A children's librarian, perhaps more than anyone else, is a person who has to cope with the realities of each reading situation. Daily she is faced by individual children who know what they want and will resolutely reject one offering after another until just the right book is found. For when a child intending to read looks at a page of print something has to happen. Something in the patterning of what he sees has to make sense *to him*. No one knows this more realistically than does the sensitive school librarian. Indeed, she sets up the library in her school as a place to which children, individually or in groups, are free to come at any time—to read, to get help, to do research, to check out books, to share ideas, to discuss books, to plan plays, to write, to ask questions, to get individual help and guidance.

Down through the years the school library has held a place of importance proportionate to the value the individual schools have attributed to it as an educational investment. During these years, the library, conceived in a more or less extracurricular sense, has served pretty much a threefold purpose: to provide a place for reference materials, to cultivate library skills, and to make possible in the school wider circulation of supplementary reading books. With currently increasing emphasis on the personal and varied nature of reading the country over, the scope of the elementary school library and the role of the trained school librarian are expanding proportionately. Even in schools lacking the services of a trained librarian—where a sixth-grade teacher and her children are still obliged to find time and ways to keep the library open at specified hours of the day—the library is coming more and more to be looked upon as essential to the well-rounded education of children.

Setting up the Library to Serve Its Users

It should be helpful in this connection to follow the story of how one school librarian, Miss Bosner, a woman of long experience with children and teachers, and of always growing insights, views the role of the library. In her opinion, the fundamental function of the library and books is that of improving human relationships. "The library should serve to improve human relations in the entire school," Miss Bosner maintains. "The relationships between teacher and teacher, teacher and children, children and children, children and parents, parents and school, all who are involved in the satisfying experience of children reading books, should be warmer and better because there is a library in the school. For books are a record of human life; out of them come keys to human understanding."

Miss Bosner came only this year to the school in which she works in so pivotal a way. She tells us how she found this combination elementary-high school quite lacking in unity, "really just a long string of rooms and hall, with little to tie it together." School-wide communication was lacking in many ways. There was a bulletin board in the elementary school office, but it was not read by all of the teachers. The library, although amply supplied with books, was unattractive and not functional. The children had to walk across the room to the circulation desk, for example. The history books and encyclopedias were kept in a part of the room that was mostly used as a runway for older children on their way to the high school end of the library.

Miss Bosner studied this long narrow room to see how it might be conceived more functionally. With the help of others in the school she made some major rearrangements. Certain dark spots in the library were painted. The catalogue and circulation desk were moved to a place more easily reached. The encyclopedias were arranged in a part of the room, set up especially for them, to which high school as well as elementary school children delighted to come. The history books were pulled out of their dark, drab shelves and put into a lighted spot which came to be known as the History Corner. With a comfortable chair or two, as well as the study table, this corner was arranged to *invite* children to come and make use of the books.

The Story Corner was set up, at the opposite side of the room, especially for children who tended to have difficulty with reading. Some extra lamps, one or two upholstered chairs, and a couple of benches helped to make it a favorite spot. The label *Easy Books* was changed to *Story Corner,* as a way of helping these particular children to keep their self-respect. Miss Bosner recounts how Dennis had come to her earlier with *Misty of Chincoteague* in his hand. "I like this book but I can't read it," he had told her. "Do you have a horse story that I can read?" Miss Bosner started to pick up *Hugo* from the Easy Books shelf, when Dennis called out, "Oh, no, not over there!" So the label was changed so as not to signify "baby stuff," and several more difficult books were sprinkled among the easy ones.

In another part of the room, set off by bookcases jutting at right angles from the wall, were the record player and cabinet, with story and speech records to be used by any who chose. The three most popular albums, Miss Bosner recalls, were *Nancy Hanks,* Lois Lenski's *Strawberry Girl,* and some readings from Edna St. Vincent Millay.

The cabinet in which the pictures were kept served a dual purpose in one corner of the library. The children would get behind it to carry on their puppet shows. There was a sign-up sheet near the cabinet, on which children would sign up for the puppets. "We kept boxes of puppets on a shelf," Miss Bosner explains, "which circulated just like the books. There were all kinds of puppets—people, clowns, cowboys, animals— which children could take to their rooms for use. The children would always add something when they returned them. Sometimes it would be a crudely made hand-puppet, sometimes a purchased one. At one time a puppet frame was brought in which, put atop the cabinet, was used a great deal."

Near the circulation desk was a shadow box or display case, set up especially to highlight books and manuscripts, anything, in fact, that had to do with the art of printing. Here would be announcements, for example, and arrangements of materials showing how to make a book—papers, pens, pictures, an engraving of an old monk, indicating with what great care the old manuscripts had been transcribed. There were displays and arrangements of various kinds, frequently changed, all designed to emphasize bookmaking, book reading, book use. A fifth-grade boy, who had lent his collection of dime-store prehistoric animals, had a couple of friends help him make a skyline and backdrop which could be lighted up to give reality to the collection. Near it the boys put together an exhibit of books about dinosaurs—especially of the new books that had come in only recently.

A great deal of reading of books went on continuously, in the library and out of it, encouraged and enjoyed the more because of the wide variety of special activities provided for. For all of these special arrangements were set up as an invitation to books, with emphasis on the participation of all who could help in any way. The children took responsibility for the charging and checking at the circulation desk as well as for some of the shelving. They were called Assistant Librarians, with specially made name cards for those in charge set out on the desk.

Of especial interest as time went along was the Writers' Corner. Partially closed off by files from the rest of the room, this was quite the quietest corner in the whole library, Miss Bosner observes. Here there were chairs of different sizes around a comfortable table. There were boxes holding different kinds of writing materials—special pens, ball-point pens, pencils, colored pencils, crayons, brushes, inks, rulers, erasers, blotters. Nearby were the dictionary shelves, with a variety of dictionaries for convenient use. There was one file labeled *Books Waiting for Authors,* in which sheets of paper of all kinds and sizes and colors and shapes, lined and unlined, were put together in folders, not stapled yet, but ready to be written upon and made into books. There were colored covers also to be completed and used, some hard, some soft—all arranged to interest children in writing and making books.

Scarcely an hour of the day went by that some one child or several children were not busily and creatively at work in this Writers' Corner. Always there would be older children available to help in ways that were needed. Older children, librarian, and many times parents would be there, if requested, to take down the writers' dictation. Everyone, from kindergartener to sixth-grader, was welcome and encouraged to be a writer. From time to time, the newly composed stories and books would be read aloud. An announcement on the bulletin board, for example, that Mary and Don B. and Emmy Lou were going to read their original stories at a particular hour, would bring an audience of interested children, even some high school students, and frequently parents.

At regular times, Miss Bosner herself would read aloud to the children. Sometimes the school principal, or a boy or girl from the high school, came in to read poetry. Always there was an eager audience, usually of mixed ages—groups of children as well as individuals who had elected to come from their classrooms. There were scheduled choice periods in the school that cut across grade lines, one for kindergarten through third grade and one for the upper grades. At this time, children could choose individually to go to shop, science, art room or library. This policy made for interesting, intermixing relationships in the library activities, which Miss Bosner welcomed. It pleased her to see a kindergartener and a third-grader stretched out on a rug together, looking at a favorite book, or younger children asking the older ones to read a particular story. Many loved to read on their own, of course. Others valued increasingly these opportunities for genuine interaction. "I'll teach you to read," a third-grader might proffer to a kindergartener. Or, a first-grader, to anyone who appeared interested: "I can read this. Don't you want to hear me read?" And someone would be sure to listen.

At one time, Miss Bosner recalls, a crowd of younger children were putting on a show, "The Elves and the Shoemaker." Mary was the shoemaker's wife, but everyone else wanted to be an elf. There was no shoemaker. Fifth-grader Steven was reading nearby. "I'll be your shoemaker," he said. The children were overjoyed, because big Steven was a wonderful actor. He carried the part well, with the younger children imitating his dramatic style and sincerity.

The use of sign-up sheets for children helped to make manageable this wide variety of activities. Throughout the year boys and girls were signing up for play production, for story telling, for story reading, for talking about books, for the production of plays or spontaneous skits.

The library, designed to cement human relationships in the school, was doing just that. "It was always orderly though seldom quiet." Children were coming and going at all hours of the day, stopping to look at the shadow box, to hear a story-in-the-making being read aloud, to comment to one another about a book that was being returned. The record-player or some form of story-telling was almost always going on. Miss Bosner remembers the day she looked up to see gangly Jimmy and four of his friends (little devils, by reputation!) "crying their eyes out" as they listened to the recorded story of Nancy Hanks. Jimmy's mother had died at about the same age as had Lincoln's mother.

As new books came to the library Miss Bosner would invite groups in to see and hear and talk about them. The books kept moving. The whole school was reading. Everyone came in to get books to read. They read them in the library. They read them in their classrooms. They read them at home. They shared them with their friends and family. Returning the books to the library, they would recommend them to others, discuss new ones, exchange opinions.

As time went by, Miss Bosner, noting which books were coming and going, discovered that poetry books were not being used. True, a few of the teachers were helping their children to enjoy poems in the classroom. But most of the school seemed not to put poetry high on the list. One day, Miss Bosner spoke about it to a group of children gathered about her. "You know, there's one thing we do not have in this library. That is a book put together and printed by you yourselves!" And there and then began the making of *Singing Willows*, the whole school's anthology of their favorite poems. One fifth-grade class set up the plan. They invited every class in the school to select their favorite poem and submit it in whatever way they liked for the collection. Each class was given special paper on which to copy the poem, in manuscript, or in cursive writing as they chose.

This was a voluntary affair, but the poems came in, beautifully copied and illustrated. The poetry shelves of the library were devastated as selections were being made. And what a collection! Everything, Miss Bosner tells us, from "The Death of Cleopatra" to "Casey at the Bat"! Some Mother Goose rhymes were included as well. The book was bound in magazine style, with authors, titles, and pages listed in the Table of Contents, followed by a carefully written introduction. It turned out to be a beautiful and attractive anthology of which the school was proud. And after each class had had a turn to enjoy it together, it came back to the library as one of its choicest possessions.

Nor is it only the children who contribute to the activities. The working principle of this library is that "the more people who give something, in time or ideas or materials, the more meaning the library will have." The Parent Teacher Association had a Library Committee, which helped in a number of ways. Thinking of them as a resource, Miss Bosner cleared out a space in the room to be used as this Committee saw fit. Not a week went by, she tells us, that something wasn't planned for the Library or brought in by this group. Because the chairman happened to be interested in science, there were frequently simple arrangements and materials set up in this field. The P.T.A. News Bulletin carried notes about new books or attractions in the school library. The *Have You Read . . . ?* column was a short but regular feature. Some elderly ladies from the town's sedate residence hotel worked long and hard on a display of Pandora's Box, which they proudly presented to the school library, together with a colorful bouquet of spring flowers. On several occasions throughout the year, special people were brought in to the library to speak on special things —on Flower Arrangement, for example, on Making Books, on Illustrating Books. Invitations to come and listen to these talks were sent to the classrooms, from which any children or all could visit.

The door to the library was always open, Miss Bosner reports. Always, that is, except for one afternoon when a sculptress had been invited in to show and talk about her work with the sixth-graders in the library. She was rather a timid person, and children looking in through the door as they passed made it difficult to hear her. So the door was closed. One other time, Miss Bosner recalls, the door was closed—when the school Superintendent had come in to discuss his experiences with American Indians, and the crowd of children and teachers was especially large. Other than on these two occasions the door to the library was always open. There were places to sit comfortably . . . fresh new things to catch people's eyes . . . always pretty flowers . . . always books, books, books, and children intently reading.

Examining the Role of the School Librarian

So the wise librarian wants children to know and use the library not as a place bound by strict rules, as libraries all too often are, nor indeed as a beautiful place to "emote" about. Rather, she wants boys and girls to know the library as an ordered arrangement of the world, in which, once you find the order, your power is tremendously increased. As one older child puts it, "All the junk of the universe is classified in an orderly way so you can get at it. If you want a book on space travel you can find it. If you want a book on horses, you find that, too. You name it, we have it! If you can't find it yourself, there's always someone to come to your aid."

"I like the children to think of me as a person who has time for one child—for one child or for many," a good school librarian will say. And she does find time for giving significant help to individual children as they come in. Not to replace the teacher in any way, but to use her own special library training and insights to help and further supplement the work which the teachers are doing.

When Mike comes into the library and asks for a good book, for example, the librarian can't simply send him to the card catalogue or even to the particular shelf where story books are kept. Not if she really understands Mike's requests, she can't. For Mike means much more than meets the ear when he says, "I want a good book." He means: "I want a good book that I can read. I want a book that makes sense to me. A book that will carry me further in my exploration of what it is like to be me and to live in the world where I live."

To answer such a request adequately requires of the librarian genuine understanding—understanding that is at least four-fold:

1. The librarian must understand the interests of Mike as a little boy and as this particular little boy.

2. She must understand Mike's spoken language patterns

which, like his interests, are developing primarily within the context of his home and neighborhood living.

3. She must know the content of books available for him in the library.

4. She must be aware of the language patterns used by the various authors for expressing the content, together with pictures which also are part of communication.

The librarian will ponder Mike's request and his possible interests. Fishing is one interest which she knows looms high in his experience. This she knows from conversations with Mike about his out-of-school living. It is not important for her to dwell on the fact that he does not have books in his home. All of his family goes fishing in the nearby lake. This is one way in which Mike's father provides food for a growing family. And if the family members fish together, certainly they talk about fishing. From such talk Mike will be familiar with language patterns which tell about fish. Simply stated patterns which tell about fish being caught, fish getting away, fish being eaten. Oh, yes, and the interminable waiting . . . waiting for the fish to bite.

Does the school library have such a book for a young boy who is just learning to read? A boy who firmly states that he wants a good book? The librarian thoughtfully ponders this, and thinks at once of Bernadine Cook's wonderful book, *The Little Fish That Got Away*. She remembers how faithfully this book, through both pertinent illustration and printed word, reflects the language patterns of fishermen, young and old.

"Then along came a great big fish. And it swam around, and around, and around and around and around. Just like this. (end of page) It looked at the worm on the pin. It waggled its tail. Then it swam around, and around, and around and around and around— Right back to wherever it came from. Just like this. Yes it did. (end of page) The little boy waited and waited—And waited."

Best of all, the eventually successful fisherman in the book is a little boy. Someone who could be just Mike's size when he is out fishing with his father—or, someone who could be much smaller than Mike, depending upon Mike's particular state of mind when he is reading the book.

Yes, the librarian does have a good book to recommend in response to Mike's request. Together they walk over to a low reading table, and the librarian sits by Mike while he tries the book out, as it were. Soon Mike's own fishing experience and the experience of the boy in the book are finding common expression in the author's faithfully organized fish talk. Important lines begin to repeat themselves. Mike has caught the pattern. The librarian can go back to the desk now. Her young friend is on his own reading a good book.

Beginning readers *need* books in which language is used to bring together the author and the reading child. This is accomplished through books in which the written words tick off experience common enough that it can be shared by both author and reader. Nor should this imply that only those children who have actually gone fishing will enjoy *The Little Fish That Got Away*. Fishing, with its widely loved element of flee-and-catch, is one of those experiences that seem to be enjoyed vicariously by children, whether or not they have actually lived through the experience firsthand. Rather, this account of Mike and his librarian is meant to highlight, as illustration, the case of a very satisfying beginning reading encounter, made possible because the librarian has been able to locate a book whose words communicate a language pattern that has grounding in the child's own experience.

In Miss Menlove's library, to cite another example, one could also find children intent on their quests, as individuals or small informal groups with a particular need. Most of the children, having grown up in the school since kindergarten days, were quite independent users of the library, greeting Miss Menlove as an understanding friend, and never hesitating to take any problem to her or to discuss any enthusiasm. Other children were less skilled in their use of the library, sometimes because they were not adept readers, sometimes for other reasons.

Fourth-grade Richard was one who had difficulty. He could

read, Miss Menlove explains, but he was not interested. "Books were the last thing he would turn to on his own. His mother had talked with me many times. She was worried but tried not to let him know it. He would come to the library with his group, but seldom take out a book or show any interest." One day Miss Menlove and another child showed Richard the Landmark Books, and after a period of exploring and leafing through the books he began to read one, then another, then another. He asked his mother to buy some of his favorites for his own library. Weeks later, having read about twelve of these altogether, he was checking out a book one day and happened to see *Commodore Perry and the Opening of Japan* on the desk. "Oh, look," he said to Miss Menlove, his eyes lighting up as he fondled it, "this was the first book I really ever read!"

There was also the case of Debbie. Debbie came into the library at her third-grade teacher's suggestion, since she couldn't find a book in the classroom that she could read. "She was a real stagey little girl," Miss Menlove observes, "very attractive but could hardly read a word." Debbie had been helping Miss Menlove in the library since the middle of second grade, and so knew her well enough not to mind asking for help. Miss Menlove went over to the shelves with Debbie to find *Dress Up and Let's Have a Party,* by Remy Charlip, in which Debbie seemed much interested. Miss Menlove listened to Debbie read some of it before the child left the library, and then said, "Why don't you come back and read it to me all the way through when you have finished it? It's a story I love to hear."

Next day, on her way up to the library with the book, Debbie stopped in dramatically to tell the principal where she was going and what she was going to do. She came on up to the library and read the whole simple story straight through to Miss Menlove. Then, clutching the book tightly to herself, she ran back down to read it to the principal. By the end of a month, Debbie had also taken out *Mr. Apple's Family*—three times because she loved it so. In this she took the greatest of pride, Miss Menlove recalls, because it was really a *fat* book—a beginning "chapter" book, too!

When Judy brought in a poem that she had just finished writing, Miss Menlove found the occasion to suggest: "Would you like to copy it on the primer typewriter, Judy, and we can put it up? It's so very very nice." Judy copied the following poem for the special display on the bulletin board:

Hello Star

Hello star, star up there
Star up there and I know not where

Twinkle with your little light
You're far away, but you look so bright

I wonder if I wish on you
I wonder, will my wish come true

Shine, shine, shine so bright
Guide the traveler through the night

Shine over the hills and over the dales
Over the sea and over the whales

Over the houses you look so nice
Over the heads of the cats and mice

How many are you, I've often wondered
I guess if there's one, there must be a hundred.

One could go on reporting Miss Menlove's ways for meeting the needs of individual children at different stages of development and in different situations. And although these anecdotes might seem to indicate rather simple solutions at first, closer investigation will reveal that basic to each, in one way or another, is the same fourfold understanding that enabled the earlier mentioned librarian to satisfy young Mike's request for a good book. In sum, this means understanding of the children's interests, of their spoken language patterns, of the content of books available for choice, and of characteristic language patterns employed by the authors to express content.

Space does not permit, of course, nor the scope of this book require, further detailed accounts of these activities. Miss Menlove's annotated check list of some aspects of her job as she sees it, a list not unlike that of creative, competent librarians in an increasing number of schools, can serve to suggest the various facets and functional nature of the school librarian's role:

WORKING WITH CHILDREN.

Help individual children to find the right book.

Give children reading help as needed (now and then reading with them or hearing them read).

Have storytelling periods and times for reading *to* children.

Help children to know where to find materials pertinent to a particular problem or interest (to know the basic arrangement of books in the library, to use the card catalogue and other alphabetical listings).

Help children to use reference materials appropriately, *as needed* (to learn to make use of tables of contents and indexes, to learn to skim when appropriate, to take notes effectively and economically "rather than to copy down the whole page," to draw up a bibliography, to make and keep a card file when needed).

Facilitate the circulation of books and materials. (Set up a regular schedule at beginning and close of school, with additional flexible and informal opportunities during the day; develop simple, effective circulation procedures, which children themselves can follow with a minimum of supervision, allowing them to take out and return books at any time . . . "If you don't like it, turn it back and we'll find another.")

Help children from different classes to develop skills as library assistants (through helping with shelving, with working out schedules, with circulation of books, with giving aid to younger children as needed, with making the library attractive, with drawing up book lists, with arranging bulletin boards, with selecting books to be ordered, with cataloguing new books—these jobs to be rotated to give opportunity to many children).

Encourage children to record and share their reading with others in effective and creative ways.

Help children to develop skills of critical reviewing. (A group of children may each choose a book from among those newly received, take it home and read it so they can tell others about it. "I didn't like this book," one might report. "Will someone else read it to see what he thinks?" After reviewing and discussing books informally, find different ways to publicize the books, as: write squibs to be typed and put on the bulletin boards; arrange jackets attractively, with caption, "Sixth-Grade Review Club likes these books"; post signed book reviews; introduce new favorites to groups of children in the library or classrooms; draw up a list of recommended books for the new sixth grade, have these duplicated for distribution in the Fall to children and parents who need them as they come to the Library.)

Provide a place for children to share individual and small group collections (dolls, hobbies, airplanes, stamps, coins— "the small valuables to be kept in the glass case"—all with appropriate captions and accompanying arrangements of related books).

Provide a place, in addition to facilities for reading, for small groups to come and work (to prepare dramatizations, start a painting or story or poem, to be finished at home or in the classroom. "Could you lend that lovely thing to the library when you get through, to put on the wall there by the cupboard or on the low bulletin board?" As the idea catches hold, through school-wide inspiration, contributions are always coming in).

WORKING WITH TEACHERS

Supplement the teachers' efforts in reading guidance and help.

Keep the teachers informed of new and valuable materials available (books, films, pictures, charts, television and radio programs, pertinent community events).

Provide continuous in-service education for interested teachers (ways of improving book reporting and recording, making maximum use of library facilities).

Help teachers select and use appropriate books (for classroom collection, for references on various topics and problems).

Help teachers and children with library skills as needed.

Discover needs children have for research skills (which teachers may not have noted in the classroom).

WORKING WITH PARENTS

Encourage family reading and sharing.

Help parents and teachers with Book Exhibits, Book Week, etc.

Help parents to select books for their children (meet with parent groups to discuss books for children, give them book lists, report children's favorite stories).

Help parents to understand methods and materials used in social studies research (as related to community studies, for instance, water supply, transportation, people of other times and of other countries).

Help parents to appreciate and further children's individual interests (as rockets and space travel, birds, animals, dinosaurs, history, current events, sports, music, travel, biography, people of other parts of the world, plays).

Perhaps this chapter needs no summary, beyond Miss Menlove's list—unless it is to say: Fortunate those children who have a well-equipped library in the school. And still more fortunate, those who have the services of a well-trained, warmhearted, sensitively tuned school librarian. Parents, administrators, boards of education, indeed all who respect children's need to read, please take note!

4

How one school system brought about change

While individual teachers scattered about the country have been individualizing their reading methods down through the years, so too the administrative and supervisory staffs of one school system after another have carefully developed their plans for giving help and encouragement to teachers who wish to work out individualized reading in their classrooms. To review a few of the ways in which one school system, among those the authors know well, sought to make such help available to its teachers, may be of profit here.

Reassuring Teachers about Individual Differences in Reading

When Dr. Ford, the new Director of Elementary Education, came into this city school system, she was not surprised to find great emphasis upon the teaching of reading. Teachers here as elsewhere were especially worried about the "slower" children in all of their classes who, in spite of everything that was done for and with them, were never able to read "up to grade." Every teacher in the city seemed to be gravely concerned about her slowest children—as indeed are teachers most everywhere. The administration as well as the teachers involved were disturbed when the standardized testing was over, and the reading scores in a number of the classes and even in one or two schools fell below the national *norm*. The children's test scores, class by class and school by school, were publicized twice a year, causing some unhealthy comparison and feelings of embarrassment on the part of the teachers. Those who taught in the "better" schools were envied or admired. Both teachers and children in the schools with a poorer showing were exhorted to try harder to do better.

In order to help meet this disturbing but not unusual state of affairs, a remedial reading teacher had been provided by the central office. This remedial specialist, herself a former teacher, worked very hard indeed, and most of the several children fortunate enough to be under her tutelage responded favorably. However, many more children from every school were referred to her for special help than she could possibly find time to see within her crowded schedule. "What we need are several remedial reading specialists," the teachers had commented to one another and to their principals. "We really could use one in every school to good advantage. How can they expect an ordinary teacher, with thirty or thirty-five children, to spend as much time as they really require with the poor readers without neglecting the rest of the class? It just can't be done, that's all. They'll have to give us more help."

This problem was put before their new director, Dr. Ford, as she made her rounds during the first month or two, meeting with each school faculty in the city over a cup of tea or coffee which the teachers generously set up in each case as a way of getting acquainted. "How would *you* teach reading to these children? What do *you* think we can do about the situation? Most of the teachers in this system, as the Superintendent had pointed out, had taught for a good many years. (Forty-eight was the average age of the teachers at the time.) Most of them had been trained two or three decades before, of course, although some were still taking courses each year at the nearby secondary training college in the hope of finishing a degree. All were sincere, hard-working, kindly people, genuinely concerned about the welfare of children and desirous of doing a good job with them.

These teachers were generous also in helping the new director to become aware of their resources as well as their problems. They explained that each of their schools had had its own library for a number of years, due especially to the indefatigable efforts of the library supervisor who had spent most of her professional life in the city's schools, and that the teachers were accustomed to making good use of it with their children. Although they hoped some day to be able to afford the services of a trained librarian in each of the elementary schools, the policy currently followed was that of having a fifth- or sixth-grade teacher and her children assume responsibility for the operation of the library. This teacher would work with the library supervisor in making out the annual book requisitions and in classifying the new books as they came in. She and her children would make out the schedule for use of the library by different classes, take responsibility for book circulation, for story-telling and reading with each of the younger classes once a week, and in countless ways try to make the library of genuinely functional service to the school. Everyone recognized the value of these libraries in the development of which their school system was a widely reputed pioneer. Still, so far as the skills were concerned, at least among those children who had the most difficulty, this seemed to have little bearing on the actual reading results. So some of the teachers pointed out, at any rate, for so the tests had shown.

The possibilities of individualizing reading were explored and discussed at this point, and considerable interest was shown. Building on the quite remarkable library facilities, a move in the direction of individualized reading in the classroom (or *individual* reading as it became known in this school system) seemed a natural one. At least it was something to think of and learn more about, said the teachers.

It also seemed important to Dr. Ford, even in these first discussions with teacher groups, to help them look at this business of individual differences within a single classroom as a wholly normal, even universal, situation. It is normal for children in a classroom to vary widely in their reading ability, no matter how homogeneously grouped or effectively taught. This is just plain fact, the director emphasized. The people who recognize these wide differences are not the ones who make them, or even who advocate that such be the case. But children are like that; they differ widely. Normal, healthy children the country over, differ widely—and usually not through any fault of their own, or of their parents, or even of their teachers. Children are children. Although alike in many ways, they are individually different—different physically, in ways which usually show, and different in every other way, which may not show as plainly at the outset. This is the way children are. And we might as well accept the fact and live with it. To expect all children in a class or school to come up to—and indeed down to—the grade or the national norm is absurd! Children do not come that way; neither does the norm. If all children did make the norm or above, it would no longer be the norm. It is the *expectations* that are wrong, not the children.

Helping Them Feel "At Home on the Range"

And so the discussions went, not only at these initial meetings of teachers, but on subsequent occasions throughout the year, and the years that followed. There were committee meetings of various kinds in this school system, meetings at the central office where teachers and principals were invited to come together to pool interesting experiences and ideas they were finding helpful. There was the monthly Elementary Planning meeting, when a committee of teachers, principals, and supervisors met with the Superintendent of Schools and the Director of Elementary Education to evaluate and project plans. It was during a discussion at one of these Elementary Planning sessions that the Superintendent made a facetious remark which was soon to become famous. When someone quoted a seventh-grade teacher's expression of dismay that some of her children came to seventh grade able to read only at fifth- and sixth-grade levels, the point was reiterated that, no matter how well the children were taught in elementary schools they would never *all* be reading at the seventh-grade level when they came into junior high school. Some would be reading at fifth, sixth, seventh, eighth, ninth, and some perhaps even higher. For always, in any class of children, it was noted, there is a range of ability of some three to five years or more, with the range naturally widening as the children go on up through the grades.

At this, the Superintendent, with a mischievous look in his eye, said: "Well, then, it looks to me as if the biggest job we have to do with our teachers is to help them feel At Home on the Range!" That said it. The statement was not as facetious as he had meant it to be. That really *was* the job, everyone agreed. Help teachers to be at ease with the wide range of abilities and interests and ways of learning they are bound to meet in their classrooms. Help them to accept children as they are, every one of them, and to help each to move ahead from there—with self-respect and satisfaction. That was the job for the whole school system—helping teachers to feel At Home on the Range. Exploring possibilities for individualizing reading would be but a part of it.

As a matter of fact, all of this was something of a restatement about individual differences which had been a concern of the school system for a good long time. Only within the past year or two there had been a change in the system of report cards for just that reason. And what a furor it had caused, innocently enough! Developed and proposed by the city-wide Report Card Committee, and subsequently approved by the administration, the new report had carried, under the caption of Reading, a space for noting the particular grade level at which the child read. Thus, a child in the sixth grade who was very adept at reading might take home on his report card the notation that he was reading at seventh- or eighth-grade level in reading, since the teacher had found from his performance with the group reading materials and from his choice of library books that this was about his level of reading. Similarly, some of the very poor readers in the class had been checked on the report cards as third- or fourth-grade in reading since the materials at that level or below were the only ones these children were able to read with a fair degree of facility and understanding.

The intent of this practice was sound, of course, but what trouble resulted! If my child is reading at the seventh-grade level, why isn't he in seventh grade and not sixth, parents would ask of the teachers. And it was worse still from the other end of the scale. Then he will not be promoted, my sixth-grade boy, since he is only third grade in reading. Why did you not tell me, and we could *make* him read better? Only *third grade*—not even last year did the teacher tell me.

Broadening the Concept of Grade Level

The Planning Committee now looked at these reporting difficulties anew. What had started as a sympathetic recognition that children in the same grade do differ had come to appear less sympathetic when it carried the old labels. Again, it was the labels that were at fault, the committee realized now, not the children. So, too, with the reading tests. They and not the children were giving the wrong impression about grade levels and children's reading status—about their teachers' status, too. True, it was standardized tests that gave proof, scientific proof, that sixth-grade children in any classroom were not all at sixth-grade level, so called, nor first at first, nor third at third. It was test scores that showed beyond a doubt that the usual range in a classroom extended from three to five or six years or more.

Had the test makers and testers only stopped there, Dr. Ford was heard to observe time and again, they could have made such a crucial contribution. "Look, teachers, parents, administrators, makers of children's books and of other learning materials," they could have said. "Look, this is the way children are. The grade level is four or five or six years wide. It's as wide as the range of abilities of the children in it, as shown on these tests! Let's plan and work accordingly!" That is what the test makers had discovered with scientific, standardized instruments. And that is what they should have told us. It would have set education on the track of reality and improvement for all time.

But they did not tell us that, although that is what their test scores said. Instead they straightaway found the norm, with 50 percent of the ability above the line and fifty below. And this narrow, narrow range, hugging closely above and below the norm, they call the *grade level,* as if that is where all of the children in any grade *should* be. Those who are not are automatically labeled at grade levels above or below. Is it the children then who are to blame for being what they *are,* instead of what the test makers and test users imply that they *should* be?

Helping teachers to feel at home on the range, then, meant taking a critical look at this whole grade-level concept and at everything so labeled. Realistically, the grade level—if there is one—must be the level at which children in the grade *are;* and that must be wide enough and flexible enough to encompass them all, whatever their abilities. Nor will it remain the same for any length of time. It should be continually changing, moving ahead for every child—at different rates, of course, and in different ways since, as repeated again and again, that is how children are. The important thing is to take every child where he is, quite as if he had a right and a reason to be there—which he has—and to do everything within the power of the school to help him to move on from there.

So . . . what did this mean in their own classrooms, the teachers were asked and were asking themselves at meetings of one kind and another throughout the year—in the field of reading, say? Didn't it mean that children, every one of the thirty in a class, should have the chance to read materials that held challenge and interest for them, and which they could handle confidently and with reasonable success? Didn't it mean, further, that to meet this demand the children must have some part in the selection of what they read? That they should have the chance to read along at their own rate, with whatever help and guidance they needed, unimpeded by having to wait while everyone in the class or group, fast or slow, had to take his turn? It seemed clear to many that some kind of individualized reading program was the only solution. How to work out such a program in a regular classroom, to meet effectively the needs of *every child,* became the major concern.

Encouraging Individual Effort and Resourcefulness

This called for resourceful and carefully thought through help and encouragement for teachers on the part of the supervisory staff. It was a more exciting venture all around, for supervisors as well as teachers, once the teachers accepted as a recognized fact—and not one of their own making—the wide range of differences at work in every classroom. It followed naturally that the philosophy of individualizing reading would be pretty much in the air, however scattered the voluntary commitment on the part of individual teachers. By this time, too, it had become quite obvious that the services of a single remedial reading teacher, working directly with individual children referred to her by the school principals, was not the kind of help the *teachers* most needed. It began to make sense that the same amount of the reading specialist's time could be given to *helping teachers set up their classrooms for individualizing reading,* finding appropriate materials, developing sensitive ways for guiding individual children's reading, keeping records, providing challenge to the variety of individual children with whom they were working, and otherwise finding ways for making their teaching more effective. In this way, so it would seem, the benefit to children as well as to the teachers would be extended a hundredfold.

So, after long, hard consideration and discussion by the Planning Committee, the supervisory staff, the principals, and various teacher groups, it was decided that both the Remedial Reading Teacher and the Language Arts Supervisor (both former classroom teachers) would become general Resource Teachers, to work with the Director of Elementary Education and the rest of the supervisory staff in any way and in any field in which they could be of service to the schools. Serving on call with classroom teachers and principals, as well as helping to develop policy in the central office, they were able to use their strengths and resources to much more fruitful ends for all concerned.

The kinds of help in reading made available to teachers were many and varied. Conferences were held from time to time, with many or few, and teachers participated willingly in those meetings which seemed to them most promising—even though they were set up on a voluntary basis. There was really something very satisfying, teachers discovered, about going to the central office for a cup of coffee and good stimulating talk with fellow teachers and friends. The supervisory staff tried in numerous ways to let them know they were trusted as teachers, that the staff had faith in them, felt they were competent, recognized the worth of their long experience and understanding of the community, as important factors in the solution of any problems that confronted the schools.

Although they were encouraged to ponder, observe, find out about, and discuss with one another the possibilities and problems of individualizing reading, individual teachers were advised to take whatever time they needed for making changes, if any, in this direction. "Teachers can teach best in ways *they* believe in, in ways in which *they* feel comfortable. Take whatever next steps you feel are right for *you* to take, since you know yourselves and your set-up better than anyone else. It's not a matter of moving too fast or too slow into new ways of doing things. Let's move just as fast as we can feel good about moving—no faster, and no more slowly. If you feel better teaching reading the way you have always done it, then go ahead with it in that way, of course—so long as you do it deliberately, studying and thinking about and observing what is happening to the children in the meantime. *You* teach in the way *you* feel is right for you and your children, and call on us whenever you think we can be of help to you—in any way."

An interesting thing was happening now with regard to attitudes toward the teaching of reading. Once the focus of help to teachers had shifted from the specialized to the more general, teachers throughout the system were ceasing to single out the few individual cases in each of their classrooms who needed remedial help. Rather, they themselves assumed responsibility for their total group, however wide the range of abilities in it, reorienting their outlook, organizing their program, selecting and ordering materials, marveling at children's changing attitudes and progress, and even asking for help within a new framework of thinking.

One way of reassuring teachers in this vein was to stop publicizing the comparative test scores, which for some schools, of course, were always high and for others not; this plan was agreed to almost at the outset. In fact, once the spread of the class or school scores came to be more expected than lamented, the usefulness of the tests did not lie in grade-to-grade or school-to-school comparisons. The relief was evident at once on the part of teachers in certain schools. Not that they let up in their concern for helping children to read—not one whit. On the contrary, they worked long and hard to find ways for more effectively helping individual children, once they were *free* to be thoughtful and searching rather than fearful.

The school system took a good look at the total testing program, about this time, and on the elementary school level finally decided to test in reading, writing, spelling, and arithmetic in fourth and sixth grades only, more as a way of reassuring themselves and their community that the school system was comfortably up to or above the national norm. In addition, any teacher who wanted her class or individual children tested at any time, for whatever reason, would be granted this service by the Research and Testing Department of the schools. The Child Guidance Bureau too was making its own appropriate uses of testing at any point in the development of individual children concerned.

Building and Valuing Support from All Quarters

A further factor in helping to relieve many teachers of long-time pressure and an unpleasant sense of inadequacy, was the growing realization that the consistent complaints of the junior high and high school people about children's varied reading abilities upon entering secondary schools, had been at least partially based on a misunderstanding of children and how they learn. Inviting the secondary school teachers and principals to join in the study and discussions about reading, as well as other professional concerns, proved helpful to all. And the discovery that many of these people, although as usual not the most vocal, had long had great respect for the elementary teachers of the system, came as a pleasant and bracing surprise to those who seemed to need just this kind of reassurance.

When some of the junior high school teachers themselves began to individualize the reading programs in their own class-rooms, as many of them did—especially in the combination elementary-junior high schools, where the help of the principals as well as the elementary supervisory staff was asked—there was a bona fide though quiet rejoicing among their elementary colleagues.

That changes in the reading program should be voluntary rather than imposed was stressed with principals as well as with other supervisors and teachers. Principals too had to feel competent and trusted in order to do their best job. Furthermore, the concept of the principal as a real leader in the school, a leader in the sense of drawing out and developing the leadership in all with whom he worked, necessitated *his* understanding the philosophy and techniques of individualizing reading, and his growing ability to help and actively support those teachers in the school who chose to try it.

Many of the meetings of the principals and supervisors were given over to exploration and discussion of such expanding responsibilities, and of appropriate ways for seeking and giving help on the part of all concerned. From time to time a classroom teacher or two would be invited in to help with these discussions. Also, principals were welcomed at whatever meetings were planned for the teachers. And always some of them came, with everyone glad for the opportunity to be working together. Usually someone from the Child Guidance Bureau joined these meetings, too, and very frequently a parent or two and a junior high and high school teacher or principal. The elementary teachers valued the interest and help of all of these people. It was vital to their progress.

Perhaps no one in the school system was more interested, more thoughtful, more genuinely supportive with regard to moving into a program of individualizing reading, than was the Superintendent of Schools himself. Whenever he could pull away from an already too-full schedule, he would drop in at a teachers' or supervisors' staff meeting, look at the problems with them, listen to accounts of progress, ask very sincere questions and ponder the teachers' responses. Whenever he happened into a classroom, for whatever purpose, and saw signs of individualized reading in progress, he would observe with interest, question or commend the children and the teacher in a friendly and interested way.

"I'd like you to watch especially those two young teachers I hired while you were away," he commented one day to Dr. Ford on her return from a summer school teaching position, and went on to tell of the interview he had had with them. "After they had told me of their ideas on teaching reading, I described our individual reading program to them. They seemed to be much impressed," he went on proudly, "and asked very good questions. I sensed a good deal of competence on the part of both of them as we talked."

It was important also that the children's parents should understand something of the purposes of the program, since they too were closely involved. This became a concern then at small parent meetings, study groups, and Parent Teachers meetings, as well as during the individual parent-teacher conferences which were coming more and more to supplement, and to a degree replace, written report cards in the system. Teachers and administrators made it a point to explain the program, to answer questions, show the quite remarkable reading records, invite cooperation, and in other ways help parents to know and be part of what was going on. Parents visiting the classrooms during the day were frequently asked by individual children to hear them read, to take down their dictated stories, to help them find a particular kind of book.

The community was also appreciative of the recommended book lists that the library supervisor drew up from time to time to help parents and grandparents select appropriate books as gifts for their children. Now and then individual schools, with the help of parents, would put on book exhibits or book fairs in their libraries. November Book Week in the schools was always a popular time with parents.

Getting Started in Different Ways

It is difficult to say what were the things that helped most in encouraging individual teachers throughout the school system to move into individualized reading. It was obvious that all of the teachers would not, or could not, crowd out old ways with new ones all at once. Genuine progress is seldom, if ever, a matter of full-blown shift. Some teachers there were who, through the years, had made much of library reading as an important part of their total reading program. These teachers needed little more than the initial discussions to get themselves going in the organization of an individualized reading program.

Furthermore, they were always happy to share their discoveries with anyone interested. Sometimes, one or two or three in a school would get started, talk with their principal and with one another as to how they were setting about finding more suitable materials, giving more appropriate individual help, keeping more valuable records, making friendly help more easily available to children. Some teachers, even in the same school, preferred to hold to their usual three-group basic book method, with only a slight change here and there—such as more emphasis on library reading, perhaps. But all of this was acceptable to the administration, who maintained that an individualized reading program worthy of the name calls for opportunity for self-selection on the part of teachers as well as of children.

In their own school staff meetings, in the meetings at the central office, in various committee meetings, teachers and principals would report with enthusiasm, listen to the accounts of others who were working in this direction, and both give and receive help in the most friendly and stimulating way. Sometimes they would ask one of the resource teachers or Dr. Ford to drop in and see if she could help them work out a particular problem. Always these teachers were willing to have interested visitors from other school systems come to their classrooms, perhaps to meet later at lunch with the visitors and supervisory staff, to answer questions about what they were doing, how much more all the children were reading, how the demand for a variety of books was increasing, how they were trying cooperatively to meet these demands, and other questions their colleagues or the visitors would ask.

Because the program was voluntary—the administration had to continually reassure those who were still using their long-practiced methods that they meant what they said—there was little reason for anyone to be on the defensive, whatever the practices honestly and thoughtfully followed. Teachers were encouraged to develop their own individual ways of working in the classroom, to keep their own records, to share them in any ways they or their principals saw fit. The supervisory staff let them know in a variety of ways how proud they were of the progress being made. How proud they were too that teachers would not let themselves be pushed into teaching in a certain way if it did not truly make sense to them. Sometimes this was hard to do, but it was considered important enough to command special effort. Indeed, it was this voluntary aspect of the program, this starting by a few and spreading as if by contagion, that seemed to account for the generally warm and constructive attitudes toward the program. Even those who took the longest time about accepting it as their own way of working, seemed to be proud that their school system was exploring new ways and moving ahead.

Organizing "In-Service Education" in Reading

The teachers were getting and giving help then in a variety of ways. There were the pooling sessions earlier referred to. There was the publicizing of good things the supervisory staff saw on their visits to the school (always with emphasis on the positive, however conscientiously one had to look for it). There were the oral and written accounts individual teachers and principals brought or sent in from time to time. There were the meetings held especially for the growing number of new teachers now coming into the system, but to which anyone else was invited to come and help—including, in addition to teachers and principals, the high school seniors interning in the elementary schools as part of their precollege and senior social studies program.

In addition to all of this, the administration provided another source of help which proved unusually fruitful. With a subsidy from the Board of Education, they invited a not-too-distant university to come and help set up a Workshop on the Teaching of Reading, to which the school people brought their own reading problems and resources and, with the help of jointly selected university and public school consultants, worked out their own indigenous solutions. The visiting consultants would usually arrange to spend a few hours in the local schools, visiting classes, talking with principals and supervisors, and with teachers, too, whenever possible, before joining the workshop.

Participation in the workshop carried college credit for those who needed it, and professional stimulation and genuine camaraderie for all who wished to participate, credit or no credit. Many teachers, principals, supervisors, a few parents, and on occasion, the Superintendent, availed themselves of this opportunity and had a wonderful time. For the entire semester the workshop met both before and after dinner once a week. This might have seemed like a long hard pull for teachers and others who had worked hard all day; but the intervening supper and singing and general good time, in addition to the stimulating discussions, exchange of experiences, lectures, and planned visits to libraries and classrooms, always seemed to give them a second wind. They loved being together at these times, and all the things they were trying to do in other ways to help improve their teaching of reading and ways of working with the children generally, were reenforced and strengthened and integrated with the workshop program. Indeed, it was found to be so profitable that similar plans, related to other areas of the curriculum and needs of the teachers, were organized for succeeding semesters.

Helping to Provide Appropriate Materials

Needless to say, this growing emphasis on individualizing reading meant a substantial increase in the number and kind of books requested for the library, as well as for individual classrooms. The schools were already pretty well stocked with sets of basal and supplementary readers from several publishers, never having adopted any *single* system of teaching reading over the years. Always the school budget had included both trade book and textbook items. Now the schools found themselves with each requisition ordering proportionately more trade books, with special attention to sufficient variety to ensure that all children in the school could select from large numbers of books those they were able to read. Classroom teachers, teacher librarians, principals, supervisors, the library supervisor, special curriculum committees, as well as Dr. Ford and others of the central office, laid special stress on this aspect of book ordering. In addition, since self-selection involved in individualized reading implies increased provision for self-selection in other phases of the school day, the administration encouraged the ordering of certain kinds of science and art and other supplies this necessitated, sometimes arranging to subsidize from the general budget particular orders they wished to promote in the schools.

All of this gave impetus to still fuller and more intensive use of the school libraries. Books were off the library shelves more than they were on, partly because of increased borrowing by teachers for classroom use. It was evident, from the way the stock of simpler books was always depleted, that upper grade teachers as well as lower were trying to provide for every child the books he was able to read—books for him to grow on. There was every kind and on every subject. There were individual demands from time to time also for books of what might be termed "high school level"—and for everything in between—as teachers helped children to find reading materials appropriate for them. There were frequent runs on favorite books as well as demands for new ones. The need for trained and paid librarians to help shoulder the responsibilities now carried by hard-working sixth-grade teachers and their children became more and more apparent as the program developed.

Organizing for Maximum Progress

Another plan employed, to help teachers of the youngest children especially to move in the direction of individualizing programs for children, was to encourage a number of kindergarten teachers to go into first grade the following year with their children. This practice of staying with the same children for two years was already being followed by some of the middle- and upper-grade teachers, to notable advantage. With the youngest children now it was found particularly helpful. It seemed to give continuity not only to the children's learning, but also to the teacher's thoughtful planning and setting up of the classroom for varied activities, to include gradually more and more individual and group use of reading. Also, the close contacts of kindergarten parents with the school seemed more apt to persist through first grade when the first-grade teacher was someone whom they and their children already knew well.

A program of individualizing reading proved to be a boon too to teachers who, because of the system's determination to keep class size down to thirty in spite of increased school popu- lation, were obliged to teach combination classes—first and second, say, third and fourth, fourth and fifth—or "mixed grades," as they had come to call them. With individualized reading it proved possible, even preferable, to work with the children as if they were one class, with the usual wide variations, rather than two distinct classes whose abilities, of course, over- lapped, sometimes embarrassingly. Indeed, teachers found it easier, with help and encouragement from the supervisory staff —including concrete help in the classroom from the resource teachers or their own principal—to extend this way of working with the children to other areas of the school day, as already indicated.

At first it bothered parents to have the grade levels or distinctions between separate grades in a single classroom erased—just as it had earlier bothered teachers. Parents, like teachers, had to be reassured that this would mean neither holding back certain children nor accelerating others. Parents needed help to see that a better program could be provided when the class functioned as one unified, if widely varying, group of youngsters, with opportunities for self-selection and appropriate individual and small-group guidance being thereby greatly expanded. Before long parents too tended to accept the philosophy as practiced. This acceptance became less wavering as time went on, of course, and they were able to note the proof of the pudding.

It was also easier for parents to accept the idea—again, as it was for the teachers and principals—when the basis for dividing a grade was shifted from that of reading or other achievement scores to the simpler matter of chronological age. That is, when part of a too-large third grade was to be combined with part of a too-large fourth, to become a combined or mixed third-fourth group, the chronological age of the children could serve as the determining factor, now that grouping children on the basis of reading ability was no longer essential to the reading plan. In this way, a serious complication that had plagued the school system for years was largely eliminated. A sensitively planned, well-provided-for individualized reading program could fit these combined classes like a glove!

Helping through Practical Bulletins

Quite obviously, then, the help the school system offered teachers in developing individualized reading was not concerned with the reading of books alone. Rather, emphasis was put on extending the functional use of reading and writing and speaking throughout the school day. A large part of many meetings, in the schools, the workshops, or the central office, was devoted to helping teachers in this way—and encouraging them to help one another. The Language Arts Committee put out a brief but helpful bulletin on Functional Writing. Another group helped the supervisory staff to revise an older bulletin, on The Teaching of Spelling, to reflect the ways in which phonics and word attack can be better taught at times when the words are already out of context, than when individual children are absorbed in a story and ask for help on a word.

The following rather comprehensive bulletin, drawn up at the central office by the Director of Elementary Education and one of the resource teachers (the former remedial reading teacher) some time *after* the individualized (or individual) reading program had really begun to take hold, was sent out to all teachers and principals. It seemed a good way of passing on genuine reassurance and of suggesting possible next steps:

DEPARTMENT OF EDUCATION
Division of Elementary Education

Some Suggestions on Individual Reading

READING CAN BE FUN

A love for books—a love for reading—is a natural outgrowth of the individual reading program which is based on the belief that "we must learn to read by reading."

Even before they come to kindergarten, many children have had pleasant contact with books and the process of reading. They have watched, maybe imitated, father reading the paper, brothers and sisters losing themselves in bedtime stories or library books. They have enjoyed books of their own. They have listened to mother or father read stories to them, have looked at the pictures and turned the pages, later "reading" and rereading their own creative versions as the pictures inspire.

In kindergarten and first grade their reading experiences have continued, pleasant and happy ones. All kinds of interesting colorful reading go to make up their classroom environment. Listening to stories together is a favorite pastime. So is perusing picture books or simple story books at the library table. Children like to read of their own experiences also—putting together things that they or the teacher have said and the teacher has written in large clear manuscript—on a chart or on the blackboard—or has duplicated for all of the children. They enjoy simple, true stories about Our Trip to the Dairy, about Mary's Baby Sister, The Little Black Dog, Making Ice Cream, Our New Playground Tunnels, and other events and experiences which they recall vividly and with pleasure. Sometimes the teacher writes their individual stories in "books" of their own which they love to illustrate; later they make their own and have fun exchanging them with one another.

At any time of the year then the first grade program is chuck-full of interesting things to do and to read. Attractive charts, some old, some new, are up on the wall or in a large book on the library table. Children like to read them again and again, individually or with one another. The bulletin board holds a large letter of invitation from the second grade to see their play. There is also a letter from

John who has moved to Florida, some of the postcards he has sent, and perhaps a copy of the children's letters to John which they had dictated to the teacher, illustrated with their own pictures, and mailed in the box close by.

Ruth's collection of shells in the back of the room carries labels she made for them. The Science Table this week is divided into two parts, with materials tested and classified under the captions "Things That Will Float" and "Things That Will Not Float." The recipe for Gingerbread is on the blackboard, in anticipation of class preparations for this month's birthday party. On the blackboard also is a caption: "Those Who Will Bring Orange Crates Tomorrow," under which several children have signed their names.

And books—books—books, of all sizes and shapes, full of interesting colorful pictures and stories that are fun to listen to, to read with the teacher, to read quietly or aloud "to one's self," or to read with one another. Some children at an early age achieve a degree of independence in reading which enables them, with occasional help from the teacher or another child, to read along for considerable periods quite uninterruptedly. Others need almost continuous help in the earliest stages, reading aloud to the teacher, taking turns reading aloud with one or two other children; and these early stages may extend throughout the entire year for some. Reading, book reading, all kinds of functional reading, based upon and grown out of their whole gamut of enjoyable, profitable experience, contribute to the program for children in the early grades, as well as later.

Of necessity the program will be geared to the wide range of differences in the abilities of the children. A roomful of normal, lively six-year-olds varies widely; so do fives, so do sevens. So do children through every year of the school.

It is as the children come to gain independence in reading that the individual reading program, as our school system is working with it, takes on especial significance. Each child, according to this program, tends to spend his whole "reading period" reading, without such interruptions as group "motivation," questions and answers, reading word lists, or keeping the place and listening while others read.

INDIVIDUAL DIFFERENCES

To repeat, within each group or grade we always find a wide range of abilities and interests. This holds true of reading as well as of all other skills. Standardized test scores the country over give scientific proof of this. Expecting all children, because they are eight years old and in the third grade, to read at a particular "third grade level" is quite as absurd as to assume that all eight-year-olds, because they are eight years old, should wear size nine shoes. The grade level of any classroom of children is always as wide as the range of abilities and interests of the children in it. This is important to remember. Using the individual method of reading, it is possible, as soon as a fair degree of independence is established, to take each child *where he is* and help him to progress in reading effectiveness to his maximum potentiality. There is no stigma attached to the slower reader because he, as the others, will be reading a book suited to his interest and level of maturity. For the more mature reader, this way of working offers untold possibilities because there are no restraining or limiting factors to hold him down to the group tempo.

MATERIALS

The individual reading program makes it imperative that each classroom be equipped with a wide variety of books and other reading materials suited to the range of interest and ability of the class. There should be a sufficient amount of material at hand to offer each child a choice. *Full* use of the school library books, the Public Library books, the books already in the room, and home resources make this possible. Reading books of different kinds and difficulty supply stories which certain children will read and enjoy.

METHOD

There is no magical formula for teaching according to the individual reading program. Each teacher will develop her own method with her class and will work out her own techniques as she experiments.

One way of starting an individual reading program is as follows:

Start with your "best" group of readers. Have them bring to the reading circle library books, reading texts, or other interesting source materials. Suggest to the group that they try a different way of working today—that each will read his own book to himself, going as far as time permits, not waiting for the teacher or other members of the group. If a child meets a word he does not know or cannot work out by himself, he will simply point to it and the teacher will *tell* him the word. He will then go right on with his own reading. In the meantime, the teacher invites one child to sit in an extra chair placed beside her and asks the child to read to her individually. This child will read in a low voice so that just the teacher can hear. This will not disturb the others who are reading.

While the teacher listens to the child beside her read on in his story from his own book, she gives him help as needed and makes mental note of his interest, ability and specific needs. At the same time she can note with little effort that others are interested and intent on their own reading and can encourage continuous reading on their part by casually telling the words they need as she glances in their direction. *Each* child is treated in a similar fashion, reading for a short time with the teacher alone and then returning to his chair in the circle to continue by himself. Because the teacher notes each child's reading needs at this time, she will find that she can follow these through in other situations within the total program which involves use of the same skills (spelling, written work, research and science, social studies, arithmetic, etc.). As teacher and children become familiar with the individual reading process, other individuals or groups are gradually drawn into this reading plan until the entire class is using individual reading. From time to time also, pairs of children, or groups of three, either in the reading circle or elsewhere in the classroom, may be reading softly to one another. Some teachers prefer at the outset to alternate these plans with their present reading program, making the complete change only as they see the value of it.

SHARING

The individual reading program places a great emphasis on group enterprise as related to reading. There is stimulation and pleasure in sharing with others, in large or small groups as occasion warrants—the exciting experiences, the thrilling adventures, the important discoveries, the choice selections we have found in books. Sometimes this may be done by dramatizations or by prepared "audience" reading. Drawing information from different books about a common interest, often opens up possibilities for wider reading from many sources. Book reports are challenging when presented in a variety of ways such as illustrated written accounts, simple puppetry, clay models of book characters for exhibit, group discussion of different books read by the same author, demonstrations of experiments described in books, creative plays, quiz programs, etc. A good test of the effectiveness of a SHARING EXPERIENCE is the number of children on the "waiting list" which follows for these books shared.

RECORD KEEPING

A record of each child's reading is kept. This contains the date, the author and the title of each book he has read, both inside and outside school, including regular readers (which also prove to be much more interesting if read without interruption.) To minimize competition and pressure this record might better be kept *by the teacher* in a class notebook, using a double page for each child. If the child, as he finishes a book, brings it with this notebook (opened to his page) to the teacher, it will conserve teacher time spent in record keeping. The reason for suggesting that the teacher keep these records herself, especially in the lower grades, is to insure accuracy, to aid the child in the appropriate selection of books, and to serve him with an example of the proper form for a bibliography. The teacher making such a record has a check on the child's reading, can tell something of his growth, of the choice and balance of interests, maturity of selections, etc. Later these pages may be detached and clipped into the child's folder as a permanent record of growth in taste and ability and as a source of information on books read for succeeding teachers.

IMPORTANT WAYS IN WHICH CHILDREN SHOW GROWTH IN READING (as compiled by our Workshop in March:)

"Lick their chops about a book"—lose themselves in a story—*love to read*

Take books home to read—read during leisure time

Recognize need and develop facility for different kinds of reading, as skimming, reading directions, rapid reading, searching for relevant materials, noting details, etc.

Read fluently and with increased understanding

Read with a sense of discrimination—recognize and make allowance for bias—not "swallow whole"—weigh or test reliability of materials

Learn difference between secondary and primary sources of information

React to functional reading in in-school and out-of-school environment

Recognize difference between fact and fancy—detect relevancy of materials—see relation of factual information to a particular problem

Develop research techniques—learn to use reference materials, card catalogues, indexes, table of contents, etc.,—learn to take notes, organize materials, speak from notes

Become acquainted with authors and illustrators—know their subjects, styles, etc.

Identify themselves as authors or illustrators through writing or making their own books and materials

Know role of publishers—where to find name of publisher, date of publication

Respond to format—know how books are made—know function of title page, end papers, and the like

React to literary beauty, apt choice of words, appropriateness of style

Appreciate current trends and changes in children's books—make demands known, as: more mature content on easy level, more and better mystery stories for boys, etc.

Select books appropriately—for individual or audience reading—choose with deepening insight

Read aloud effectively to others—vary style and manner to suit audience situations

Develop wide interest in reading—help work out well-balanced program for themselves—keep record of books read

Share books enthusiastically—tell or write about them to others in unique and effective fashion—work out dramatizations, radio programs, posters, book exhibits

VALUES

The following statements of values come from teachers who are using the individual approach to reading:

1. Being able to read on his own interest level, a child is stimulated to read widely and his enthusiasm remains high.
2. Using individual reading, a child can finish a book he is interested in because he can use the same book for reading period, for outside reading, or for free reading time. (Some children under other plans have never had the personal satisfaction that comes from being able to read completely through a story or a book.)
3. The opportunity to share with others books enjoyed by individuals stimulates wider reading for all.
4. There is more practice in reading, for each child reads almost every minute of the reading period, in addition to other times in the day's program.
5. Generally, children read much better and show more growth in reading skill because they are reading more and thoroughly enjoy reading.
6. The "slow" reader enjoys individual reading because he has

the close attention of the teacher when she is working with him. Many others are enjoying easy books with him. He does not suffer embarrassment by having to read poorly before others—when he does audience reading he has time to prepare so he can read well.

7. The quality of oral or audience reading is improved.

8. There is more attention to author, title, and type of content because a child who reads and enjoys a particular book wants to find others written by the same author or about a similar interest.

QUESTIONS

There have been many questions from teachers about the individual reading plan. The following is a sampling of these questions and answers:

Question: Is there a time when children work in groups?

Answer: Yes, many times. The purpose for grouping, however, is again a functional one. For instance, a group might meet to share experiences with books, generally, or on a particular interest.

Individuals, pairs, or small groups may read choice selections to each other or to the entire class (participants will be *prepared* so that pride in accomplishment will result). There might be a group formed to practice a specific reading skill, to do research in social studies or science, to plan and prepare a particular report, a chapter in a class book, a play for the Book Week program. Very often the slow reader and the skillful reader will be members of the same group. These are but a few examples of possibilities for grouping. Grouping will be flexible, and all groups should be purposeful to the children.

Question: When do we check such skills as noting details, selecting relevant thoughts, answering questions which test comprehension, anticipating outcomes, etc.?

Answer: These skills acquire a functional setting when developed in relation to such activities as science, social studies, arithmetic. Here children have a real purpose for achieving them.

Question: How are phonetic skills accomplished?

Answer: Much of the phonetic work may be done profitably in relation to spelling when the words are already isolated and when children are dealing with words already familiar to them. Every effort should be made to help children carry over the skill developed in spelling and reading. Individual work on word attack may also be given when the teacher is hearing the child read.

Question: When will a teacher find time for this kind of reading?

Answer: The individual program need not take more time than any other. As the program gets under way, there will be some children whom the teacher will want to hear read every day. There will be others who will not need this because they will be independent enough to work by themselves with only occasional guidance. When we had group reading from the same book, the teacher would usually try to meet each group daily and give each child a chance to read in his group. In many instances, then, the individual reading places less demand on teacher time.

READING, in this analysis, as well as other language arts, becomes an integral part of the total school program. Why not label *all* the reading we do READING? It will please the parents and give all of us, too, a sense of security.

Part One: Summary

All of the chapters in Part One have expressed in one way or another the following significant facts:

• Children need to read.

• Individual children vary widely in their ways of approaching reading.

• There is no one best way for organizing the individualized reading of books by children in the classroom.

• Teachers must give children the particular kind of help they need to learn to read.

- Children need to feel good about themselves and reading.

- Children need opportunity to read uninterruptedly from books they can read.

- Children need sensitive friendly help available—to be told the words they do not know.

- Help in analysis of words can be more useful to children at other times of day, when it does not interrupt the story or content.

- Children need opportunity to select from a variety of good books from the beginning.

- The more of the reading period individual children spend *reading*—not discussing and not listening to other children take turns reading—the better they are apt to read and to comprehend what they are reading.

- Word drills, motivation discussions, other step-by-step group procedures at the time of story or book reading are sure to be a waste of time for many children.

- Teachers and administrators should accept the fact that children of the same age differ widely in reading ability.

- Expectations that all children in a class will or should read at the narrowly-defined "grade level" are unscientific, unrealistic, and unfair to children. It is the expectations, not the children, that are at fault that they do not all come up to the norm or above.

- Every child should be genuinely accepted and respected as and where he is in reading and helped to go on from there.

- Teachers do not have to give children tests to find out where they are in reading. Opportunity for them to select from a good variety of books those which they find they can read, will give the teacher much more reliable information about her individual children and their reading.

- The opportunity to read uninterruptedly from a choice of books he can read and enjoy is important for children, not only in elementary school, but on up through junior and senior high school as well. Their range of abilities and interests in reading will naturally grow wider as the children grow older.

part two

HELPING CHILDREN READ

*...through individualizing
ways of teaching and learning*

5

How the reading skills look in individualized learning

All of the teachers in the previous chapters are helping children learn certain reading skills. The children are learning these skills when they are reading books and they are learning them at other times of the day not described in the chapters. To better understand which kind of skills are learned in which kinds of situations, let us take a look in this chapter at the reading skills as such.

Reading Skills Must Be Viewed as Individual Behaviors of Children

While the reading skills have been variously described— although in any genuine reading situation they function all of a piece—for consideration by teachers they group quite naturally into three categories: orientation skills (usually referred to as readiness skills), analysis skills, and comprehension skills. The learning of any of these skills is commonly thought of in terms of teacher-directed sequences of activities which all children must perform in systematic fashion as necessary steps in learning to read. The ability to recognize initial consonants, for example, is frequently listed as one of the several word-analysis skills. The teacher is provided with a collection of graduated drills for recognizing consonants that all of her children must go through.

Actually, however, in order to be realistically understood the reading skills must be viewed, not as systematic steps in the teacher's manual or the children's workbooks, but rather as individual behavior in the living of specific children. We are gradually coming to realize how individual an affair reading is. When a person reads *he* is the one who seeks. He is the one who has the responsibility for bringing his own experience to the author's words—for stretching his own mind as far as it will go in his attempt to find out what the author is saying. Hence, individual children will use and require different reading skills at different times, depending upon unique factors in each of their experiences and ways for learning. In the pages that follow the reading skills will be considered in terms of how they function in the lives of the children who are doing the learning to read.

Orientation Skills Are a Matter of Continuous Development

All people have the problem of learning how language operates in reading. Even after a person has learned to read, he has, with each new piece of reading, the job of determining how language is operating this time. He knows general characteristics of the behavior of language in reading materials. He knows, for example, that the author has used the medium of print to convey an organized message to him, the reader. This in itself is a tremendously important concept. He knows, furthermore, that the author has used not only culturally standardized symbols to help him, the reader, make out the words, but certain signals as well to help him know when to stop and start as he attempts to recreate the author's message. By this time he automatically knows to move his eyes from left to right across the page. All of this information has been part of his gradual orientation to reading—an orientation that began with his first reading experiences, with his earliest realization that written symbols have meaning both for author and reader. With successive reading experiences he has had to continue to orient himself to the job at hand. If he is reading poetry he will expect the author to use signals (punctuation) somewhat differently from the way in which these same signals are used in prose. If he is reading a mystery story he will put himself in tune with the author's meaning, as it were, by anticipating the mood of a mystery.

Children Begin Orientation to Reading Long before School

It is easy to see that children acquire gradually the skills which are necessary for successful orientation to reading. It is also easy to see that in this day and age, and in our particular culture, this process begins very early for most children. Certainly it is not the first-grade teacher, nor indeed the kindergarten teacher, who *introduces* children to reading, or to reading readiness. Born into and growing up in a world shot through with the printed word—a world of television, billboards, neon lights, traffic signs, put-it-together-yourself and ready-cake-mix directions, not to mention the striking bombardment of books of all kinds, fliers, newspapers, magazines, catalogues, comics—most children today get a running start in reading orientation, or readiness, long before they ever see the inside of a classroom, or indeed a readiness book. With so much advertising aimed directly at children, what first-grader does not come to school already knowing, and in many cases recognizing, the written symbol of his favorite breakfast food, peanut butter, make of car, with perhaps a lengthier choice of brands of coffee, beer or cigarettes? This is not by any means to suggest that it is healthy for children to have advertising aimed directly at them, nor that all or most of the books and comics and other printed material coming across their paths are good. It is simply to highlight the fact that most children nowadays come to school having already encountered the written word in a variety of situations. And they have pretty well accepted the fact that written words do represent something real in their living.

Five-year-old Billy, excitedly hugging his model airplane kit, comes running to his teacher. "Help me put this together, will you, Miss Pappas? I tried, but I don't know where all the things go." "I'm sorry, Billy," his teacher answers. "I don't either. I just wish I could help you, but I don't know anything about putting model planes together. Maybe we can get some-one else . . ." "But Miss Pappas," Billy cuts in. "Read the directions! Here they are. Read the directions and that will *tell* you how to do it." Even at this age Billy has a clear con-ception of one of the functions of reading. He knows it is some-thing that serves people, that can tell them how to do things.

Children Need to Sense and Respond to Different Kinds of Reading

It may seem that modern children have less need for learn-ing orientation skills, surrounded as they are by written words. This is not the case, of course. Children today need more than ever to become aware of the different kinds of reading material to which they are exposed—aware of the various kinds of responses expected on the part of the person reading. All chil-dren need to acquire the habit of looking long and searchingly at materials, asking themselves as they look, "What does the author expect of me this time?" And, as they look, they need to determine just how far they intend to go along with the author's intent. For reading, as already emphasized, is a two-way transaction. And while it is necessary that the reader cooperate with the author far enough to figure out his meaning, it is also important that the reader remain aware of his own identity— of his own meanings and values and responses. Much of this he learns to do as he organizes for himself the author's meaning; in this sense the skills involved are actually comprehension skills. There are also orientation skills involved, however—the skills a child develops as he learns to take an initial glance at reading material, sensing and responding to the general mood.

Children Learn Orientation Skills Differently and at Different Times

How and when do children learn their orientation skills? is a logical question to ask. Differently and at different times, is a logical answer. John, for example, has never had any difficulty with moving his eyes from left to right across a page of print. When his teacher wishes to test his eyes for dominance, she rolls a piece of paper into the shape of a telescope and asks John to try to see their classroom clock, using one eye to sight through the telescope. John immediately chooses his right eye. He chooses the same eye when his teacher makes a small hole with a pencil in the center of a sheet of paper and again asks him to try to see the clock. Judging by these simple tests, John is a right-eyed youngster. He also writes with his right hand and kicks with his right foot. When his teacher asks him to draw a third line between and parallel to two lines which she has already drawn on a sheet of unlined paper, John takes the pencil and immediately starts on the left side of the paper, drawing his line from left to right. Children who are right-eyed, right-handed, and right-footed, seem naturally to prefer this left-to-right pattern of eye movement. And of course this makes beginning reading much easier for them. When such children pick up a piece of reading material, they do not have to consciously alert their eyes to begin on the left. The message seems automatic. They just *do* begin on the left.

While this is true of many children in our culture by the time they come to school, all of them do not naturally move their eyes from left to right. Margaret, for example, seems to be left-eyed, right-handed, and left-footed. She immediately uses her left eye to sight through the telescope and to look through the little hole in the sheet of paper. She writes and colors with her right hand, and when her teacher asks her to pile several blocks on top of one another to make a high tower, Margaret uses her right hand for the difficult job of placing the final blocks on the top of her tower. Margaret kicks with her left foot and when her teacher asks her to sit on a chair and "write" her initials on the floor with her foot, Margaret chooses her left foot for this new and skill-demanding task. When she draws her third line between the two her teacher has drawn, Margaret carefully places her pencil on the right side of the paper and meticulously draws from right to left.

While there is nothing final about these simplified tests used by John's and Margaret's teacher, they do alert her to certain behavior that may have significance in a child's reading. In Margaret's case, the teacher has become sensitive to this problem of establishing a left-to-right pattern of eye movement. She watches Margaret when she first picks up a book, and when she sees Margaret's eyes naturally moving to the right side of the page to begin, she carefully takes the child's right hand in her own and touches her finger to the left side of the page saying, "This side of the page is where the story begins, Margaret." This does not mean that Margaret will always have to be reminded or to remind herself to begin on the left. For her, just as for John, the reminder will become automatic. The response of beginning on the left will come to be associated with reading and nothing more will be required. But Margaret will have to work harder than John to acquire this skill, and she will need sympathetic understanding and help from her teacher while she, Margaret, is teaching her body to perform in a way different from the naturally preferred behavior.

It is essential to realize here that not all left-eyed youngsters prefer the right-to-left pattern of eye movement. Sometimes a left-eyed, left-handed, and left-footed child will seem naturally to read from left to right. Sometimes a child will seem to have no preferred pattern, beginning at the left on some occasions, at the right on others. There is a great deal that we do not know about left and right dominance in human behavior. The important thing for a teacher to do is to observe children when they are engaged in activities which reveal their preferred patterns of behavior. No one can tell better than the child himself what his preferred pattern is. And he cannot tell this information reliably in words. He has to tell it through his behavior. When children tell a teacher what she needs to know, she must accept this information without placing harmful labels such as "immature" on the children who prefer the right-to-left pattern. Margaret and other children are *not* immature simply because their eyes prefer to move from right to left. If we wrote from right to left in the English language, as indeed people do in some languages, Margaret is the one who would seem automatically to have the necessary orientation skill. In that case, John, whose eyes seem naturally to move from left to right, is the one who would have to spend time teaching his eyes to move differently. No, in spite of the fact that materials for teachers frequently label children immature if they do not automatically begin reading on the left, it is not a matter of immaturity to prefer a pattern different from the culturally standardized pattern. The person whose body expresses this preference simply has to work harder to pick up the pattern standardized in the language of his particular culture.

Children Learn Readiness Skills through Informal Use of Varied Books

Quite obviously, as in the situations described in the first four chapters of this book, children are continually learning and refining their reading skills as they read books and other materials provided them in the classroom or library. Reading good books will help both John and Margaret to develop the habit of moving their eyes from left to right across the page. What better motivation can a person have than to follow the author's trail in a good engrossing story? Sad but true, in this connection, not all books designed for young children encourage eyes to move from left to right. This is especially true of the preprimer type books in which phrases like "Oh! Oh! Oh!" and "Look, look! Oh look!" are repeated over and over again. Indeed, there are some pages in these books from which it seems a child could get just as much sense of the written story by reading it backwards or even from the bottom to the top of the page!

But where young children, or indeed older children, are free to select from a wholesome variety of attractive, interesting books, and to read uninterruptedly, with friendly help as needed, they do perfect their skills as they read. They do learn skills at the time of reading. From pleasurable exposure to and supervised informal use of a large and varied selection of books in the kindergarten, say, or first grade, young children easily learn the beginning reading orientation skills, or further refine these skills if they have already picked them up. This includes all of those skills commonly consigned to the more formal lessons of the readiness exercise books. While some children already have selected from the inviting possibilities and are reading on their own, other individuals or small groups of friends choose to "read the pictures," one after the other in a favorite book which the teacher, a parent, or older child may have read to them, perhaps over and over again by request. They quite naturally take on the skills of turning the pages one at a time, from front to back, to follow a story they know or would like to know. If some child seems to have difficulty with the skill, certainly this is the appropriate time and place for the teacher to note it and to give him help. Now, at the point of real need, is the time he can best use the help, rather than in some unrelated drill designed to get him ready.

Indeed, at whatever stage the individual children are in

the exciting learning-to-read-process, there are some pictures or stories or books in the varied selection to invite and engross them and carry them further. Their own current interests, their growing stock of personal meanings, developed variously from a wide range of experience such as shopping, travel, television, neighborhood play, and heaven knows what, they draw upon now to help make sense of the content and variety of books on their classroom shelves and library table. Beautifully illustrated books available today about dinosaurs, cowboys, butterflies, horses, pets of all kinds, children, family ventures, space, machines, travel . . . all of these, through picture or printed word, are bound to strike a spark in one child or another. They are bound to meet these modern children where they are and to carry them off into various questioning, curious pursuits, their individual sensitivities and meanings and conceptual orientation to reading developing as they go.

Particularly is this so because the teacher is there. A word of encouragement, a skillful question, spontaneous discussions listened to and joined in from time to time, a bit of specific help just at the point of need—all of these can help children further their learnings and deepen their insights. One could go on. The important point here is that individual children have the freedom for reaching out, for learning and developing and conceiving of the reading skills in context, where and as they are used, where and as they make sense. A child's orientation to reading, as already emphasized, consists of certain self-initiated skills and understandings which help to put him in tune for the job at hand. Self-initiated, that is, within an environment set up and planned for by the teacher to invite such behavior. And the teacher, herself freed from always being in the driver's seat, is in a better position to learn the unique dispositions and needs of individual children, and to think through appropriate ways for helping them with next steps. Responsible access to a good collection of books, at any age and in any classroom, is for children one essential condition for learning these important skills of orientation.

Children Learn to Select Books only through
the Actual Experience

The growing awareness of one's self, the increasingly dis-
criminating judgment and sense of responsibility required for
intelligent rejection or selection of a book to read on one's
own, for whatever purpose, cannot be learned apart from the
actual experience, apart from this responsible access to a good
variety of books. Barry does not perform some isolated drill to
teach him to sense the mood in printed materials. He looks
through several books as he goes about the important job of selecting his own next book to read. One by one he rejects books
which do not serve his purpose of the moment. As part of this
selection and rejection process he may talk with other children
to get their reaction to certain books. He may try out a paragraph or two with his teacher to see whether he has chosen a
book that he can read independently. And when he finally
settles on Slobodkina's *Caps for Sale,* it is he who is in the
driver's seat. He has carefully selected a book that will suit his
purpose. While he hasn't actually read very far ahead of time,
he has tested enough to have a hunch that he will be satisfied.
This contemplation of satisfaction becomes part of his over-all
mood as, with eyes aglow, he opens the book and turns one
page after another in his reading. His painstaking period of
orienting himself to this and other books before making his
final choice is rewarded. He wanted a real story in his book,
and he has found it. Here is a peddlar who can't sell his caps.
Barry eagerly joins him in his adventures.

Ten-year-old George is in an entirely different mood as he
begins to read seriously his selection. He is reading sports equipment advertisements in the morning paper, and his mood reflects his anticipation of what the material expects of him.
"What will they try to get me to buy this time?" George wonders, as he girds himself for the critical kind of reading which
he has learned by now is demanded if a person would read
advertisements intelligently. George's friend Franklin is al-

ready engrossed in a biography of Mahatma Gandhi, the fourth book he has read in pursuing his currently all-consuming interest in India and countries of the East. Joanie of course is still reading every good horse story she can lay her hands on.

The School Helps Children Expand Their Concepts of Reading

Important though it is, this use of a good collection of books is not adequate by itself for helping children develop their skills of orientation to reading. Kindergartener Billy must soon learn to read his own directions for building the model airplane. As he goes on through school his teachers will provide him with further opportunities for knowing reading in this way and in many others. They will so plan the school program, year after year, that Billy and his classmates will need and use reading in an infinite variety of ways to meet their purposes. Billy will continue to know reading as a worthwhile tool to own as he, with his friends, reads to enjoy his favorite stories, to follow the notices on the bulletin board, to send and to receive letters, post cards, invitations, to work the Space Club's newest crossword puzzles, to make some of his own for the others to work, to play Spelling Bingo, to find answers to his many questions, to keep up on the news of the latest rocket, to make his own newspaper and ditto copies for all of the children, to find out how to make a good working doorbell for the kindergarten playhouse, to sign up for the gym equipment that he wants, to write to the United Nations for a UNESCO pamphlet on Mexico, to learn about his favorite subject, dinosaurs, to do research for the book, *Stories of the Northwest Territory* that he and his friend Mark are writing . . . But enough now of Billy's ways for seeing reading in a larger context. Some of the exciting activities that children and teachers are doing in this connection will be given in more detail in the chapters to follow. Suffice it to say here that orientation to reading—even for children—is orientation to a whole dynamic world full of inter-related people and places and things.

Analysis Skills Focus on Language Patterns

Four-year-old Jenny stands up on the bus seat beside her mother and pulls the cord to signal the driver to stop at the next corner. Then as they walk down the aisle to leave the bus, Jenny announces to anyone wishing to hear, "I ringed the bell." Jenny's particular use of *ed* with the word *ring* is not new to anyone who has heard young children similarly announce, "I runned all the way home," "I falled out of the wagon," or even, "I spillded the water."

Where do these youngsters learn to add *ed* to their spoken words? we might ask. Certainly Jenny has not heard any of her influential grownups say *ringed* so she is not merely imitating what she has heard. No, children do not simply repeat what language they hear from others in their world. Even young pre-schoolers use important analysis skills where language is concerned. Because language is so highly patterned and because human beings are equipped to notice pattern, children do not simply hear words in the world about them. They hear arrangements both within and among words, and they try these arrangements out for themselves. Thus while Jenny has not heard her grownups say *ringed,* she has heard them use *ed* on certain familiar words. And from listening to them and responding to pattern, Jenny is beginning to generalize about the kinds of situations in which a person adds *ed* to a spoken verb.

When Jenny begins to read she will go right on analyzing words and groups of words. For her as for other children, this is a well-established habit with regard to language. Looking carefully at words which she has been hearing all of her life, Jenny will be saying in effect, "Hmmm. So that's how that word looks." She will notice everything she can about written language. It will be fun to see in print what she has been hearing.

When Jenny looks at words in books and in other writing in her classroom, she will begin to generalize about written words just as she did about her spoken *ed*. She will expect certain things to happen. For example, when she sees the familiar beginning *B* she will expect the word *Baby* to sound something like the often-seen name of her friend Barbara. She will notice that the written names Billy and Timmy end like hers, and she will probably say the names aloud—checking with her dependable spoken language to see if they all really do end alike. Gradually she will expect to see and hear the endings of words—perhaps even to expect any word which ends in *y* to sound in its ending like Billy and Timmy and Jenny.

Jenny's generalizing will be influenced a great deal by the materials made available to her by her teacher. If she is lucky, she will have materials which reward her long and thoughtful look. She will find written patterns which compare with her own spoken patterns—dependable written patterns which respect children as competent analyzers of language. And if she is lucky she will have a teacher who will listen to *her* way of noticing patterns in words. She will have a teacher who will help her to look better—who will give just the right hint when she and Jenny are reading together. She will have a teacher who will select interesting books for children, who will take down the children's own stories and make them into books, who will invent interesting puzzles and bulletin board signs to help children in their self-initiated investigation into language.

And when the situation is right, this is how children learn to read. They encounter written language in books and stories and on bulletin boards in their classrooms. They talk with sensitive teachers about what they see. Their teachers pick up the cue from each child and help the already inquiring child to go further. "Joel asked about the period today. Tomorrow I'll see if he remembers." "After reading, 'A fish swims in the river,' Mary figured out, 'A tree grows by the river,' all by herself. She looked at the accompanying picture, referred back to the previous page in her book, and she had it." "After asking the word *this* once, Dave read the entire book, *Is This You?*"

And so the teachers' comments run—comments which grow out of valuable reading times with individual children.

Teachers who work with children in this way know how important timing is when it comes to giving children help. Because, when the time is right, one little hint in response to a child's question or observation about written language can refer that child back to and make him consciously aware of his whole store of knowledge about spoken language, which he has been gathering in self-initiated research all of his life. This helping a child to become aware of his store of knowledge about spoken language includes the important facet of correction also. Just as Jenny learned by continued observation to say *rang* instead of *ringed,* so children learn to broaden and correct their growing store of knowledge. And because *they* are the ones to do the important connecting of the new with what they already know, their new learning makes sense. It is orderly because it is related by particular individual children to what they already know. In this sense, language analysis is not some totally new activity which a child must take on lesson by lesson as part of learning to read. Analyzing *written* words is merely an extension of his on-going research in language, and for human beings, research in language is the job of a lifetime.

Analysis Focuses on Whole Words when Children Are Reading Content

Six-year-old Erling is at the library table reading a book which one of his classmates has written. When he comes to an unfamiliar word *damage* in the story he pauses momentarily and then points to the word so his teacher nearby can see and tell him the word. "*Damage,*" repeats Erling after the teacher, half to himself. "That word *looks* like damage. It reminds me of the hurricane in Westport." And he goes on with his reading. In his own way, Erling has made a useful analysis of the word. Who is to say what caused Erling to say that the word reminded him of actual damage? And who is to say exactly what reminded

Erling of his earlier experiences with a storm in Westport? The important fact to be noted is this: Erling is the one doing the reading. He is the person who did not know the word *damage* when he came to it in his story. And having asked his teacher to tell him the word, he is now the person who fixes the word in his mind in his own personal way. This is how it is with word analysis, just as it is with other aspects of reading. It is a very personal thing. Different children have different words that they do not know. They have different ways of seeing words. They have different ways of weaving new words into their experience to make the words and their meanings their own.

Erling's teacher, Mrs. McKinney, is not disturbed when Erling says that the word *damage* looks like actual damage he has known. She knows that Erling is not saying that he always expects words to look like the reality that they represent. He is simply responding to the fact that there is some kind of a meaningful pattern to written English. And he is verbalizing his recognition that his own meanings are closely related to the words which he sees and hears.

Mrs. McKinney had other choices open to her when the child pointed to the word he didn't know. She could have made him sound out the new word—reminding him if need be of other words that start with *d,* or perhaps requiring him to find the familiar small words within his unfamiliar longer word. But this teacher long ago discovered that such procedures would only have interrupted Erling in his reading; and, interestingly enough, they would not have helped him to make his useful, meaningful analysis of the specific word *damage.* He makes this useful analysis once he is told the *whole* word. All of his responses are then made in relation to this new whole word; consequently they all help him to fix the new word in his mind.

This does not mean that Mrs. McKinney does not help children to sound out words. To begin with, she uses her own knowledge of language patterns each time she writes something which the children will be reading. "Bulletin board notices, arithmetic materials, labels and signs—really everything I write in the classroom—becomes, from my point of view although not theirs, a reading lesson," Mrs. McKinney observes. And the children respond to this deliberate planning of their teacher.

"Look, Mike, you'd better be careful which slip you sign your name on," warns Tim. "This one says, 'I *want* to go to the park' and this other one says, 'I *will* go to the park at 10:30 today.' Sure, I want to go to the park sometime, but not at 10:30 today when I can be finishing my boat. I'm going to sign the *want* slip, so she'll know I want to make plans for another time. But I'm not going to sign the *will go* slip. Not today." And Tim carefully signs the proper slip.

Thoughtfully looking at the two important phrases, Mike compares them. He too notes especially the words *want* and *will,* remarking, "You could certainly make a mistake there. They even start alike. You sure have to look clear to the end of some words to know what they're saying."

"Yes, and sometimes you need to look at the other words a word is used *with,*" adds Mrs. McKinney who has noticed Mike's and Tim's absorption in the sign-up slips and is standing near in case help is needed.

The important consideration is that, like the teachers in earlier chapters, Mrs. McKinney does not interrupt the children in their reading to help them figure out word construction. She does not deny children the opportunity to make their own personal analysis of words as *wholes.* Telling a child a word when he is in the midst of reading a story invites him to bring his own experience to the word quickly so that, as he and the author can both claim the word as theirs, he can go on without losing the continuity of the story.

When she tells him the word *damage,* and Erling makes his response, Mrs. McKinney is careful to note this response. She believes that teachers need to know a child's way for analyzing words. Just as there are some children more interested in taking objects apart and others in putting them together, so it is with word analysis. Some children prefer to analyze their words by taking them apart. Others prefer seeing them whole. When Erling responds as he does, he is telling his teacher that in this instance, at least, he is a boy who prefers looking at words whole. This is legitimate word study, as Erling's teacher sees it—both for him and for her.

Certain Analysis Methods Distort Meaning and Slow Down Reading

On the other hand, seven-year-old Hilda, new to this interage group of youngsters, has already learned to use a quite different method of word attack. She has recently come from a traditionally graded school where she would have been in the second grade this year. Now she is in Erling's group—a class of six-, seven-, and eight-year-olds who are grouped together without the label of grades. These children are simply called Mrs. McKinney's group; and within this primary unit each child works ahead at his own pace. Hilda is reading independently, as is Erling. But Hilda does not ask her teacher for unknown words when she comes to them. To her this is not proper behavior for a child. Hilda has her own well-learned, if quite inefficient, system for sounding out new words. It is the only system she knows—the system she was taught in first grade. When Hilda comes to a new word in her reading, she immediately begins to look for familiar *little* words in the unfamiliar longer word. It makes no difference where in the word these familiar little words are. The trick, as Hilda has learned it, is to find the little words. When, in reading the same story, she comes across the word damage, an unfamiliar word to her as well, her eyes light first on the word *age,* a word she knows well from filling in blanks on her various worksheets. Hilda thinks of her own age, seven, as she makes note of the familiar word, and also remembers a test form where she had to fill in her age . . . Shifting her thinking, she returns to the job of figuring out the word *damage.* "Dam," says Hilda softly to herself, and a look of hidden mischief crosses her face. *"Dam, dam, dam,"* she repeats, obviously enjoying herself. By now the content of the story is forgotten and Hilda is absorbed in her word play.

Finally she puts the two little words, chock-full of meaning, together and she too claims the word *damage*—whose meaning of course has nothing to do with *dam* (damn) or *age*!

Erling's and Hilda's teacher now, Mrs. McKinney, wishes that Hilda had not learned this time-consuming way for sounding out words. Looking for and recognizing familiar little words provides so many distractions for a child from the real job at hand, which is reading the content of the particular story. Carried to its logical conclusion in attacking new words, it is easy to see how confusing this technique can be. Instead of concentrating on the meaning and pronunciation of the new word in the story she is reading, a child may well have the meanings and pronunciations of a whole host of small words cluttering up her mind, quite because of this well-learned technique.

It will take time and patience to help Hilda change, Mrs. McKinney realizes, now that this behavior pattern has become a habit which she associates with reading. Particularly is this true since, along with the inefficient technique for word recognition, Hilda has been taught to feel guilty about asking the teacher or another child for help on a word she doesn't know. Asking for words carries the stigma of "baby" for Hilda, unfortunately, while the system for sounding out words through finding the little words has been equated with "grownup" reading. In the opinion of Mrs. McKinney, this is why Hilda does not seem able to lose herself in a story. Her earlier experiences with reading seem not to have given her the opportunity to build the habit of reading good books for the sake of the story the author has to tell. The expectancy in Hilda's mind when she picks up a book has to do, to serious degree, with the ritual she has learned for sounding out words.

It is important here to repeat that Mrs. McKinney is not critical of all methods of attacking new words. She too sees value in helping children gain independence through sounding out unfamiliar words they meet in their reading. Indeed, it is natural for children to develop their own systems of word analysis, which operate so quickly in the act of reading that they need never be made articulate. Given the opportunity, children simply read, seeming to use intuition to weave together what they already know about spoken language and relate it to written language. For a teacher to insist that children arbitrarily use other people's workbook ways of sounding out words or learning rules for attacking words, as a prerequisite for reading, is in effect asking children to back up and "learn" steps which they have already taken or, in fact, do not need. For many children this backing up means being cut off from their own developing systems of language analysis and being placed at the mercy of systems that do not have intrinsic meaning for them. In short, it can make problem readers of children.

Focusing on Whole Words, in Context, Children Can Sound out Words

Mrs. McKinney does not approve of those awkward, slowing-down methods that force children to take their minds off the meaning of what they are reading. When a child is reading a story, he knows that it is accepted classroom procedure to point to a whole unknown word and have a teacher or other child pronounce the word for him. If he chooses to sound out the word, he looks at the beginning first. In a significant sense, he is ready for the word because he has learned to read for content and not for mechanical word study. He picks up the beginning sound, pronounces the first two word parts, say, looks quickly toward the end, and more often than not, the context will do the rest.

In reading the word *damage,* had Hilda not already learned her cumbersome system, she would not have looked at *age* as a little word at all. Neither would she have looked at *dam* as a little word. She would have started with the *beginning d,* the next part *am*—or perhaps immediately *dam*—and while pronouncing this to herself, would be glancing quickly to the end of the word, to blend the letters *a g e* together, almost automatically choosing the soft pronunciation for *g*. For Hilda would not have been looking for little words at all. Rather she would look for the one important whole word that she needed to go on with her story. And the context of the story itself would have her so ready for the word *damage* that she would not have to laboriously put the parts together to make the whole. If the word had seemed to require such laborious putting together, Hilda herself, having learned to accept the friendly help available to these children, would have chosen simply to ask the teacher and thus get on with her reading.

Comprehension Makes its Demands on the Individual Reader

Reading a book or other piece of written material is an adventure between two people—the author and the person doing the reading. Each has certain responsibilities which must be assumed if the transaction is to be a satisfactory one. The author must have patterned the words and punctuation in such ways that the person reading will know when to begin, when to pause, when to feel amused or frightened or mystified. The person reading must have the expectation that the author will use language and punctuation to guide him, and he must free himself to follow the author's trail. More than that, the person who is reading must recognize when meaning has been transmitted to him. No one can do this *for* him. He is the one who can personally know when he knows what the author has written for him.

In other words, comprehension in reading—and if there is no comprehension there is no reading—is a personal, an individual affair. When a person reads he is the one who figures out meaning, as already stressed. He is the one who seeks, who brings his own experience to the author's words to find out what the author is saying. And again, this bringing together of his experience and the deliberately used symbols and patterns of the author, is not something which can be done *for* the reader. Otherwise, he is not the reader. When a story is "developed" by the teacher before a child is allowed to read it, the child never does have a chance to develop the story himself, which is the heart of the reading process. The teacher keeps him or protects him from reading, as it were.

The point to be stressed here, then, is that the *comprehension,* to *be* comprehension, has to belong to the individual child who is doing the reading. When a teacher asks the class or the reading group a series of questions to make sure they comprehend the story they have been reading together, calling on one child after another, and then judges the comprehension by the responses of the few children called upon, or by the number of waving hands that her questions elicit, she is overlooking the important fact that it is each of the individual children doing the reading—not the group as a group—who has to get the meaning. And comprehension involves something more than being able to answer a factual question or to repeat what has been read in the teacher-directed lesson.

Many of the exercises provided for classroom use under the label of "comprehension" are in actuality exercises designed mainly to take up time. Teachers may have problems, then, not because the children do not comprehend what is written, but rather because they more than comprehend the over-simplified materials provided for their reading. Frequently the problems become discipline problems rather than comprehension problems.

It is one thing, furthermore, for a teacher to help a child acquire a questioning mood with regard to the author's content and purposes. It is something else for the teacher methodically to become the asker of questions which a child must answer. In the former situation, the child is himself the asker of questions, and the teacher's role is to help him become a better question-asker. In the latter situation, it is of course the teacher who constantly assumes the responsibility for asking questions. Consequently if anyone's skill is improved, it is hers.

When seventh-grader Dan reads a book on the Antarctic for his social studies report, he is aware that the author has a purpose in mind. He is trying to give information. Dan thinks of this purpose and he studies all of the author's techniques for accomplishing his goal. As he studies these techniques, Dan also studies his own responses to the material and he makes more than one judgment on whether or not the author uses language skillfully. He also passes judgment on the author's purpose. Is this author trying to put across a certain point of view in giving out information? Is it a point of view which Dan accepts? If Dan rejects the information which the author has to offer, is it because the author lacks skill in organizing this information or is the rejection due to the quality of the information itself—due perhaps to a difference in beliefs which exists between reader and author?

Dan's teacher is helping him to form these judgments which are a necessary part of understanding what an author has written. Sometimes she suggests guide questions for Dan. Not the kind of questions which simply ask him to repeat what the author has written to prove that he read it, but questions which help Dan to do the complicated job of organizing the author's meaning for his own comprehension. "Learn to ask yourself questions about what you are reading," his teacher may propose to Dan and his classmates. "What techniques does the author rely on to put his point of view across?" "Does the author *tell* his reader what to believe or does he invite the reader to think for himself?" "For what purpose does the author give information? Is he trying to sell a point of view? Does he succeed?"

There are other questions also with which Dan is concerned. These are questions his teacher helps the children to point up one morning in a lively current affairs discussion. They really start Dan off on his serious reading about the Antarctic. Why are some of our government officials so eager to put through a world-wide Antarctic peace pact? Why are others just as strongly against such a pact? What are the issues involved? What historical factors? Are there other countries who have interests in the Antarctic that would be endangered by such a pact or the absence of one? If so, then why should the U. S. and the U.S.S.R. seem to be so much more concerned than other countries? What is at stake? Dan and a couple of friends are seeking out reliable information on this matter from a variety of sources, including some abstracts they have found available at the library, and a professor Dan knows who was with Admiral Byrd on one of his Antarctic expeditions.

Young children are not and need not be too much aware of their role in relation to the author's purpose. A young child reads a story and responds to the story. It is good. It is funny. It makes him think a new thought. As children grow older, however, like Dan, they can and need to develop their own individual skill for recognizing and doing something about the two interrelated roles.

Children and Teachers Develop Their Skills in Real Reading Situations

"The children in my reading group are fine," student-teacher Dianne explains to her classmates in seminar, "so long as we're reading the story. It's when we stop to discuss what we've read that the trouble begins." When someone brings up the question of why the children *should* stop to discuss what they read, Dianne ponders, with a suddenly amused look at where this line of thinking will take her. "Well, I don't know," she answers. "We're only supposed to read a story a day, I think . . . Otherwise, I'm afraid the book wouldn't last more than a week."

"Then what would you do?"

"We'd read another one, I guess."

"And after that?"

"Still another . . . and then another . . ."

"And under which of these circumstances do you think the children would learn to read better?"

"Well, when they read more, of course. And I'd have a wonderful time . . . But what about the skills? How would you know if the children were comprehending what they read?"

A good question (except for the faulty but rather common

assumption that the reading skills are somehow apart from the reading)! How *would* you know? How can you tell if children are comprehending what they read? Generally, what do you see when you look at children who understand what they are reading?

If they are reading interesting stories, particularly self-chosen ones, as with the children in the earlier part of this book, you can easily tell, say the teachers. The plot and the style and the mood, together with the children's expectations, just seem to carry them along. The occasional child who asks for words as he goes does so almost automatically, hardly changing his intent expression as he holds the book up to you, pointing to the word. So, of course, you can tell. Without questions or required book reports, really, you just know that comprehension is there.

What about other situations, though, not as simple as good story-reading? What do individual children look like when they are having to try to figure out the meaning? Observe second-grade Billy following directions for making that model airplane, say, reading and rereading a single step . . . selecting a particular piece which seems to fill the bill . . . trying to fit it in crosswise as the directions say, then going back and reading again to make sure. Now, taking the next step . . . holding the specified strip in his hand as he reads . . . Any doubt that Billy is figuring it out all right? Any signals for help? Perhaps Billy goes to his good friend who knows about these things and interrupts him for a moment—just to ask about this one step he is not quite sure of. And the friend reads the particular point of instruction with him, getting him past the difficulty. Or it could be that you, the teacher, see he is in difficulty and seems to have no place to turn on his own initiative. So you capitalize on this point of need to say, "Perhaps I can help you." Unless, of course, he comes to you first and makes his own request. Or maybe Billy and a friend are working it out together from the beginning and help each other. In any case, he gets the help he needs at the time he needs it and goes on about his business.

Or take a look at several children at odds about the rules of a table game they are playing in the back of the room. To settle the matter they turn to the printed instructions, and one or two, even three, may read the essential points, aloud. Maybe Alden, who has laid his claim hardest, will insist on taking those instructions himself and rereading the rule in question. "Aha . . . see!" And the boys are back again at the game. Their teacher has no doubt that these children have figured out the necessary meanings on their own.

Or look at Madeline, taking a folded note with her name on it from the mail box just outside the class door, unfolding and reading it on the way to her seat, maybe stopping stock-still for a moment as, with furrowed brow, she ponders what her friend has written to her. Then may come the look of disgust and, quite to herself, "What does she think I am? Why doesn't she come to *my* house and watch *our* television for a change?" And maybe she stamps her foot as she takes her seat, getting out the materials at once for writing her answer. Madeline may or may not share this experience with the teacher. But the teacher has eyes and ears. She knows that Madeline has comprehended the written message.

Or there is Hugh, trying to find information about a particular kind of dinosaur. Hugh selects the encyclopedia from the shelf, searches for the name in the appropriate alphabetical category and obviously finding the word, reads the several inches of description, checking it perhaps with the drawing he has on his desk already in process. Then with the encyclopedia still open, Hugh picks up *The Book About Dinosaurs* which he has lying on his desk. He looks through the table of contents, scratches his head, turns to the index of the book, checks back on the spelling in the encyclopedia, moves on down through the index . . . and his teacher, with an eye on all of this, knows that Hugh is pretty much aware of where he is going. He too may come to the point where he needs her help or someone else's, at which time he will let her know by word or action. But that time is certainly not now.

A sensitive teacher can tell what *lack* of comprehension looks like also. Miss Floyd in an earlier chapter is a case in point. When her children are trying to increase their number of books on the reading chart, you remember, Miss Floyd can tell that Ronnie is not reading with comprehension—not reading at all, in other words. She notices that his eyes wander about the room during reading time. She watches him turning the pages of his book rather craftily, looking off into space from time to time. Miss Floyd doesn't need to ask Ronnie about the pictures in his story to know that he doesn't know what they are about.

It doesn't take Miss Floyd long to discover the cause of Ronnie's trouble either, in this case the reading chart and the competitive pressure it inspires. Something wrong in the classroom set-up, unsuitability of the material or the task, a personal problem that has the child worried—there is always a cause. What may look like inability to comprehend may be something else. Lack of interest because the material is too easy. Discouragement because the job is too difficult or the pressure too great.

The important thing to notice is that Ronnie is telling Miss Floyd that he doesn't comprehend. Miss Floyd is not the one telling Ronnie. To be sure, in Ronnie's case he is giving this message to Miss Floyd through his behavior rather than telling her in simple words that he does not understand what he is reading. If it were not for the reading chart, in a classroom like Miss Floyd's where children read for meaning, Ronnie would simply tell his teacher, "This isn't the book for me. I can't read it." Or, if the problem is comprehension, "I can't understand it." For in this kind of classroom it is the children themselves who are figuring out meaning in the reading. And Miss Floyd knows that it is the individual reader, not just the teacher, who needs to know if he is not understanding what he reads.

Not only is it the individual child who knows he does not *understand,* but being in a classroom where he is expected to solve his own problems, each child finds unique ways for improving his reading skill. Take for example seventh-grader Louie. After diligently working for a good part of the reading period, he calls his teacher to his desk, mainly to verbalize the problem he is facing and attempting to solve. "Look," he exclaims, indicating the two pieces of reading material he has open on his desk—one Dumas's book, *The Count of Monte Cristo,* the other a comic version of the same story. "Look! I can read the comic, but it doesn't tell me enough of the story. And I can't read too much of what's in the book." "Do you want some help, Louie?" his teacher asks. "No, it's O.K., I think. I'm getting it. I go back and forth from the comic to the book, and it's getting easier to figure out." And Louie does get it. In his intelligent, satisfying way, he lifts himself up by his own bootstraps, so to speak, improving his own reading skills until he is able successfully to read the book, *The Count of Monte Cristo.* In this situation, as in others throughout the book, teacher and child are communicating in significant ways about his—the child's—development of useful methods for learning to read. This intercommunication is at the heart of helping children learn the reading skills.

6

The teacher's role: gearing children's choice toward learning the skills

First, what do we mean by individualizing the learning of the skills? We mean simply that the teacher deliberately sets up situations in which children are the ones who do their own learning. That the teacher acts upon her knowledge that the individual is the one who organizes and internalizes his own learning. Each child has his own unique ways for looking upon an experience he has actually lived through and for organizing this experience in the light of his previous learnings, thus making it available for him in future situations. Equally unique are his ways for looking upon the recorded living of other people and integrating into his own store of usefully digested experience what he reads or figures out—his learning.

Arranging must be a key concept when we think about individualized learning. And to repeat, it is the learner, not the teacher, who can do that arranging—within a framework of possible choices which the teacher sets up. The child is the one who needs to see patterns, to experiment with arrangements, gradually to make generalizations about the arrangements which he encounters. This is true whether the arrangements occur within his own first-hand living or within the patterns of printed words which he reads. How important it is that his teacher provide for this active reaching out, so that learning may be kept where it belongs—in the hands of the learner.

It is the deliberate structuring of real situations—in which, with this chance to express their own choices, children need and learn their important skills—that becomes the major responsibility of the teacher. There are several aspects of this responsibility for deliberate structuring, each of them worthy of treatment in a separate chapter, yet ideally so closely integrated that they lose their true meaning when looked at in isolation. There are the written materials which teachers select or prepare to help children respond to and use the skills of reading and writing in the solution of real problems. There are the teacher's ways of setting up the classroom so that these and other materials can best serve to invite children's self-propelling activities, and make next steps available for them without the teacher's directly taking over. In other words, this is the problem of organizing space and materials in the classroom in those ways which enhance genuine intercommunication. Another aspect, closely related of course, is the time factor—the arrangement of time schedules that allow for children's whole rather than piecemeal learnings. And through all of this, as already noted, is the continuous problem of providing just the kind of help needed at just the time it is needed and can be of most value to a child's learning. All of these aspects, sensitively and resourcefully interrelated, define "teaching." All of them together spell out the deliberate role of the teacher in a program of individualized learning.

This chapter, *Gearing Children's Choice toward Learning the Skills,* will center around that phase of the teacher's deliberate structuring which has to do primarily with the preparation and use of materials for children's purposeful written communication. Chapter Seven, *Setting Up the Classroom to Invite Whole Learning,* deals with the organization of time and space and materials to invite self-initiated learning, and with ways of providing other kinds of help children need.

The content of Chapter Eight, *A Closer Look at Children as Authors in a Planned Situation,* could well be part of this chapter, as will be quite evident. So indeed could the content of Chapters Nine and Ten. That is the way with *whole* learning. It does not easily lend itself to part-by-part consideration. Some compromises have to be made. Realizing this the reader will not be surprised or too much disturbed, it is hoped, as he finds what seems to be repetition, separate treatment where treatment should not be separate, and other inadequacies which this finally devised plan of organization is bound to give rise to . . . . But on with the business of the chapter now, *Gearing Children's Choice toward Learning the Skills.*

Teaching takes on a realistic air when we insist that the teacher respond to motivation as it is felt by individual children. This is true, provided the teacher makes use of materials and other resources which help her to see and understand and do something about this motivation. Accustomed as many teachers are to seeing motivation written up in oversimplified paragraphs in teachers' manuals or education books, how are they to recognize motivation, one wonders, in the unparagraphed living of children? In other words, if teacher- or textbook-prepared motivation does not bring the teacher and learner together, what can be relied upon? Obviously it is not the laissez-faire, unstructured "What shall we do today?" relationship which has been tried and has not worked. Genuine human communication is too complicated for such oversimplified verbalizing. More subtle and intricate ways for communicating are called for, if really significant messages concerning human needs and wants are to pass between two people, between child and teacher. Experimenting with a wide range of communication possibilities has led to the discovery that human beings will give out vastly important information about themselves when they are in a situation that has been so structured that they are free to select among alternatives. This is true whether the alternatives be material objects, such as food, toys, or construction tools, or abstract ideas.

It is not that human beings select only when the situation has been structured to enable them to behave in this way. On the contrary, human beings always select, in the sense that each personality internalizes in terms of himself—of his own way for seeing and using that which comes in from the world outside him. But when *learning* is the activity under consideration the importance of the relationship between learner and teacher becomes highlighted. This is when the structured choosing situation becomes crucial. As earlier chapters bear out, when a child is encouraged to choose between alternatives which the teacher or he and the teacher together have made available, he tells her something important with his every choice.

Planning for Learning through Real Use of Reading and Writing Skills

An increasing number of teachers are coming to realize that planning for children's choices through the functional use of reading and writing—since all writing involves reading—is a basic part of helping children learn to read. Being on the alert for and setting up situations in which children will need to use these skills in achieving real purposes, such teachers are expanding their own concepts of reading and writing as legitimate tools of communication in the classroom. They know that among children's other important learning, related to reading and writing, basic words can be learned as part of managing one's daily affairs:

> If sign-up slips and other materials are especially prepared with this in mind.
>
> If materials are changed as children are ready for new learnings.
>
> If activities such as signing for choices are a part of regular routines and not something brought in spasmodically in the hope that once or twice will do the trick.
>
> If materials and activities are planned *to involve all children* in the actual using of the words. Effective language is not learned by watching another person do all of the using.

Learning and Using Written Communication for Planning and Organizing

Teachers are devising ingenious ways and materials to give children opportunity, through written communication, to be in on the planning and organizing of their own learning from the first years in school.

SIGN-UP SHEETS AND CHECK LISTS.   Mrs. Williamson uses the sign-up idea from the beginning. Even with the youngest children she finds it to be one of the routines which they come to respect and use. The attendance report is about the first sign-up notice she puts to work in the classroom. On a sign on a large low bulletin board, which the children can reach easily, she prints in large letters:

I am here today.

On the first day of school she gives a name card to each of the children, since many of them are not able to read their names.

Before long, however, she spreads all the name cards out on a table before the school day begins and, as the children come in, gives them the help they need in finding their own names and putting them on the bulletin board under the sign. Mrs. Williamson does this spreading out of the name cards with care, for she sees this as an important time to help the children unlock some of the secrets of written English. She takes advantage of every possible opportunity to help the children see patterns in written words, one day arranging the cards in terms of names that begin alike, another day taking advantage of names with common endings (Tommy, Billy, Nicky), and still another day combining names having like word parts (Ted, Fred). And because names matter so much to children they are quick to notice, and gradually claim as their own, the many learnings which their teacher makes available to them. "You can be sure I have to make more than one set of name cards during the first month of school," Mrs. Williamson says. "There are so many times during the day when individual children wish to use these cards—inventing their own games as they arrange and rearrange these important written symbols which name every person in our group."

Gradually the process of finding one's name for the bulletin board becomes automatic. The children become less curious about the arrangements of names which Mrs. Williamson lays out in the mornings as they exhaust the potential learnings from their printed names. So from time to time Mrs. Williamson changes the plan and thus introduces new learnings. As the children are able to sign their own names, a large sheet for the purpose replaces the use of name cards and Mrs. Williamson uses her ingenuity to find thought-provoking ways of using this device. To the children the act of using one's name to indicate "I am here" becomes an efficient and businesslike way to start the morning—a way of indicating to the world that they are here today. To the teacher this practice is one of her best ways for significantly helping children learn to read.

A further step for her children in knowing reading and writing as convenient, worthwhile tools, is the sign-up sheet used for popular equipment in the classroom or on the playground. Mrs. Williamson runs off on the ditto machine a supply of sheets with the picture of the desired piece of equipment at the top. This may be a limited kind of sign-up sheet at first, with perhaps only two lines for names. "Two people can use it today and two more tomorrow." Or it may involve something which many will want. Some children need this assurance more than others do, Mrs. Williamson finds. "Just to say to a child, 'I've put your name on the list, so you'll have a turn,' may be enough to let him know that the world has order," she observes. "He may forget all about wanting the thing later on and not even come back for his turn. On the other hand, he may keep asking for it until his turn actually arrives. The fact that his name is put down for his turn means something important in both instances."

With very young children the sign-up sheets are for one desired object at a time. It may be the blue tricycle, say, or a new set of pulleys for which the children sign or the teacher writes or checks names. Or it may be a treat—a bowl of oyster crackers, raisins, or fruit put on a table. The teacher has the sign-up sheet, or perhaps the class list in this case, and says, "Do you think you will want one (or some)?" If the child says Yes, she checks his name as he watches.

"I always run off many copies of the class list," Mrs. Williamson explains as an aside. "It's handy for this and for so many other purposes . . ." And then, "Just the name of the thing wanted at the top of the page will be enough in most cases. For children to know that there are order and fairness in the world is so important. If Bert complains that Nickie has had many turns already, I can just say, 'All right then, we'll cross Nickie's name off the list because he's had his turn.' Once the routine is established, you will hear children saying to each other, 'Mrs. Williamson will put you on the sign-up sheet if you tell her.' "

In another school Mrs. Barnes allows her six- and seven-year-olds, most of whom live in apartment houses nearby, to take home certain items of classroom equipment for use after school and over the weekends. The parents understand this and are more than pleased to cooperate. Mrs. Barnes makes sign-up sheets for the children to use in this connection—first separate sheets with drawings of the particular toy, along with its name, at the top of the page on which they sign, later a list of the words only. This means that the children need to know the words so they can be sure to sign up for the right toy. To help them Mrs. Barnes provides a supply of carefully planned worksheets, usually dittoed pages. From time to time children who feel they need this help—or who want to prove to themselves that they do not need it—will select the sheets and, individually or with a friend, give themselves practice (see Figs. 6.1–6.3).

To be sure, some of these words would not appear in a so-called first-grade reading vocabulary. They are an important part of the vocabulary of these children, however, because they are words that have meaning for them and serve a real need.

As another very early way of giving her children a conscious part in the planning of their own learning, Mrs. Barnes writes on the board in large clear letters:

`I want to go to the gym today.`

`Yes                    No`

She reads this with the children, discussing the choice this first time, and invites the children to write their names or initials

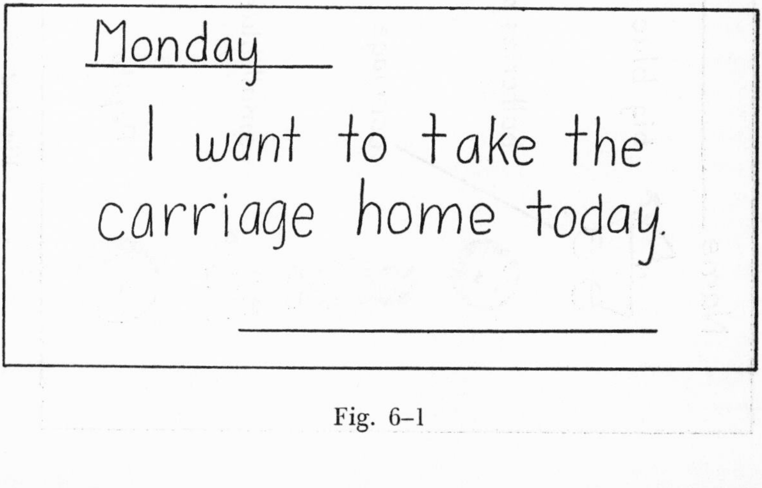
Monday
I want to take the
carriage home today.

Fig. 6–1

Name _____

big blue ball

batteries and wire

carriage

small blue ball

Pepita

Fig. 6-2

Sign here _____

Day _____

carriage

Pepita

large blue ball

small blue ball

batteries and wire

green stilts

unpainted stilts

pulleys

jump rope 1

jump rope 2

football

Fig. 6-3

under Yes or No. As some children learn to write *yes* or *no,* they can either write the appropriate word and sign or just sign, perhaps as they come into the classroom. The statements take different form as time goes on, sometimes written on the black-board, sometimes on a large sheet for the purpose.

Shall we go to the park today?

Yes   No

I want to hear a story today.

Sign here

Do you want to go to the gym?

Yes   No

The children come to know simple punctuation as they meet it in this way, too, including the question mark and the "excite-ment point," as the children call it, which they love. When they mean "Oh yes, I *do*," they write *Yes!* or even *Yes!!* Sometimes they write *No!* If a child writes *No,* and Mrs. Barnes finds that he really doesn't want to go to the park for some reason, she respects the sincerity of the written communication and makes other plans for him. Otherwise, she knows, the children would come to see this as a superficial exercise, which would defeat its very purpose. It is important, then, that the teacher write only those things regarding which there can be legitimate and real choice for the children.

That Mrs. Barnes is sincere in her belief that children can help her in deciding the kinds of activities suitable for her to plan for them is shown in other ways. Resourcefully bringing into play their growing skills of written communication, Mrs. Barnes makes available from time to time a variety of thought-fully planned materials to give children opportunity for expressing their choices. In each case, unless there is something all of the group should be in on, those children who can read without help are free to go ahead on their own with filling in their choices, while Mrs. Barnes sits down with the other children to read the sheet and give individual help as needed. If there are student teachers or other grownups in the room, they too can give help as requested. A few examples of such worksheets, always printed large or typed primer-size, are shown in Figures 6.4–6.6.

It is important to note how Mrs. Barnes uses her knowledge of word analysis in writing the sign-up slips for the children. As stated earlier, she knows that children do not learn to read simply by associating words and pictures. She respects the patterned nature of language and helps the children to become skillfully aware of this pattern in the very way she words their important notices. Note, for example, the first three items on the "Hallowe'en Plans" worksheet. Comprehension and word-analysis skills come together as each child is helped to figure out the distinctions that exist among the three words which represent the very different acts of *wearing, bringing,* and *making* a costume.

Mrs. Barnes is aware, of course, that the way children answer questions on their preference check lists today may not be the way they will answer them next week, next month, next spring. Many factors will be at work in the meantime. But anything that helps her to know her individual children better— including their ways of coming at these tasks—she welcomes as useful. She is glad to have information against which to note changes in children's attitudes and interests as they occur, as well as some helpful information for her more immediate planning.

Thus children have valuable language learnings when they make or use the sign-up sheets or the sign-up idea in any of its forms. Once again they see reading and writing as tools to help them solve their problems in acceptable, orderly ways. A teacher can deliberately arrange the sign-up slips and kinds of equip-

1. Please check the things you would like to learn to do better.

_____ cook

_____ sew

_____ swim

_____ write

_____ sing

_____ play baseball

_____ play basketball

_____ read

_____ get along with other children

_____ get along with grownups

_____ climb the ropes

_____ make pictures

_____ make things with clay

_____ arithmetic

_____ make maps

2. Winter is here. We hope to have some good days for winter games. Please answer yes or no to the following questions to help with planning.

_____ Do you like to ice skate?

_____ Do you have ice skates?

_____ Do you like to go sledding?

_____ Do you have a sled?

_____ Do you like to throw snowballs?

_____ Do you like to make snowmen?

_____ Do you like to make snow forts?

Fig. 6-4

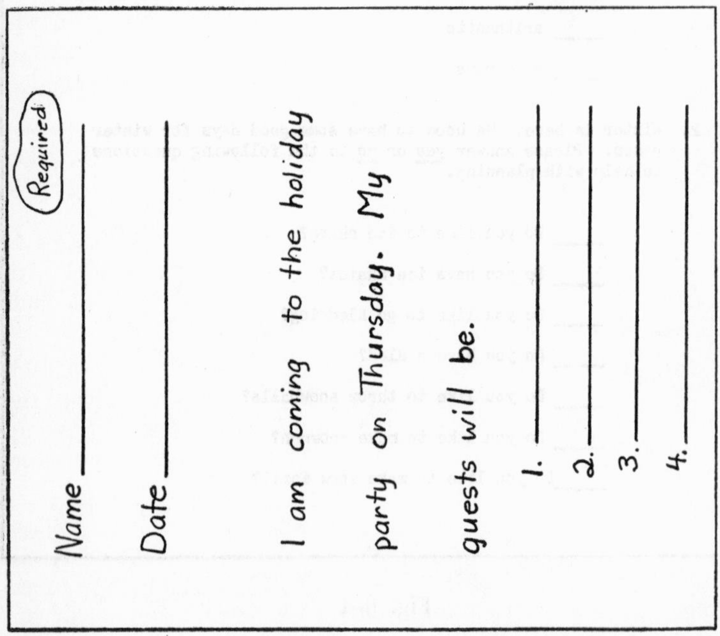

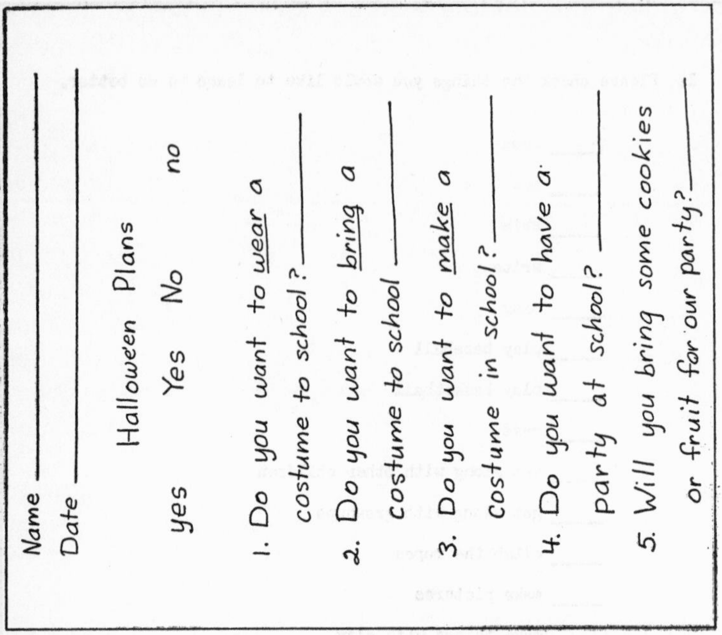

Name _____

Date _____

Halloween Plans

yes   Yes   No   no

1. Do you want to <u>wear</u> a
   costume to school? _____

2. Do you want to <u>bring</u> a
   costume to school _____

3. Do you want to <u>make</u> a
   costume in school? _____

4. Do you want to have a
   party at school? _____

5. Will you bring some cookies
   or fruit for our party? _____

Fig. 6-6

(Required)

Name _____

Date _____

I am coming to the holiday
party on Thursday. My
guests will be.

1. _____

2. _____

3. _____

4. _____

Fig. 6-5

ment to help the children acquire a basic reading vocabulary, including the vocabulary of *fairness,* which is very basic to children.

And whatever the specifics of the plan, teachers are finding that when a child can read and think through the possible alternatives, especially if the list includes those he has helped to explore or suggest, and can sign his name for the job or the material or the committee he chooses, then something happens to the degree and quality of his involvement. This becomes a very meaningful communication between him and his friends, between him and his group—a sort of contract or declaration of his intention to do a job, to carry out a responsibility. Before he signs he has to think what this particular choice will commit him to. It is a plan he is accepting with his signature. It is a reminder, too—a reminder that some friend or some group is counting on him now to do a particular job and to do it well. To a child this can bring reassurance and self-respect.

Hence children of all ages, as well as their teachers, are using the sign-up sheets as a convenient and sensible tool for seeing the selected word patterns they are also hearing in the affairs of their everyday world. In whatever form, it is a wonderful way to register one's own request or choice, and to find out from one another:

Who wants to go . . .	(to the Planetarium, on a hike with Iva, to the vegetable farm after school with Mother and me, to see "Nature's Half Acre"?)
Who will help . . .	(me write a book on A. Lincoln's Childhood, feed Crissy next week, wire the playhouse for the Kindergarten, set up the Science Exhibit, plant the nasturtiums?)
Who wants to use . . .	(the film-strip projector, the hot plate, the doll carriage, the new World Atlas, the green stilts, the red bike, the United States puzzle?)

Who will come . . .	(to hear Howard's story, to watch "Meet the Press" Sunday at my house, to the Valentine Party, early in the morning to help finish the scenery?)
Who wants to play . . .	(a musical instrument at the concert, on the fifth-grade ball team, with Peter and Pepita over the week-end?)
Who wants to be . . .	(in the Wild Animals Study Club, on the U.N. Committee, on the Hallowe'en Refreshment Committee, the first committee to give its report?)
Who wants to read . . .	(with Miss Steffan at 11:00, at 1:00, at 2:00, my new book *Nobody Listens to Andrew,* these books we have written, the latest *Jack and Jill,* Schneider's *Under the City?*)
Who needs help . . .	(on word study, on reading, on riding a bicycle, on learning the Morse code, on batting the soft ball, on playing the piano, on writing music?)
Who wants to have . . .	(a copy of this newspaper, a conference with Mr. Carlson, some of my baseball cards, a stamp from the U.S.S.R.?)
Who wants to . . .	(dictate a story, paint, learn ballet from Judy, cook, read, work with clay, have your clay things fired, trade airplane cards, fish for minnows to sell?)

Who wants to make . . .   Who needs . . .   Who has finished . . .
Who knows how . . . ?   Sign here.

. . . And all of this without the whole group's talking about it. Without the necessity of holding up the class to find out the plans of this child or the other, this committee or the other. Without the teacher having to serve as the clearing house for all of the plans and ideas, when a bulletin board especially reserved for such genuine written communication can do the job so much more efficiently. "Children can sign up for what they want and go right to work when they come in in the mornings," comments Mr. Watson, whose youngsters have just begun to use sign-up sheets for their Morning Work Time. "So much more sensible than having the whole class sit and wait and listen to whose turn it is to use the different materials. Here it is the children involved who are talking and reading and writing significantly among themselves, re-enforcing basic language patterns. And this frees me to move about and help where I'm needed."

WRITTEN PLANS AND AGENDAS.   When classroom conditions are right, then—because teachers have set them up that way—children come to use speaking and reading and writing to facilitate their planning and moving ahead. Children have a variety of ways, in addition to sign-up sheets, for listing and checking jobs to be done, individually or as groups. If it is the plan of a committee or group it may be posted on the bulletin board for easy reference or, if the need warrants, duplicated and made available for use by the individuals concerned. Such lists may include:

Questions for Mr. Ashdown When He Comes

Things to Complete before Our Report Date

Plans for the Puppet Show

Books to Consider for the Book Week Play

Agenda for the Mystery Writers' Club

Program of the History Committee

Plans for Interviewing Older Citizens

Space Club Newspaper Plans

Jobs to Be Done for the Science Show

Things to Take to the Park

Tentative Baseball Calendar

Catskill Animal Farm Trip Booklet

Schedule for Reading *Cotton in My Sack*

Children make their own individual plans as well, such as What I Need for my Bookcase, My Christmas Gift List, Table of Contents for *The Story of Maple Sugar Products*. A child can be helped to work out his own efficient ways for initialing, crossing out, or otherwise checking off the items as given precedence or completed. In this way he learns to set realistic timetables, survey progress, propose new directions, and otherwise assume increasing responsibility for himself and his group.

Alert to possibilities for using reading and writing in a variety of situations, a teacher sometimes takes the lead with a group. "I made a list of the suggestions we put on the board for the play yesterday," Mr. Sanders tells a group of his sixth graders, "and here are copies for all of you. I thought they might come in handy for a check list as we go along." "Gee, thanks. That's a good idea," the children agree, as they read them through and make additions. For the next discussion of progress and further plans for the play, Merri Lou and Lettie proffer to keep the record and to put it on the ditto carbon for duplication.

LABELING THAT HELPS.   A further use of the written word by children and teachers to insure better organization as well as planning, is functional labeling. Not even for younger children is this the *floor, chair, cupboard,* and such obviously non-informative variety, but the genuine, purposeful kind of labeling that can actually make classroom living smoother and more responsible. Labels such as Song Books, Mystery Stories, Our Own Stories, Travel Books, Biographies, can help in the arrangement and use of the Book Corner. *This is Molly's Shell Collection, Leaves from Central Park Trees, Specialized Agencies of the United Nations, Letters from our Friends in Kyoto, Japan* (and translations by Kyosh and his mother), *Kenneth's One-man Water-color Exhibit, Photographs from the Picnic— Where Are You?* and similar communicative titles indicate other possibilities. Because they stand for concrete arrangements in children's minds, most children learn to read these words more easily than the carefully controlled words in their readers. Labels such as *Mystic Tape, Stray Pencils, Leather Tools, Old Christmas Cards,* keep supplies conveniently accessible. Other readable labels (on white paper or tape, perhaps) used on file or desk drawers, supply shelves, tool boxes, scrap boxes, victrola records, can similarly serve. So at times, when tables are arranged primarily for gift-making, let us say, can labels such as *Basket Weaving, Pottery Painting, Jewelry and Leather, Sewing and Knitting.* (See Doris's report, especially pp. 240–241.)

Where there is a class store, such things as price lists, goods labels, special signs, sales slips, checks, various accounts and records, can invite reading and writing that are important to the store's effective functioning, as well as to the children's concepts of useful language (Figs. 6.7, 6.8, 7.1, 7.2 on pp. 242–43).

Imaginative labels made by the teacher or children can suggest and make more realistic children's building and dramatic play also (Figs. 6.9 and 6.10).

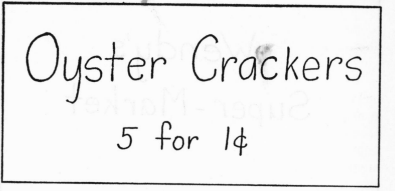

Oyster Crackers
5 for 1¢

Fig. 6–7

The Sixth B Bank   No. ____

Date ____

Pay to ____ $ ____
Amount ____

Signed

Fig. 6–8

TRIP PLANS AND PREPARATIONS.   The potentialities for children's useful written communication in the planning and preparation for class trips are almost limitless in scope and variety. If carefully structured, the thinking and study that go into the preparations for a trip can extend and deepen considerably the learnings which the children will experience from the actual trip. To suggest concretely a few of the many real possibilities, apart from the usual writing of letters in preparation, several pages are reproduced here of a trip booklet, worked out by one teacher page by page with her group of children (Figs. 6.11A–H). It is evident that while the teacher has designed the

Wendy's
Super-Market

Fig. 6–9

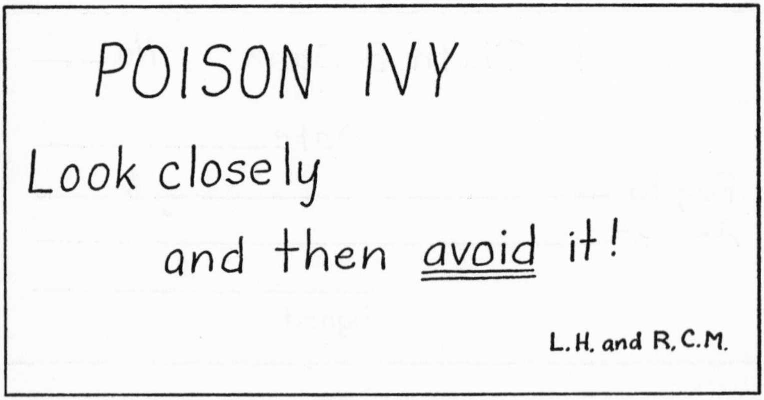

POISON IVY
Look closely
    and then <u>avoid</u> it!

L. H. and R. C. M.

Fig. 6–10

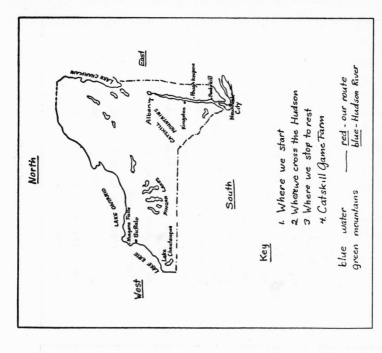

Key

1. Where we start
2. Where we cross the Hudson
3. Where we stop to rest
4. Catskill Game Farm

blue water —— red - our route
green mountains —— blue - Hudson River

Fig. 6-11-B

OUR TRIP

TO THE

CATSKILL

GAME FARM

Fig. 6-11-A

Money Planning
(Budgeting)

$1.00

Key

red — entrance fee
blue — rides
yellow — animal food
green — animal milk
purple — treat

Color in the pennies to show
how you plan to spend your
dollar.

Entrance fee	30¢ children
	85¢ adults
Rides	14¢
Animal food	5¢
Animal milk	10¢
Swings	free
Fire engines	free

Fig. 6-11-C

About Our Trip

When we drive along the
Hudson River to the Catskill
Game Farm, we'll be driving in
history! Henry Hudson sailed
up this river in 1609 in his boat
the Half Moon. No one knows if
he was attacked by wildcats, but
he named the mountains on
the west side of the Hudson
River the Catskill Mountains.
This name Catskill (Kaatskill)
means Wildcat Creek.

This is also the country
of Rip Van Winkle and his 20 year
sleep on a rock.

Needless to say, things were
different in Henry Hudson's day!
America did not belong to
America. Hudson was hired by

Fig. 6-11-D

About The Catskill Game Farm

The Catskill Game Farm raises animals to sell to zoos. There are about 700 animals on display. Visitors are invited to come right on in and be friendly with the animals. It isn't at all unusual to find a big llama rubbing his nose down your neck! In the animal nursery are baby deer and sheep and other animals crying for the already prepared bottles of warm milk.

The farm is off Highway 32 between Palenville and Cairo.

Fig. 6-11-F

the Dutch East India Company to explore this newly discovered river and claim it for the Dutch people.

This he did and little by little Dutch people came over and settled this colony called New Netherlands.

But then as now people were having wars to claim land! After 40 years of Dutch rule, New Netherlands was taken by the English people. They changed the name of the colony to New York in honor of the Duke of York. For over 100 years New York was ruled by the British.

Fig. 6-11-E

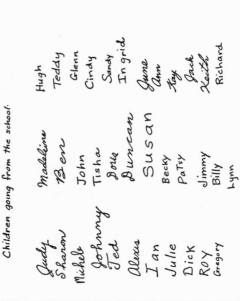

Trip to the Catskill Game Farm

May 21st

Leave school: 7:30 am.

Transportation: Chartered bus from A. Transit Company
Tel. KI 7440

Destination: Catskill Game Farm
Tel. Palenville 3350~

Children going from the school:

Judy	Madeleine	Hugh
Sharon	Ben	Teddy
Michele		Glenn
Johnny	John	Cindy
Ted	Tisha	Sandy
Alexis	Dora	Ingrid
Ian	Duncan	
Julie	Susan	June
Dick	Becky	Ann
Roy	Patsy	Kay
Gregory	Jimmy	Jack
	Billy	Keith
	Lynn	Richard

Fig. 6-11-H

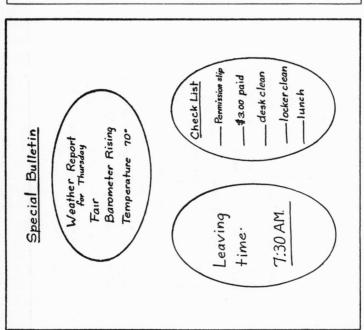

Special Bulletin

Weather Report
for Thursday
Fair
Barometer Rising
Temperature 70°

Check List
____ Permission slip
____ $3.00 paid
____ desk clean
____ locker clean
____ lunch

Leaving
time:

7:30 A.M.

Fig. 6-11-G

booklet with a number of good communication uses in mind, uppermost is her aim to make sure that the children's own individual involvement will enable them to find meaningful reading in the words and sentences and paragraphs that relate to their trip.

Learning and Using Written Communication in a Broader Context

Perhaps at this point in the chapter, lest the one-by-one consideration of these ways of structuring for the learning of reading and writing skills in the classroom take on an air of unrelatedness, it will not be amiss to inject some reference at least to whole learnings. From a series of informal letters written by our friend Mrs. Barnes to the parents of her class, we can get something of a picture of the ways in which some of these uses of written communication, for which she so sensitively sets up her classroom, take on meaning in the exciting, dynamic everyday living of children. The role of children's choice in the plans for class trips, for example, as well as in other areas of their individual and group planning, has particular pertinence here. The letters follow:

October 26

DEAR PARENTS,

This is one of the brief news reports we mentioned at our evening meeting. It is by no means a complete account of "life in Room 202." As we said then, it seems better to send accounts from time to time, mentioning different items of interest.

There are many important learnings in connection with reading. Here are some we are stressing now in our room:

1. *Reading is a kind of communication.* Children are learning that reading is concerned with real and important messages. Each morning they sign up for selected materials to take home in the afternoon. "I can tell where to sign up for the carriage because it starts like car" is typical of the conversation as each one makes certain that he is signing for what he wants. Recipes for cooking

are serving the same purpose, now that we have our hot plate. They are printed on a large card on the wall above the plate. When we were deciding on our first trip, I gave all the children three mimeographed pages, one describing a trip to the airport, one describing a trip to the zoo, and one describing a trip up the river. They read each page carefully. Then each child was given a page with "My first choice is" printed across the top. Each one filled in his choice and indicated his line of reasoning. When we go to the park we put a sign on our door (printed by a child) telling where we are. Each morning children sign up for choices, such as "We want to go on a hike with Iva," "I need wheels for my scooter." When we decided that the zoo trip should come first, the children wrote information about the trips for their parents.

2. *Reading is fun.* As often as we can during the day, we find time for children to read or hear stories of their choice. At morning snack time they look at books, ask to have stories read, and read to one another. Whenever a child writes or dictates a story we ditto copies for all the children to have in their folders, and we find times to sit down and read these stories together.

Those parents who have asked about helping their children at home can do a great deal to help children know that reading is communication and can be fun too. "Dear Henry, Look under your plate for a surprise" links reading with both of these. A short, simple, printed note on the door or some other familiar place saying, "Dear Bobby, I have gone to the store. Please wait for me. Mother" —or whatever message is appropriate, has the same value that our school messages have. All children love mail. A post card with a short message mailed from a city shopping trip can be fun. "Dear Henry, Do you like this funny card? I thought you would!" links reading with friendliness, love, fun, and security. Perhaps you are having other interesting experiences with reading as communication and fun that you'd like to share.

DEAR PARENTS,

Whenever a group of people live together, the problem of how to encourage disciplined action from individuals arises. Children learn most efficiently through the kind of activity that challenges them. It is important therefore that they do not associate discipline with "sitting still," "being quiet," "doing nothing." They must see disciplined action as an integral part of activity. With this in mind I have included the following kinds of activities:

1. In the afternoons we spend at least an hour in the gym or outdoors when the weather is good. We may use more than one place during the hour, including our own room. The very act of changing from one place to the other calls for disciplined action. In the big gym, children must first sit on the red line and then move into action; in our own room there is not enough space and equipment to move without considerable planning and sharing. Half the hour we call "work time," which means that children are disciplining themselves to learn to follow verbal or musical directions, use new equipment, and learn rules for games. The other half is "free time," which requires even more discipline in child planning.

2. When we go on trips, disciplined action is particularly necessary—planning, writing letters, reading for information, figuring and keeping within our budget of time and money, and following rules of every kind. Parents are welcome on our trips. You will hear more about this soon.

3. Equipment in a room calls for disciplined behavior too. The children's Inventing Corner looks like fun when they are busily at work. Close observation, however, reveals the thoughtful planning the children have to do in order to keep their materials available and ready for use. So it is with the balls, the hot plate, the maps, the games, the piano, and the phonograph.

4. The free work period may look as if the children are free from restrictions, but here too close observation shows how much discipline is necessary when there is no pattern laid down for all to follow.

Enclosed is a copy of our most recent program.

I enjoyed our meeting, and the visits with you also. Please feel free to come in at any time and to make suggestions.

DEAR PARENTS,

We have planned our first three trips. All of the skills come into real use on trips—planning, figuring time and money, following rules of all kinds, reading for information, writing letters. Parents are welcome (!!!) on any or all of our trips.

1. Bronx Zoo. Tuesday, October 30. We shall leave school about ten o'clock. Before we go each child will fill out an information card to have in his pocket should he get separated from the group. We'll take with us a small first aid kit and check to see what the weather prediction is before leaving. The telephone number at

the Zoo is Fordham 7-2000, should you want to send a message any time during the day. I'll call that number just before we leave for home. We'll take the Broadway-Seventh Avenue Express to the end of the line and walk two blocks to the Zoo entrance. Then we'll break into small groups, depending upon how many grown-ups are with us. We'll meet again as a group at the Zoo Bar which is just outside the children's zoo. We'll eat there. Children can buy their entire lunch or milk to go with whatever they bring. I suggest that they bring sandwiches in a paper bag, that they plan to buy milk, *that they do not have lunch boxes or thermos bottles which are breakable or must be brought back home*. We'll plan that the morning time *not* be spent in the children's Zoo. We'll meet there at twelve-thirty for lunch and spend the rest of the time in the children's zoo until 2:15 when we'll meet to leave. There is no charge to get into the zoo. The children's zoo cost 12¢, the train in the zoo 10¢ each way for a ride, the pony ride 15¢, the subway 15¢ each way. Most things that cost money are in the children's zoo—one reason for not spending the whole day there. Each child will need from 50¢ to 75¢. depending upon how much of his lunch he is buying and what he plans to do.

2. *Up the River*. We'll ride up the river on a train—a stream-liner, I hope. At Yonkers we'll take the ferry boat across to the New Jersey side. We'll come back by bus across the George Washington Bridge. Details later.

3. LaGuardia Airport. Excellent services are provided for school groups. Details later. (We'll not fly!)

I enjoyed our meeting and look forward to others. Please feel free to come in at any time and to make suggestions.

Sincerely,
KATHERINE BARNES

Learning and Using Written Communication for Finding Out and Keeping Records

INDIVIDUAL READING RECORDS.   With a good deal of varied reading going on in classrooms such as those reported in all of the preceding chapters, teachers face the problem of effective record-keeping in this connection. Here they recognize the importance of the children's being in on this responsibility, as well as of the opportunity for them to select from among alternative ways of keeping an account of their reading. Teachers are continually seeking ways to accomplish this, making sure the requirements are not so demanding that children will almost prefer not to read the books in the first place, and yet to allow for whatever genuine reactions the children want to share from time to time. Keeping track of numbers of pages read from day to day may also, in the case of some children, be their indications of having read from different parts of the book.

Mr. Carlson meets this problem, you remember, through the agreed-upon use of a card file, into which a child finishing a particular book may insert a card with author, title, child's name and date of reading, together with any reaction which he may have. (See page 38.) This is done partly to stimulate the spontaneous discussion that can follow contradictory reactions, or indeed similar ones, as they are recorded, thus encouraging other children perhaps to select the book in question. It is also meant to help children see how different people, with different experiences behind them, can interpret the author's message in different ways.

Other teachers and their children are finding other ways to accomplish the purpose. Some prefer, depending upon the age of their children and other specific conditions taken into account, to provide a variety of record forms from which the children may select, and from the reactions to which the teachers can get invaluable insights into the thinking and ways of working of individual children. Figures 6.12–6.16 show a few examples.

BOOK LISTS AND BIBLIOGRAPHIES. Book lists to serve one purpose or another are drawn up by teachers and children, frequently with the specialized help of the school librarian, and *read* by children and parents or whoever is concerned. *Favorite Books Read This Year, Books That Make Good Gifts, Books Recommended for Summer Reading, Books I Would Really Like to Own, Books Written by Authors in This School,* are suggestive of possibilities here. Also, of a somewhat different

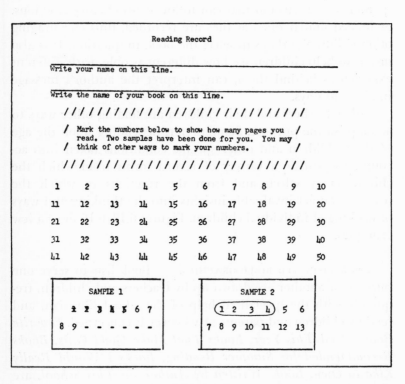

Fig. 6–12

Fig. 6–13

Name_____

Date_____

Reading Record

Signs and words you may need for your answer

✓ yes	no	to have fun
to read better	to get information	
I don't know	required	

1. I read alone._____

2. I read with_____

3. My Purpose:_____

_____

_____

_____

_____

_____

4. Book or other materials used:_____

_____

_____

5. Follow-up:

   Questions   _____

   Puzzle   _____

   Fact Cards   _____

   Report   _____

   Word Study   _____

   Other   _____

Fig. 6–14

Fig. 6–16

Name _____
Date _____

Reading Record

Hi! Would you like to know about a good book I am reading?   I will tell you something about it.

_____
_____
_____
_____

Fig. 6–15

Name _____
Date _____

Reading Record

When I read today I _____

_____
_____
_____
_____
_____
_____

nature: *Books about Abraham Lincoln, Good Reading on Space and Space Travel, Wonderful Horse Stories, Bibliography for Our Study of Emerging Africa, United Nations Bibliography.* It is not only books that appear on such lists, as the following titles indicate: *Sources of Information for Our Study of Early Coalville, Chapter Six: How We Checked Our Facts, Where and How You Can Get Information About Turtles, Where I Got Information for Writing This Book, Sources for My Report on the Sit-Ins.*

GUIDE QUESTIONS AND STUDY HELPS.   Many teachers find that good guide questions and thought-provoking study helps, such as Dan's teacher in the previous chapter aids him and his classmates to work out (see pp. 111–113), can give point to children's reading and add depth and focus to their individual and group investigations. Samples are shown in Figs. 6.17 and 6.18.

New Friends and New Places   pages 59-78

Name ——————————————————————

Date ——————————————————————

Follow-up

Information **please**! Why do so many people seem so disgusted with the little helicopter? Why do you talk about the helicopter and laugh and make fun of what the helicopter does? Why do you finish the story if you don't like it? I need some **facts**. Is this a good story or isn't it?

——————————————————————
——————————————————————
——————————————————————
——————————————————————

Fig. 6–17

Name _____ Date _____

<u>TWINS</u>

    This is me. This is when I was just powdered. This is my sister. She is littler than me. Now she is crying because I was powdered first. Mommy went out so our nurse Mattie had to powder us. She also put Baby Oil on us. My name is Patricia. My sister's name is Mary. We just had a bath before we were powdered. Guess how old I am? I am four months old. Now my sister is crying again because I didn't say how old she was first. She is my twin sister.

About the Author

Yes No ?

    1. The author is 4 months old.

    2. The author is using Patricia and Mary to tell about a feeling.

    3. The author probably knows what it means to feel jealous.

    4. The author wants the reader to know how it feels to be jealous.

    5. The author doesn't like jealous people.

Fig. 6-18

Figure 6.18, in which a child's own story is used as the base, is an example of one teacher's method of helping children to read between the lines. Important in such worksheets is the expectation that the children will answer only those items which make sense to them. The teacher purposely plans her questions—some calling for factual answers and some for reading between the lines—so that no one answer is the *right* answer. Any answer that a child writes helps his teacher to note his increasing depth of understanding in reading.

LANGUAGE AND WORD STUDY.   Miss Floyd and other teachers in Part One of this book, as well as Erling's teacher Mrs. McKinney in the preceding chapter, know that word study at

---

Name   Date

Find a picture that shows the word *summer.*

Is there a girl in the picture? _____

What is she doing?

_____

Is there a boss in the picture? _____

What is the boss doing?

_____

Would you like to be someone in this picture?

The boss _____

Another person _____

Fig. 6–19

times other than book-reading periods, can be of value to children in helping them understand the mechanics of their own language. From familiar words or parts of words they learn how words are constructed. They even surprise themselves at times to discover how quickly beginning with a word they know, they can figure out how to spell many other words closely related in structure. Children feel a growing sense of power as they manipulate words, discover language patterns, and, particularly older boys and girls, actually *discover the rules* of language—of spelling or grammar or whatever else—which once upon a time their own parents and teachers had to memorize! (See Figs. 6.24 and 6.25.)

Name   Date

Find a picture that shows the word *family*.

Draw a line under the words that tell who is in the picture.

_____ father

_____ a nice father

_____ a little girl

_____ a happy little girl

_____ a frightened child

_____ a girl who loves her father

_____ a crying girl

_____ an unfair person

_____ a cruel person

_____ a teacher

_____ my teacher

Fig. 6–20

In the worksheets, Figures 6.19–6.22, the teacher makes use of pictures to help the children read deeper meaning into the words, to help them see that the meaning of a word is dependent upon the context in which the word appears. Sometimes she provides a choice of pictures from magazines and other such sources. More often she has the individual children simply select their own pictures from familiar reading materials. And because of the way the worksheets are constructed, the children's answers give the teacher important insight into the personal meanings that each child brings to the common words that he meets in his reading. For example, one child looking at a picture of a man, will see him simply as *a father,* and will

Name _____ Date _____

Find a picture that shows the word <u>people</u>

Draw a line under the words that tell who is in the picture.

_____ father

_____ a nice father

_____ a little girl

_____ a happy little girl

_____ a frightened child

_____ a girl who loves her father

_____ a crying girl

_____ an unfair person

_____ a cruel person

_____ a teacher

_____ my teacher

Fig. 6–21

check the blank accordingly. Another child will see this same man as *an unfair person, a cruel person,* or perhaps *a nice father.* The child who does not see these further qualifications for the man will not have the feeling that his answers are wrong because he did not check more words. To him what he sees in the picture *is* what is there. And the teacher takes this as bona fide information about this child's perception. When a child's perception is shown to be harmfully limited, and when it is in an area about which the school can do something (as when a child tends always to see the teacher in the picture as an unfair person), the teacher makes plans for new experiences that will help the child have new perceptions. This is a far more basic way for improving reading vocabulary than is the method of simply showering the child with lists of new words, on the expectation that words can be learned apart from the living context. That learning to read or sound out new words is a complete process within itself, or can be accomplished without accompanying experience.

```
 Name                      Date

Find a picture that shows the word _____ .
Mark x by each word that tells who are in the picture
  man        lady        girl        boy        dog

Do you think this picture could really happen?
_____

Do you think it did really happen?
_____
```

Fig. 6–22

Again, it is the child's perception that invites him to see a boss in a picture which, to another child or group will not have a boss at all. The difference between these teacher-constructed materials and many of the commercially made materials commonly in use is just this: in the commercially prepared materials, generally speaking, there is one right answer for each question. And *right* is determined by the perception of the adult who prepared the materials. No provision is made for the reading between the lines which always goes on when a human being brings himself to the printed page and tries to organize meaning in what he finds there. When a child does bring his own meanings to such materials, and comes up with his own answer, different from the one expected by the person who created the materials, the child is the one labeled *wrong*. In this case, instead of insight passing between him and his teacher with regard to his way for reading, this evaluation of wrong is the only communication that passes. And wrong is of course a barrier rather than an invitation to communication.

Children, even younger ones, love to experiment with words and sounds and new language patterns. Along with using their own stationery, exchanging notes with their own close group members, they are fond of inventing signs and codes and sometimes a quite new language of communication.

Fig. 6–23

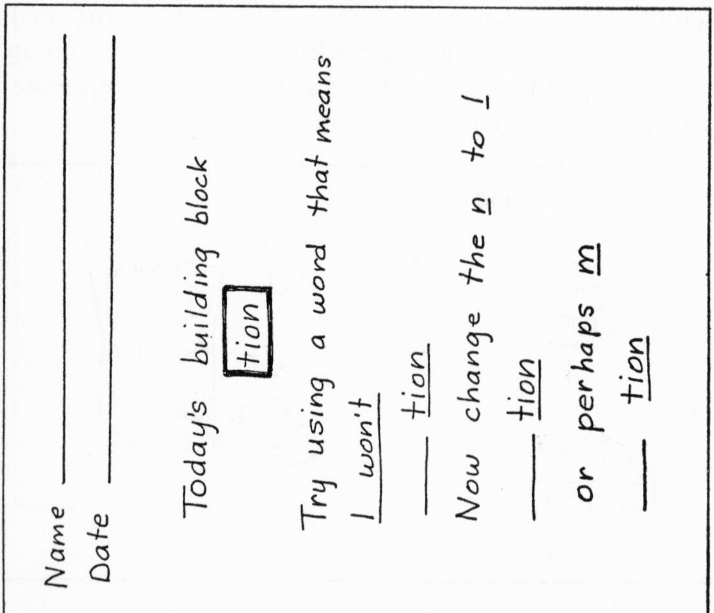

Fig. 6-25

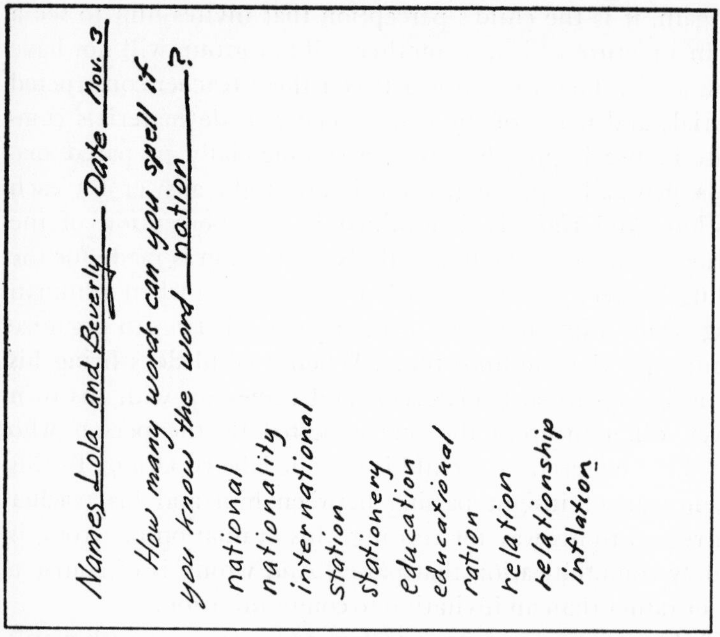

Names Lola and Beverly   Date Nov. 3

How many words can you spell if
you know the word __nation__?

national
nationality
international
station
stationery
education
educational
ration
relation
relationship
inflation

Fig. 6-24

Name _____
Date _____

Today's building block

[__tion__]

Try using a word that means
I won't

_____ __tion__

Now change the __n__ to __l__

_____ __tion__

or perhaps __m__

_____ __tion__

Name_____

Date_____

Word Study Record

Signs and words for your answer

✓   yes   no

Today I am studying these words.

_____

_____

Ways for studying:

Writing_____

Spelling_____

      to myself_____

      with_____
                   name of person

Tracing_____

Thinking_____

Testing_____

Other_____

Fig. 6–26

A single word is also given importance when a child can respond to its wholeness. Spelling and pronouncing the word "as the world spells it," and defining it in terms of its meaning to him, is one way for achieving this feeling of wholeness. Teachers, and children too, discover the varied meanings individual people have for words when children are given opportunity to respond spontaneously to a given word—*happy, sad, afraid, bored, good, bad, unfair, friend, mother*—by simple drawing or by word definition. (See Figs. 6.27–6.31.)

Individual children show their fascination with language in delightfully spontaneous ways. It is during the Morning Work Time, when his classmates are engaged in a variety of undertakings, that ten-year-old Ben, restlessly moving about at first, suddenly has an idea—an idea that calls for action. It is the language patterns of another time and place, currently investigated by Ben's own study club, that give him food for thought. By the end of the period, obviously having had a very enjoyable frolic with words, some traditional patterns of which he knows well enough to deliberately distort them, Ben comes up with the following piece:

The brave knight will rideth
Where the path guideth
To slay the knight in gold
And goeth the tale
The knight did not fail
And slayeth the knight so bold
A hero he was
And his honor and pride
Was valiantly won
From his gallantry ride
So in gold the knight is no more
A ruthless killer they could not endure

The king was a man proudeth of him
He had a black beard neither bristley nor slim
He said to the knight with a glare in his eyes
You deserve this right well, here is your prize
The knight bowed low and thanked the king true
And looked at his prize as any man would do

A bag full of gold, and a bag full of silver, and
   a bag full of money o' brass
He packed and mounted his horse
And went without force
Through the mountains and valleys agrass

At inn he stayed
And he talked all night
Of his gallant fight
And the knight of gold armor he slayed
The innkeeper listened with eyes on the gold
He was too clever for it to be stoled
So made he prices right high
And when came the morn the knight said in sigh
Fifteen pounds and twenty groats and sixpence down the drain
It's the innkeepers fault
With his giant full vault
By the blade of my sword this will mean assault
En garde thy villain no coward ist I
Fight for your life and die for your lie
How now said the innkeeper frightened
I'll fight you to the end, and his grip on sword tightened
Calleth me coward now I shall slayeth
But at the end the innkeeper layeth
And so the tale must to an end
For I have no more paper or poems to lend.

Fig. 6–27

Fig. 6-29

Fig. 6-28

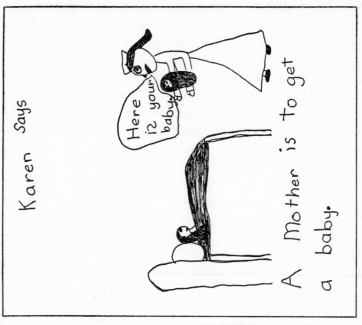

Fig. 6-31

Fig. 6-30

NUMBER SYMBOLS.   Words are not the only written symbols where form is necessary to communicate meaning. Arithmetic or number symbols also depend upon pattern, which teachers help children to learn from the beginning. Usually in combination with words, number symbols are met very early and come to have meaning to young children as they find them in, or as they are related to, their own real experiences. The variety of budget-planning falls into this category. Furthermore, the happy personal could-be-true little stories about children which teachers write quickly on a ditto carbon to give to children to read, can frequently take on more interest and challenge if the closing sentence or question gives children a reason to fill in a blank with a number, or in some other important way to register their number thinking. (See Figs. 6.32–6.39.)

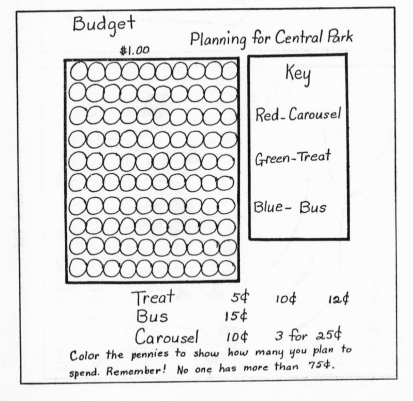

Fig. 6–32

MY IMPORTANT NUMBERS

Name   Date

MY IMPORTANT NUMBERS

I am _____ years old.

I live _____ from school.
       blocks   miles

There are _____ children in my room.

There are _____ windows in our room.

There are _____ boys in our room.

There are _____ girls in our room.

Here is a number story about our room.

     .....boys   .....children

     .....girls   .....teacher

     .....teacher   .....people

     .....people

Fig. 6–33

CALENDARS.   Calendars too serve to help children see that numbers and words (or letters) carefully placed—even carefully placed by the children themselves—can represent a great deal of very useful information. The teacher runs off a large supply of blank calendars, such as the one below. She helps the children to write the name of the month in its proper place, the appropriate letter for each day of the week, and, as they find

Name _____   Date _____

MY IMPORTANT NUMBERS

I am _____ years old.

I come _____ to school.
      blocks   miles

I wear size _____ shoes.

My sweater is size _____.

I weigh _____ pounds.

I am _____ tall.
    feet   inches

Here is a number story about me.

Once upon a time I weighed _____ pounds.

Now I weigh _____ pounds.

Once upon a time I was _____ old.
      years   months

Now I am _____.

Once upon a time my shoes were size _____.

Now they are size _____.

Fig. 6–34

where the first day of the month is to fall, the rest of the numbers. Furthermore, when a child keeps track of his attendance on a calendar form, he is helped to understand that *he* is the one who is moving through time and that *he* is the one who can use number language to keep track of his movement. The

Funny Anne!
She had 7 balloons.

She stuck 4 of them
with a pin. Bang!!! Bang!!!
Bang!!! Bang!!!

Now she has _____ balloons.

Fig. 6–35–A

Lucky Tuckie! He has two

apples.   He wants to give Billy

$\frac{1}{2}$ of an apple. Then he will

have _____ apples left.

Fig. 6–35–B

calendar numbers in and of themselves can't tell how many days he has been in school. The calendar is simply one of the culture's special arrangements of numbers—a mathematical form invented by people to help themselves keep track of where they have been and where they are going in TIME. All of the numbers on a calendar describe *TIME* in terms of days and weeks and months and years. But these numbers do not tell PEOPLE where they are in Time. Each individual person must still bring himself to this arrangement of numbers—*must still find himself* in TIME. This a child does when he keeps his own daily attendance record. Coloring *red* for days when he is not in school and in other ways using mathematics to make the calendar talk to and for him, a child is putting his personal claim on the culture's generalization of TIME. (See Fig. 6.36.)

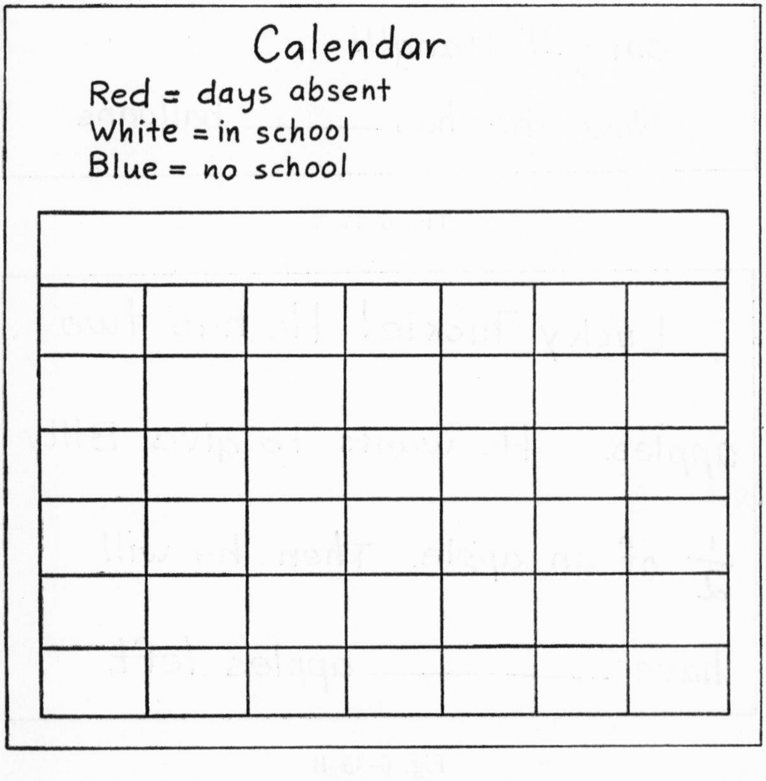

Calendar
Red = days absent
White = in school
Blue = no school

Fig. 6–36

THINKING ABOUT ROOM ARRANGEMENT

There are _____ boys in our group.

There are _____ girls in our group.

There are _____ students in our group.

We could sit together in groups of 6.

We would need _____ sixes.

There would be _____ students left over to form a smaller group.

Picture language:

Number language: 6) _____

Here are other plans which I can see in picture language, word language, and number language.

Fig. 6-37

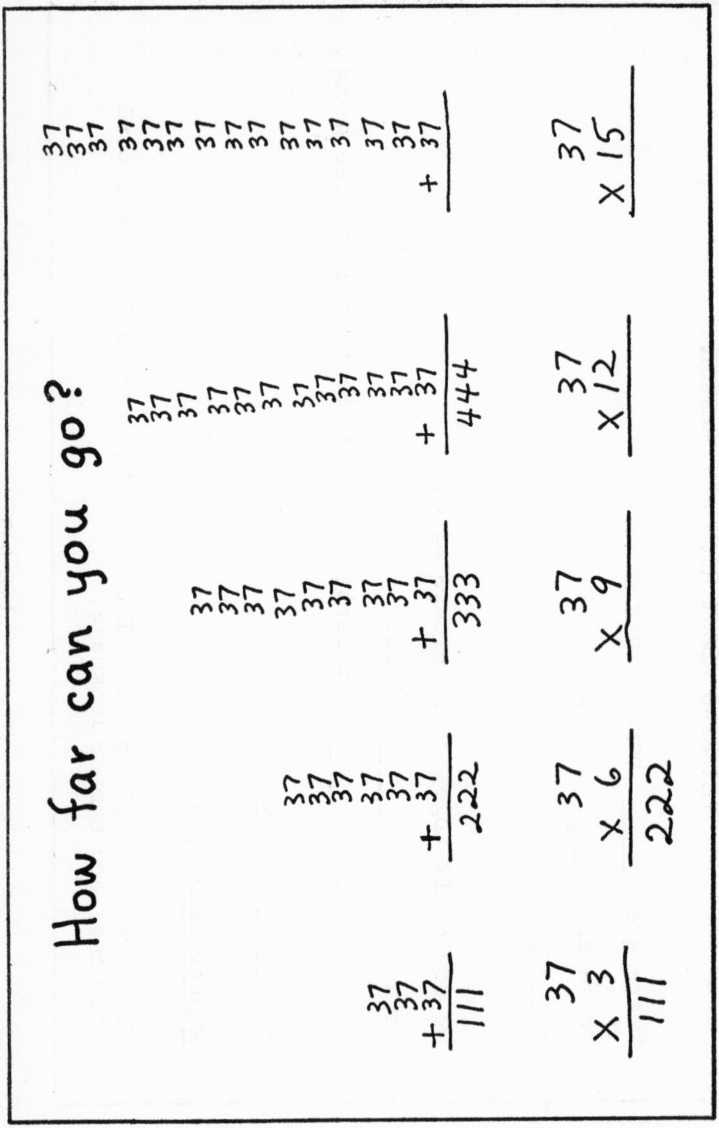
How far can you go?
37 37 + 37 111
37 × 3 111
37 37 37 37 37 + 37 222
37 × 6 222
37 37 37 37 37 37 37 37 + 37 333
37 × 9
37 37 37 37 37 37 37 37 37 37 37 + 37 444
37 × 12
37 37 37 37 37 37 37 37 37 37 37 37 37 37 + 37
37 × 15

Fig. 6–38

Learning and Using Written Communication for Sharing Ideas and Fun

LETTER WRITING.   Writing letters on one's own self-designed stationery helps many children learn to read:

> If writing and receiving letters is a regular part of the school day.
>
> If children are free to ask how to spell words and copy words which are spelled correctly so that valuable drill is not wasted on writing and seeing words spelled incorrectly.
>
> If children are helped to organize letter-writing words into card files or notebooks where they are easily available.
>
> If the letters are sincere expressions of feeling and not school exercises in writing only those feelings which fall within some adult's basic vocabulary.

Miss Bradshaw's class has set up a mail box just outside the door. Letters, notes, invitations, and announcements from outside the classroom are deposited here to be collected, distributed, or posted on the bulletin board, as the case may be, at particular times of day. Inside the classroom too, the children find reasons for writing to one another. From time to time they drop in letters which they wish to have delivered. Rather than being frowned upon, this writing to one another during the school day is accepted by the teacher as a very worthy kind of communication among friends. (See Figs. 6.40–6.44.) When, in the course of individual or group correspondence, children use words to hurt one another, when strong club or other group rivalries bring forth written language that is meant to repress others, this is Miss Bradshaw's opportunity to discuss with the children certain limitations on individual freedom because of the framework of their situation. The classroom belongs to everyone. The mailbox belongs to everyone. Language cannot be used to enhance the living of some at the expense of others.

These are very important learnings for growing children, as through real experience they are helped to build socially useful meanings about the communication skills at their disposal. The realization that a respectable member of the Dinosaur Club would have certain limitations as well as certain guarantees with regard to his freedom does not come through verbal lessons about democracy spelled out in advance. Rather it is a socially useful meaning acquired in this classroom through the opportunities the teacher provides for using language in the day-by-day working out of problems. As such it is a meaning whose social usefulness is not confined merely to this concrete experience within the specific classroom. Future reading from books

Name

My Important Numbers

I am ____ years and ____ months old.

I am ____ feet and ____ inches tall.

I weigh ____ pounds.

My apartment number is _____.

My phone number is _____.

I live on the _____ floor.

There are _____ people in my family.

My favorite number is _____.

Fig. 6–39

Letter Words

Dear

thank you

present

happy

just right

Christmas

Hanukkah

wonderful

your friend

love

Fig. 6–40

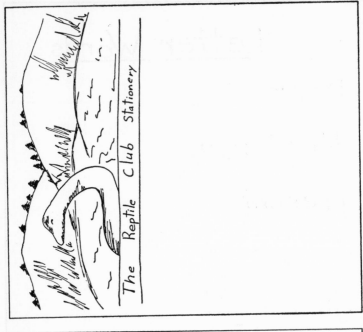

Fig. 6-42

Fig. 6-41

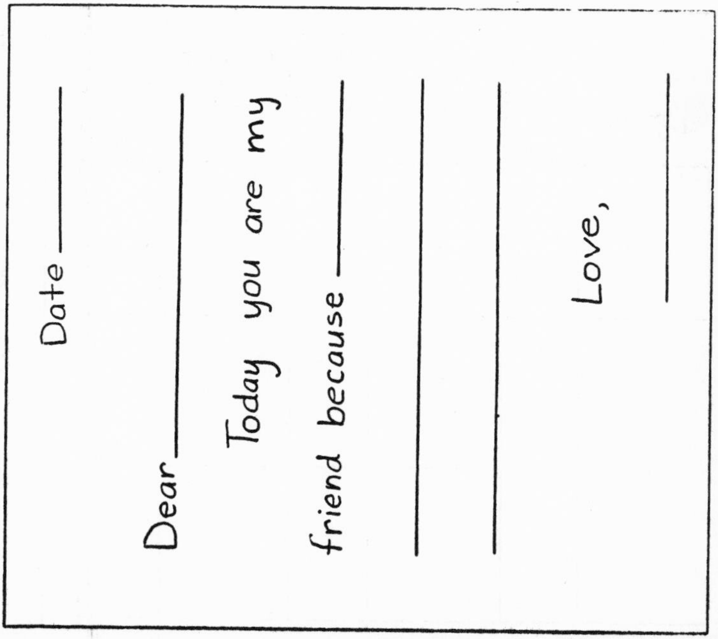

Name _____
Date _____

My birthday wish for you
is that _____
_____
_____
_____

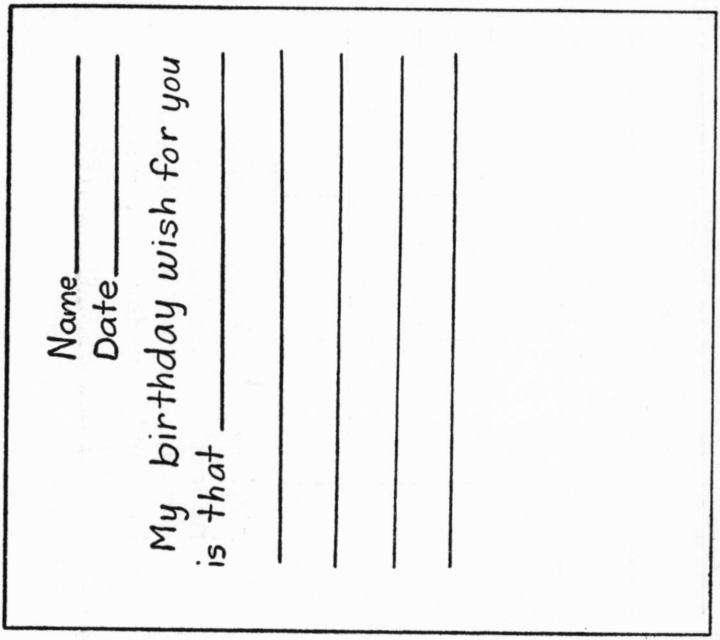

Fig. 6-44

Date _____

Dear _____

Today you are my

friend because _____
_____
_____

Love,

_____

Fig. 6-43

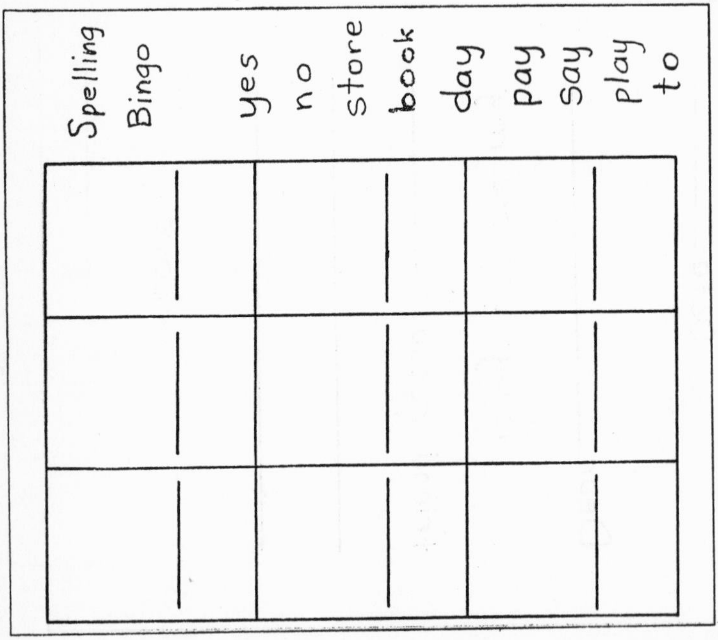

Spelling
Bingo

yes
no
store
book
day
pay
say
play
to

Fig. 6-45

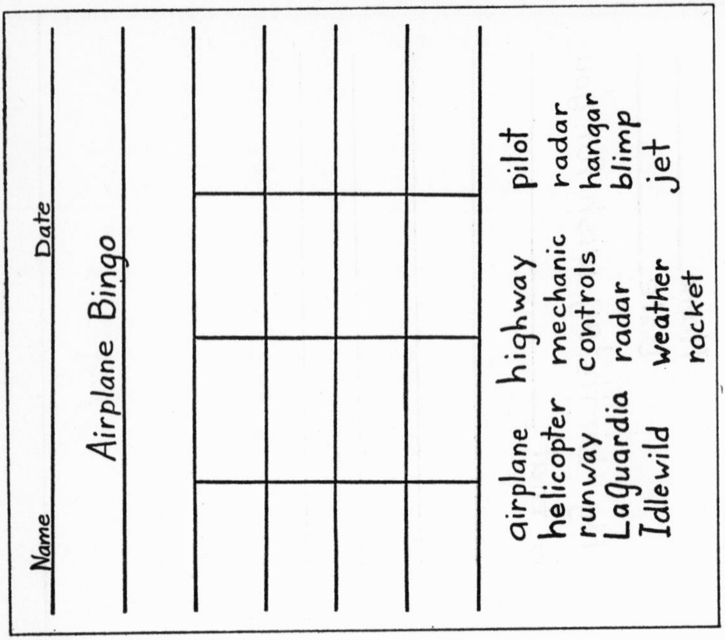

Name   Date

Airplane Bingo

airplane   highway   pilot
helicopter mechanic radar
runway   controls   hangar
Laguardia radar   blimp
Idlewild   weather   jet
           rocket

Fig. 6-46

WORD BINGO

When a child chooses a Spelling Bingo sheet, he copies the words at the side of the page into the squares in any order he chooses. When all of the children playing together (usually a group of five or six) have their words copied, one child acts as caller. He calls the words off one at a time. As he calls each word, the children mark that word where they have written it in a square. As soon as a child gets a row of words marked, he wins. Usually the children like to go on and play until everyone gets a row marked. Sometimes they prefer to begin another new game immediately. This flexible material is useful for the following reasons:

1. Children can bring their own stages of learning to the material and find a comfortable way to move forward.

2. Because the words are written correctly on the paper, the time spent copying these words is worthwhile drill time. The children do not guess at the spelling.

3. Children of varying academic but similar social skills can play together. One child may copy the words and ask what they say. Another may know how to read and spell several of them. Either way of getting the words down allows successful completion of the game.

4. Children can easily prepare stencils, thus making even more provision for "finding themselves" in the work materials provided. This also provides for invitations to be tempted beyond one's own interests and achievements into Bingo games suggested by friends.

Fig. 6–47

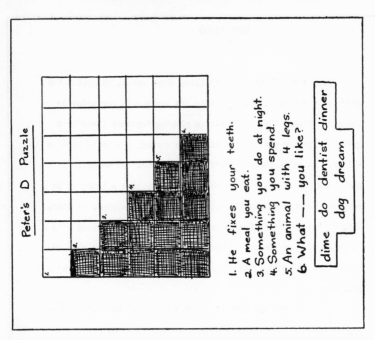

Peter's D Puzzle

1. He fixes your teeth.
2. A meal you eat.
3. Something you do at night.
4. Something you spend.
5. An animal with 4 legs.
6. What —— you like?

dime do dentist dinner
dog dream

Fig. 6-49

Johnny
Name

1. What flies in the air on a string?
2. Who is going to be a mother soon?
3. What did we use as bait for the fish?
4. Who always wears Patsy's pretty hats?
5. When we went rowing we spent 15¢
   to ride for ½ ——.

Fig. 6-48

Jerry wrote two cards.

And he read two books.

After lunch he played on the roof.

After school he took off his shoes.

Then he got some water.

And he washed the windows.

Fig. 6-51

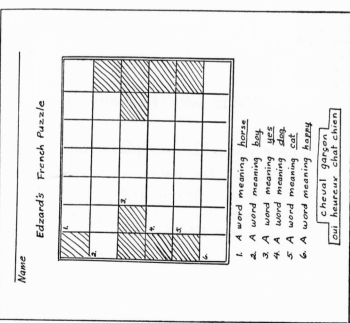

Name

Edzard's French Puzzle

1. A word meaning <u>horse</u>
2. A word meaning <u>boy</u>
3. A word meaning <u>yes</u>
4. A word meaning <u>dog</u>
5. A word meaning <u>cat</u>
6. A word meaning <u>happy</u>

cheval garçon
oui heureux chat chien

Fig. 6-50

and newspapers, or listening to broadcasts about freedom of communication in a democratic society, will to some degree be interpreted by these children in terms of meanings grown out of these thoughtfully structured firsthand experiences.

PUZZLES AND GAMES. A variety of games, the idea for which initiates with the ingenuity of the teacher but is soon picked up and extended by the children themselves, makes good use of and practice in word skills. Mrs. Dunn's *Word Bingo* is a favorite with her children because it is both challenging and fun. It is a favorite with Mrs. Dunn because it invites so much learning on the part of individually differing children and lends itself to so many profitable uses. Figures 6.45–6.47 show one "issue" of Word Bingo, together with Mrs. Dunn's explanation of it, as well as another sample of Bingo sheet made and used by older children:

Simple, horizontal-only *crossword puzzles,* made by teacher and children together, also provide good word study. They help children to focus on whole words and their meanings in

Bingo Was His Name-o

There was a farmer had a dog
Bingo was his name-o
B-i-n-g-o   B-i-n-g-o
B-i-n-g-o
Bingo was his name.

Fig. 6–52

relation to their own everyday interests and experiences. Quite like many grownups in their culture, boys and girls of any age enjoy the challenge of figuring out, as well as of making and dittoing, such puzzles, which of course increase in complication as the children grow older. Three of these crossword puzzles, each suggesting a different type of content, are reproduced in Figures 6.48–6.50.

COMIC SHEETS.   Jerry and his classmates enjoy reading again and again the comic which their student teacher makes for Jerry, depicting in word and picture, some of the actual experiences and skills of this friendly, outgoing little boy. (See Fig. 6.51.) All the children are glad to read such comics on the bulletin board, together with an offer of dittoed copies for the individual folders of those who would like them.

WORDS TO FAMILIAR SONGS AND RHYMES.   Children have good reading practice too, although they do not think of it as reading, when they are given typed or printed copies of familiar

---

A Jump-Rope Rhyme

My mother and your mother
Live across the hall
Every night they have a fight
And this is what they call
Icka bicka soda cracker
Icka bicka boo
Icka bicka soda cracker
Out goes you!

Fig. 6–53

Bow, bow, bow, Belinda
Bow, bow, bow, Belinda
Bow, bow, bow, Belinda
Won't you be my darling!

Right hand round, bow, Belinda
Right hand round, bow, Belinda
Right hand round, bow, Belinda
Won't you be my darling!

Left hand round, bow, Belinda
Left hand round, bow, Belinda
Left hand round, bow, Belinda
Won't you be my darling!

Both hands round, bow, Belinda
Both hands round, bow, Belinda
Both hands round, bow, Belinda
Won't you be my darling!

Do-si-do, bow, Belinda
Do-si-do, bow, Belinda
Do-si-do, bow, Belinda
Won't you be my darling!

Cast off, bow, Belinda
Cast off, bow, Belinda
Cast off, bow, Belinda
Won't you be my darling!

Fig. 6–54

songs to enable them to follow along as they sing. It makes sense to older children especially if, when learning a new song, or groups of songs for a school festival, say, they can be handed copies written by one person only and duplicated, instead of all being requested to copy the words laboriously and inefficiently from the blackboard, as is still common practice. Collecting and compiling favorite songs or poems or rhymes, as well as writing their own, is a hobby many children can enjoy and share with their friends. Figures 6.52–6.54 show samples from two different types of collections.

Sometimes a small group of youngsters on their own will get together and work very hard on a poem they have selected for the fun of reading in chorus fashion. This may get other children in the class going also, hunting up exciting rhythmic poems for the purpose and giving themselves practice in reading them aloud together. Student teacher Doris S. encourages such activities among the children in her classroom by bringing in dittoed copies of poems such as the following:

RAILROAD REVERIE*
By E. R. Young

The little boy stopped in the middle of the hayfield
And cocked his head and listened for the sound.
It was there, it was coming, it was growing,
   it was coming
It was coming, it was growing all around.
Far away, but growing nearer, growing nearer,
   growing nearer,
Coming closer, coming closer, coming closer
   all the while;
Rumble-rumble, rattle-rattle, clatter-clatter,
   clank-clank,
Chugger-chugger, chugger-chugger, and it reached
   the final mile.

The little boy, rooted in the middle of the hayfield,
Cupped his eyes to shade them from the sun,
And heard the far-off whistle and the far-off rumble
And the far-off rattle of the railroad tracks

As the heavy giant train roared on.
Catch-a-teacher, catch-a-teacher, patch his britches,
Patch his britches, catch-a-teacher-patch-his-britches,
Catch-a-teacher   Whoosh!

Chugger-chugger, chugger-chugger, smoke upon the hayfield,
Cinders in the boy's hair and soot upon his face;
Laughter in the boy's heart, joy in the boy's feet,
Laughter in the engineer's face.
Chugger-chugger growing fainter
Catchateacher patchhisbritches
Catchateacherpatchhisbritches
Chuggerchugger sssssssssssss.

And the little boy turns to other business of the day
As the heavy giant rumble rumbles out and fades away.

WRITING ABOUT ONE'S SELF.   To the sensitive teacher, it
can be useful to encourage children to write about themselves
and their personal choices. Such writing is usually kept in a
private folder for each child, and the contents of these folders
is not available for others to read unless a particular child wishes
to share what he has written. Reading and writing become
effective tools for communicating about one's private world
when worksheets such as those shown in Figures 6.55–6.59 are
provided.

Mrs. Bennett is pleased to note that her children are becoming increasingly sensitive to the fact that choices are not always
easy for people to make. That sometimes there are conflicting
forces at work that make choices difficult. As situations arise,
she helps children to look into the motives which people may
have for making decisions or taking action, and which at first
glance may seem unkind or unwise. Once in a while, too, she
makes a worksheet for them that helps to point up the problem.
If children are not themselves too closely checked on, she finds
that they can be helped to build an internal system of checking,
a growing awareness that people have different motives for their
actions. Figure 6.60 is one of the sheets Mrs. Bennett's children
take to their desks to fill out, but not without a good deal of
pondering and spontaneous comment among themselves, which
too she is interested in noting.

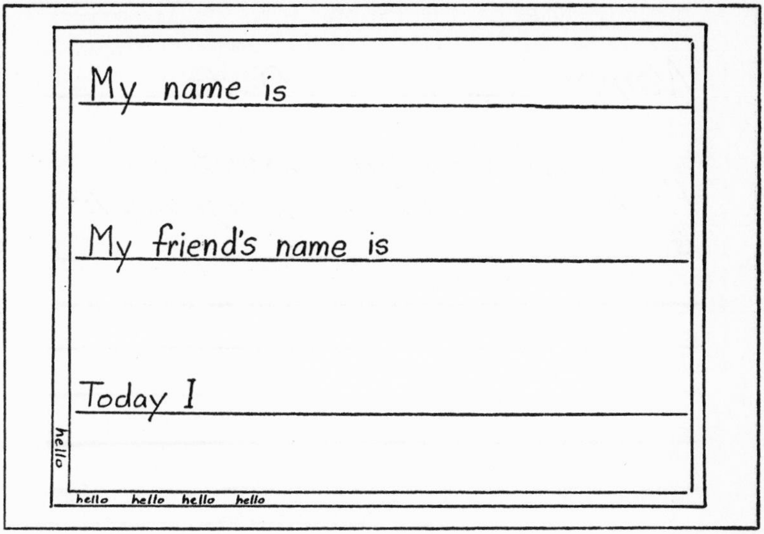

My name is _____

My friend's name is _____

Today I _____

hello   hello   hello   hello   hello

Fig. 6–55

HI - What are you

doing today?

Fig. 6–56

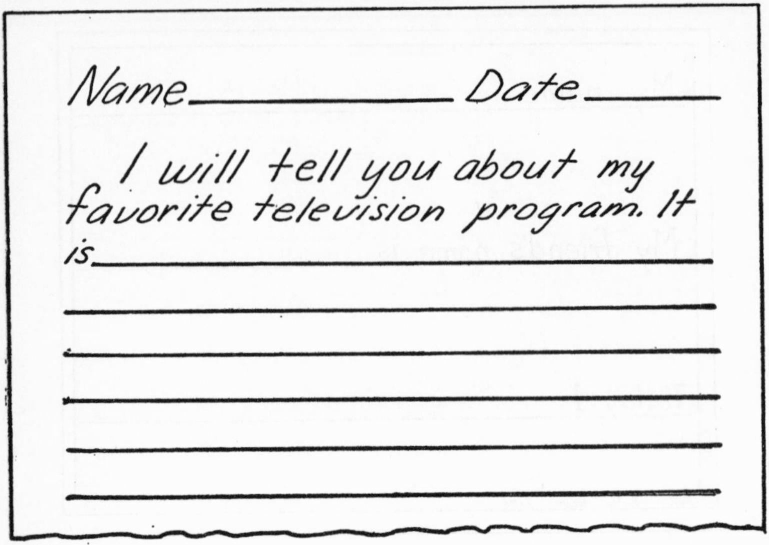

Name_____ Date_____

   *I will tell you about my favorite television program. It is*_____

_____

_____

_____

_____

_____

Fig. 6–57

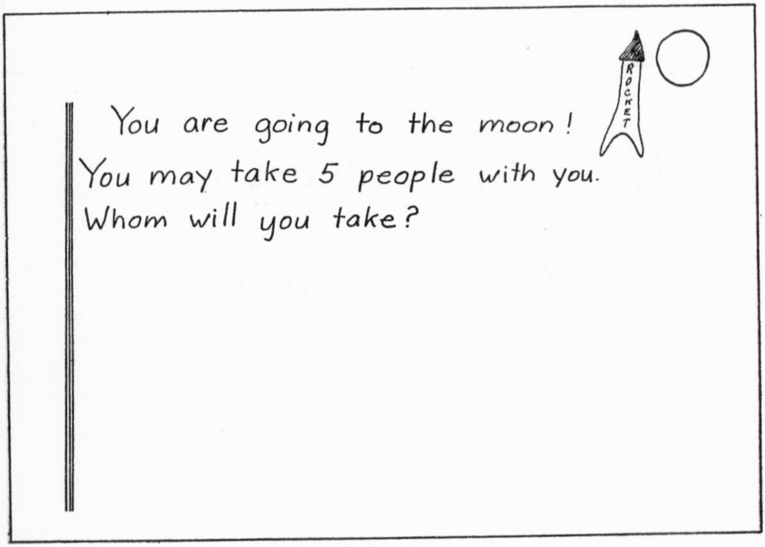

You are going to the moon!
You may take 5 people with you.
Whom will you take?

Fig. 6–58

ABOUT ME

1. My name is _____

2. I feel good when _____

   _____

3. I worry when _____

   _____

4. I feel happy when _____

   _____

5. I feel important when _____

   _____

6. I like to _____

   _____

7. I don't like to _____

   _____

8. I feel jealous when _____

   _____

9. I think _____

   _____

10. When I grow up I want to be _____

    _____

Fig. 6–59

Name_____

Date_____

    A storeman bought some tops to sell to children. He

tried one out on the sidewalk in front of his store. It flew

into the street.

    "This is a bad toy for children! They'll run into the

street after the tops. I'll send them back."

    This storeman_____

    1. was foolish. He lost money.

    2. was a friend to children. He didn't want them hurt.

    3. was not a friend to children. They would like tops.

    4. I don't know.

Fig. 6–60

Editor
Tish

202 News

Musicians Come To School

Program

Haydn	String Quartet
Ravel	String Quartet
Bartok	Jack in the Box
	The Life of a Fly
	POP Goes the Weasel

Sing along with the String Quartet!

All around the
    cobbler's bench
The monkey chased
    the weasel

The monkey stopped to
    pull up his socks

POP! goes the weasel.

Peter, Harry, Dike, and Walter came to entertain the children at our school.

We laughed at Peter and Dike when they said funny things.

The time flew by because we were having fun.

Fig. 6–61

January News

Brooks changed
her name to Tim.

Sambo gave
a report
about Russia.

Betsy's hamster
had babies

Andy made
a clay map.
He painted
it.

Barbara made a
beautiful clay girl.

Marion has a new brother.
Tommy brought his swords
to school.
Elsie put on her wraps in
four jumps of the clock
one special day.

Fig. 6-61-A

Once upon a time there was a
beautiful dog that lived under
my sink. It was a mother
dog and it was getting puppies
One nice day she got the puppies
and my mother said I had to
divide them in half with my
neighbor. There were 12 puppies
so I gave her 6 puppies and I
had 6 puppies left.
                              Vicki

I went to La Guardia Field
I had dinner there Every
six minutes we would look out
doors and watch the airplanes.
It was cold I was shivering.
                              Ann

Fig. 6-61-B

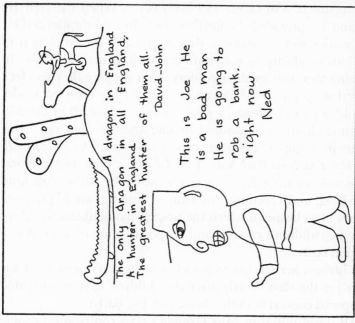

A dragon in England.
A dragon in all England.

The only dragon in England
A hunter in England
The greatest hunter of them all.
David John

This is Joe He
is a bad man
He is going to
rob a bank.
right now
Ned

Fig. 6-61-D

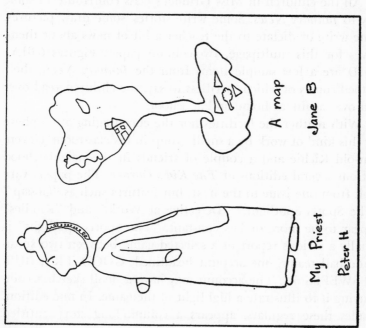

A map

Jane B

My Priest

Peter H

Fig. 6-61-C

INDIVIDUAL AND GROUP NEWSPAPERS.   When children are free and are provided the facilities to write and duplicate their own stories and newspapers, they respond to the wholeness of this human ability to communicate with written symbols. In so doing they also let their readers in on the way they see, feel, and value people and things and events of their everyday world. A child, a pair of friends, a small group—maybe all of these in the same classroom, reassured by one another—put out newspapers in single or several successive editions. *The Space Club Weekly, The New Park Star, The All-About Newspaper, Horse Sense, Science Club News* suggest some of the titles. This kind of writing, and certainly this kind of reading, are highly contagious in a classroom which the teacher has deliberately set up to invite children's creative and cooperative use of the communication skills.

Tish gets her teacher to help her make this one-event newspaper for the class shortly after the children have participated in a special concert at their school. (See Fig. 6.61.)

All the children in Miss Grumet's class contribute in some way to *January News.* Some write stories, some draw pictures, some write or dictate to the teacher a bit of news about themselves for this multipage, two-column paper. Figures 6.61A–6.61D are a few sample items from the *January News,* their dittoed copies of which, needless to say, the children read over and over again, at home and at school.

With neither the facilities nor the encouraging atmosphere for this kind of work by a small group in his classroom, eleven-year-old Richie and a couple of friends in the neighborhood put out several editions of *The Kid's Corner.* The papers vary a bit from one issue to the next, but features such as "Gossip," "The Sports Spotlight," "Detective at Work," and "Riddles" appear to be more or less constant. "The Sports Spotlight" is usually a serious report of a selected game between two sixth-grade ball teams, one account headlined, GOOD TRY, BUT 6-2 SWEEPS 6-3. The account may have a small sketch accompanying it to illustrate a highlight of the game. In one edition, besides these regulars, appears a column-long story entitled

"Deer Deer Counselor," which good-naturedly exaggerates a long strenuous hike which the boys at camp have to take. ". . . When I finally regained consciousness from the shock of him telling me I was to walk ten miles without a rest, I found out that I would have to walk with a twenty pound pack on my back. (At that moment I realized how Santa Claus must feel.) At first I refused, but he said if I didn't (go), I would get thirty straight days without missing one meal and with our food I would rather walk . . ." It ends with, "When the hike was over I finally died. The Cheerful End."

There is also a column of rhyme called—quite typically for this ambivalent age—"I Hate Goils," and two comics, "Micky the Zooloo" and "Modern Family." This newspaper reflects a modern child's environment, including the last paragraphs of a humorous column, to wit: "But, because of my vast experience in cases such as Master W. I have cured him of schnupur, compa lumpa, pampa, nomaitez. If you send in the coupon on the other side, plus a medical book I will send you free a pack of Wheaties box-tops. Thank you for your cooperation. I leave you with this thought: A hole in the head does not always indicate an open mind. The End." Directly across in the next column, there is the boxed three-line label (Fig. 6.62).

Here are Richard and his friends using their language skills and persistent time and energy (and his secretary-mother's typewriter and access to a ditto machine) on a cooperative, good-humored project that for several weeks brings them and their

> Offer Coupon for Box Tops
>
> And Don't
>
> Forget Medical Book.

Fig. 6–62

readers a good deal of satisfaction. It is well for many children, whose homes are not thus equipped or thus conducive to such resourceful activity, that an increasing number of teachers are taking their tips from such instances and providing ready access to the required facilities for individual and group newspapers in their classrooms.

Thirteen-year-old Benji quite spontaneously types out his own paper, *The Benji Blab,* with tongue in cheek. His second issue carries as its introductory item the following, obviously designed to get the writer and his readers in the mood for what is to come, and spaced to reach across the two-column page:

THE RETURN OF ULYSSES

Recently we put out that extravagant, enlightening magazine, "The Benji Blab," and the reaction was so magnificent that we finally got a second edition out of the proof-reader's and censorer's offices. We shall commence the scripture."

The scripture is commenced with "The Nutnick," a wry, column-wide, single-paragraph bit which identifies Benji quite unmistakably with the age in which he lives, at the same time clinching the mood of *The Benji Blab*. It reads:

History has been made. My recent article on a trip to the moon has been outdated since for the first time people have stopped talking and started doing. Our first step toward commerce with Mars has been achieved. A satellite has been sent around the Moon by itself. It is called the Nutnick. It weighs 5 grams and is 34 millimeters in diameter. It can be seen by the unaided eye as a faint star in the sky. However, anyone who claims he has seen it is seeing things or else is more remarkable than the Nutnick itself. Prominent scientists are combining forces to beat this remarkable scientific feat. Their minor inferior shell is going to be called the Potato-Nik and is going to be 20″ in di. and weigh 140 lbs. HaHaHa! DO NOT LAUGH AT SCIENCE. What did they do to Fulton when he let off steam in his fish market & Macaroni when he invented the wireless terrier, and Watt when he invented the what? They laughed but they were sorry when he walked off with their stock. Never say impossible. It is impossible for anything to be impossible.

Under the heading "Jobs," there are such entries as:

Wanted . . . novice sensational hit-and-run singer. Don't call us we'll call you.

Wanted . . . Mug the Bug $10 reward for information leading toward the conviction of Big Louie, wanted in 68 states and United States, too.

Secretary for no pay. Find me that one!

After "Today's Puzzle," comes an item, "Big Bank Robbery," which goes:

Readers, readers, gory, blood-enthralled readers, we have managed to get at last one of our wonderful stories of crime.

The report has just come in that the Gatville Bank has been robbed. The intrepid robbery took place at 2:30 apm Eastern Sittard Time. Two men with masks over their faces came in and said, "Trick or Treat!" Immediately they took the loot consisting of 10¢, two apples and a krrrrrunchy candy bar.

Then they ran outside on a bicycle built for two and were off before the bank clerk realized that it wasn't Hallowe'en.

It just goes to show you that you can fool some of the fools all the time, all of the fools all of the time, but you just can't fool all of the fools all the fool time.

Then comes:

TEAMSTERS UNION EXPELLED

This morning Jimmy Haha, Leader of the teamsters union was fired for his criminal dealings with a group of men called the Johnny Trio. The question put before the labor busters was should the teaming teamsters be expelled or should they be allowed to finish smuggling baseball teams out of New York City? Last week it was the Lodgers who inhabited reserveed seats in Central Park. A report has just come in. The extra e in reserved is to give you more for your money. Another service of the Blab. Just yesterday they smuggled out the Huges and they've been yankin' on the Crankees.

FLASH!

The Blab has started again.

WEATHER

Could be better. The temperature in the low 1,000,000,000,000. Whoops! That's the solar report. Humidity so Cousteau informs us is 200% but the sea affects his readings being too accurate, since he's in it. Snow and heat wave expected sooon. Emphasis.

Individual newspapers made by a ten- and seven-year-old are reproduced in Figures 6.63 and 6.64. They also help to show the wide range of opportunities for good reading and writing that children's making of their own newspapers can provide.

CHILDREN'S POEMS AND STORIES.   When young children make their own arrangements of written symbols which have meaning to them, they are helping themselves understand that form does make a difference in a written symbol. They are learning to read.

Susan likes to write free verse, enjoying her freedom from the usual punctuation requirements and focusing on vivid word pictures:

My Dream

>Two terrible boys on Parkway Road
>A dog with a head higher than a great Dane
>A bicycle so weak it crashed
>But a girl lifted me high
>Just in time . . .

Robert, in another school, having cut out pictures that serve his purpose from the supply of old magazines kept on a handy shelf in the back of the room, begins his collection of *My Own Stories* with a table of contents that reads: "The Airplane," "Our Trip," "My Daddy's Truck," "Our T.V.," "Our Car," "My Pet," "At Night," "Kim," "The Rooster," "The Tractor." Identifying the pictures as illustrations of his own personal world, he writes among others, the following stories:

The Airplane

See this big thing.
It is an airplane.
It goes high in the sky.
The man will not fall out of it.
He can drive it.

My Daddy's Truck

I wish I could drive my Daddy's truck,
but it is too big for me. Daddy says
I must grow tall. Then I can drive
it to school.

At Night

Every night before I go to bed, my
mother reads a story to me. Then I
jump in bed, kiss mother and go to
sleep.

Kim

[This is written below a large picture of a young child sitting on his father's shoulders, and holding tight to his father's forehead.]

Get off Daddy, Kim.
You are hurting his eyes.

Robert helps his friend Joana find a picture, too. The one she selects shows a man at work painting. He has blotches of paint on his overalls and cap, of course—apparently advertising a particular brand of house paint. Joana's story reflects the values she has already learned to hold (see Figure 6.65).

Robert's and Joana's teacher helps the children who write stories to put them in good big substantial books, with tape-bound pages and gay, colorful covers. It doesn't take their class-mates long to learn to read these stories with great enjoyment, one after the other, again somewhat more easily than the stilted stories in their primary readers.

For the history book, *Once Upon a Time in Cache Valley*, which their class is making of true stories told them by old

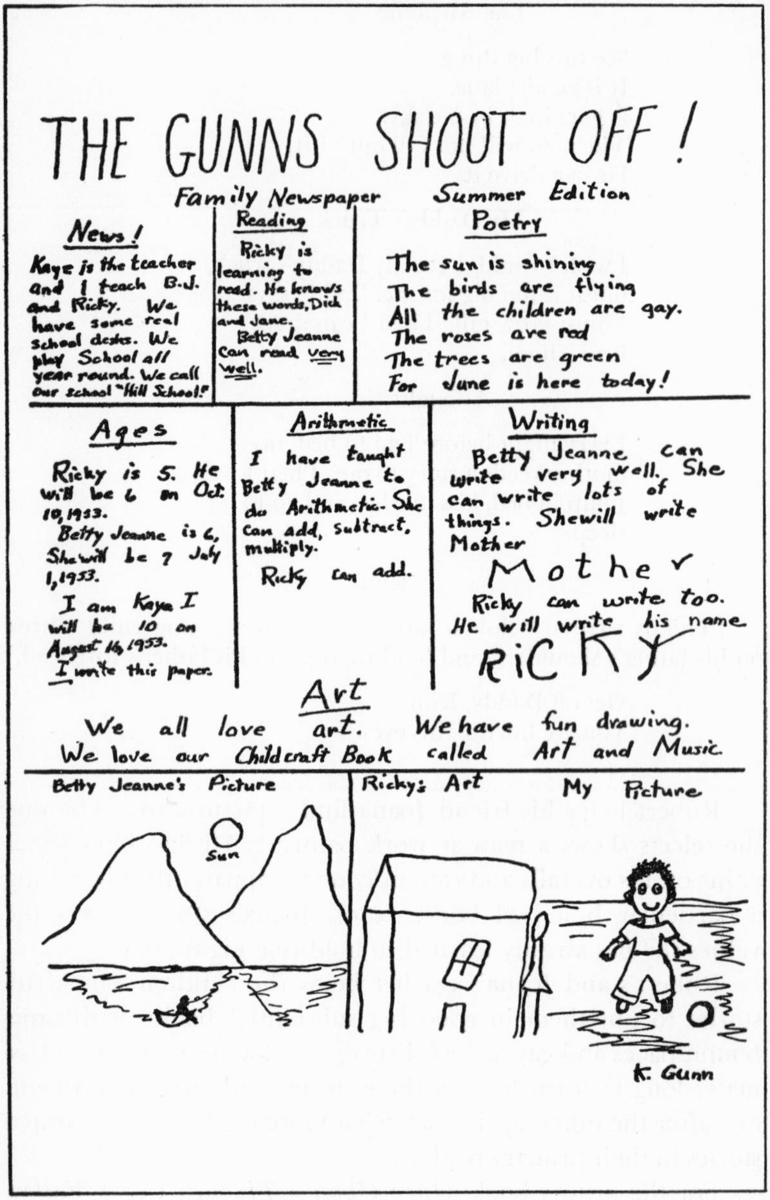

THE GUNNS SHOOT OFF!

Family Newspaper   Summer Edition

News!

Kaye is the teacher and I teach B.J. and Ricky. We have some real school desks. We play School all year round. We call our school "Hill School."

Reading

Ricky is learning to read. He knows these words, Dick and Jane.

Betty Jeanne can read very well.

Poetry

The sun is shining
The birds are flying
All the children are gay.
The roses are red
The trees are green
For June is here today!

Ages

Ricky is 5. He will be 6 on Oct. 19, 1953.

Betty Jeanne is 6. She will be 7 July 1, 1953.

I am Kaye I will be 10 on August 14, 1953.

I write this paper.

Arithmetic

I have taught Betty Jeanne to do Arithmetic. She can add, subtract, multiply.

Ricky can add.

Writing

Betty Jeanne can write very well. She can write lots of things. She will write Mother

Mother

Ricky can write too. He will write his name

RiCKY

Art

We all love art. We have fun drawing. We love our Childcraft Book called Art and Music.

Betty Jeanne's Picture   Ricky's Art   My Picture

Sun

K. Gunn

Fig. 6–63

Fig. 6–64

pioneers invited to the school, Jeannette and Bettie Mae combine forces to make this account as interesting as old Mr. Smith had made it in the telling:

Riding on the First Train

One morning in the Valley of the Willows a little boy named Joel went into the house. He had heard that the first train was going to be in the valley. It was going to come to a town ten miles away.

"Oh Father, may I go down to Hampton's and see the new train that is coming tomorrow? Can I go?" said Joel very excitedly.

Father said, "My son, you have been a good boy, so you may go. You will have to get up very early."

That night Joel went to bed very early. All night he dreamed about going and seeing the train. At last morning came.

"Oh Father, is it time to get up?" said Joel as he got up to see if the sun was up.

"Yes, if you want to," said his father sleepily.

After all his work was done and his breakfast was over, he ran over the fields as fast as he could. His feet hurt him. The hot sun burned them, and the rocks cut them. Still he kept on. Finally he got to Hampton's and there was the train. People were shouting. What a busy town!

"Get on," said the engineer as the train was ready to leave. Joel was happy at this and got on the train.

When it started going five or six miles an hour, Joel thought that it would jump the track. But when he looked at the other men, Mr. Thatcher and Mr. Ormsby, who were also on the train, he saw that they were talking and didn't seem frightened at all.

"I will not let them know I am afraid," said Joel under his breath.

When they got to the place where they were to turn back, the conductor said: "Come and ride home with us, Joel." But as soon as he was off he stayed off. And what do you think he said?

Joel said: "Not on my life will I ride the blamed thing. It might jump the track." And so home Joel went, walking all the way.

From *Long Ago in Cache Valley*

Figs. 6.66A and B are other pages from the same lovely book, an artistic integration of all the skills of communication, spoken as well as written and, in this particular project, spanning several generations.

Mrs. Golden, a teacher of long experience in a large school system, is much excited about the wide variety of really good stories her children are writing now. She types and dittoes copies of these stories, and the children put them into books for their own use. This is the first time Mrs. Golden has had her children write stories and make books in this way. "My principal lets me do it all right," she explains. "He reluctantly gave me permission to use the typewriter and even the ditto machine in the outer office. But he thought it was all a waste of time—and ditto paper too—until he saw that the children were really reading these books, eating them up, in fact. Children who can't read their readers can read their own and each

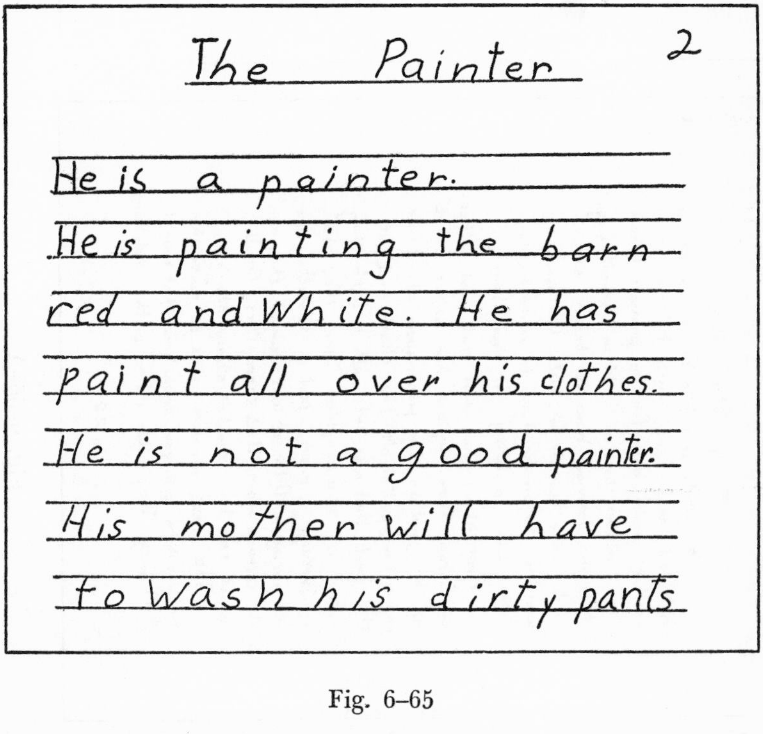

> The Painter   2
>
> He is a painter.
> He is painting the barn
> red and White. He has
> paint all over his clothes.
> He is not a good painter.
> His mother will have
> to Wash his dirty pants

Fig. 6–65

Making Straw Hats

How would you like to make straw hats all day? Lucy Smith helped her mother make hats for the pioneers. When her mother was a child in far-off England she learned how to braid straw and make wonderful hats. And now she was in Logan she had to make hats to help get a living for her family.

First of all they went out and gathered straw. Then Lucy and her mother cut it at the joint so the pieces were about five inches long, pulled off the sheaf and cut the part that was left with a little thing called a straw-splitter. Then they ran it through a press, that is something like a wringer. After it was braided they ran it through again. And then Mrs. Smith would sew the braided straw into hats.

The next problem was to make the hats white and you know how that would thrill Lucy. They made a fire with sulphur,

28

Fig. 6-66-A

put the hats around it to soak in the steam, and covered them up until they were bleached.

When they were ready to wear, Lucy would go around showing her hats to people. But she couldn't have all the hats because they had to sell them for a living.

—Bettie Mae Harper
Sabra Whatcott

Fig. 6-66-B

other's stories. This Mr. S. can hardly believe. Now he's telling *me* how to make the books better: Leave a neater margin on the pages that I type. Cut instead of tear the sheets for the pages. Have the children put the illustrations so they face rather than follow the pages of printing. Have them staple the pages more carefully; also cover the line of staples with mystic tape. You know . . . he's really proud of what we're doing, and is bringing visitors to my room for the first time in years.

"One of these days I'm going to get up courage enough to talk with him about a *second* ditto machine for the school. A number of the teachers are picking up the idea now, and to preserve the peace and efficiency of his own office, he'll be forced to get another one. Seriously, when he considers how it will help all of us to teach reading better, I think he'll give it thought. There's a kind of supply or store room down in our wing of the building, where it would be much handier for most of us than the office . . . Well, we'll see."

A particular shelf in one school's library holds a variety of books which from time to time have been contributed by class or individual authors of the school. These are treasured and circulated with pride. There is *Story Book Time,* for example, which Miss Kenyon's fourth-grade class had such fun writing and compiling. Held together in a stout spring binder simply but colorfully decorated, it consists of stories of every conceivable interest. Thirty or forty of them are listed by title and author in the Table of Contents. "Riders of the Golden West" by Dorothy J. "Saga of the Wild Horse" by Nancy Ellen D. "The Robin's Return" by Martha G. and her mother. "The Little Lost Colt" by Reed R. "A Trip to the Moon" by Sammy B. and Leonard O. "The Run-Around: The Story of a Spy," by K. S. B. "Easter Poem" by Genevieve I. The titles run a wide gamut.

"We really had a run on writing stories," Miss Kenyon recalls. "I took down the dictation of two or three of the children whose ideas came so much faster than they were able to write. Then my little ole Nancy Ellen, whose several chapters of an exciting 'western' were already being read and reread to and by the children, asked me to take her dictation. 'Why, you rascal, you,' I said to her privately. 'You can write as well as I can. Why should anybody take your dictation?' 'Because I could think better, and write better stories,' she answered. I gave in.

"When I had time I took Nancy Ellen's dictation. And it was a rare experience. I could just watch the wheels go around in that head of hers, as with her eyes shut to a slit and a faraway look on her face, she would dictate: 'The long eerie shadow of a wolf rose up onto the horizon . . . no, rose up into the night . . . Now, read me what you've written," she would say every so often without changing her expression. Anyway, her stories were the more remarkable because she didn't have to think about writing and punctuation.

"By this time others were wanting me to take their dictation. I was swamped. They would also greet any visitor, parent, teacher, or principal, who came into the room with, 'Will you please take my dictation?' Finally we worked out a plan. I talked with two of the sixth-grade teachers, and they agreed that it would be a good use of skills for their children, if a few of them could come down to take the dictation of my youngsters. So the last hour of school, and the desks in one section at the back of the room, we set aside for those who wanted to write. If six children wanted to write on a particular afternoon, we would send up for six sixth-graders, alternating between the two sixth-grade classes. Some days it would be ten children. Sometimes eight. Sometimes only three. No one felt any pressure.

"From time to time as the business progressed, the children would read their stories to others who wanted to hear. 'Oh boy, let's hear the next chapter of Howard's mystery. It's a scarey one, he says.' Of course, even with sixth-grade help, there were misspelled words and poor punctuation in these rough manuscripts. I was pleased that children were using words and expressions far beyond their ability to spell. I copied a few of the finished stories on the typewriter, in my hunt-and-peck way, and put them on the bulletin board. The children all came at me. 'Please type mine next, Miss Kenyon.' 'No, I've waited longest.' 'O.K., then mine after Marian's?'

"About this time an idea hit me. I went to John Garrett, who teaches typing in the high school. Sure enough, he was looking for practice work for his classes. And we both thought it would be very valuable experience for them to take the children's rough manuscripts, spell and punctuate them correctly, and type them up in shipshape form—'edit' them for publication, really. When I told my class about this they were beside themselves with anticipation. We agreed to ask for carbon copies of the stories. The original would go into the class book, *Story Book Time,* which we would keep in circulation in the neighborhood. And the carbon copy would become the author's own property.

"The book got thicker and thicker. We decided to include a section of correspondence we had received from many different people. Chief among these was the answer from our new school superintendent to our invitation for him to speak at a school assembly that we were planning. He had answered it all in cartoons—bless his heart!—and the children treasured them. So into the book those went, as you would surmise. Several children tried their hands at cartoons too, as well as the perfectly beautiful drawings with which many of them illustrated stories or poems.

"And the book went the rounds as it grew. A couple of children made a schedule and each of us had a turn. Then we began on the second round, as parents and grandparents and brothers and sisters put in their requests. Of course the sixth-graders had a chance at it too. And the high school class kept it for several days, I remember. After that, we gave the book to the school library, where from then on we took our turns along with everyone else. . . .

"But this all happened a long time ago," Miss Kenyon exclaims, suddenly bringing herself back from some obviously pleasant reminiscing. "If we were doing it today? Yes, if we were doing it today, we'd probably do two things differently. I think we'd compile the stories into several books instead of the one great large one. And no doubt we would ditto and bind them for still wider reading."

Learning and Using Written Communication through Use of the Ditto Machine

The term *dittoing* is used in this book to mean any duplicating process in which the carbons used are such that teachers and children can print, draw, or typewrite directly and easily on them, and mistakes can be corrected quickly and without spoiling the carbons. A process in which the machine itself can be operated by teachers or by a couple of children with care but without special technical skill: that's dittoing. The ditto machine (or reasonable facsimile thereof) has opened up many new possibilities in working with children, as these pages are continually reminding.

Dittoing makes it possible for the teacher to gear reading and writing materials to her particular children's needs, a claim which even the best of commercial materials, necessarily directed to all children of a certain age or stage, cannot make. Children like to see their own names in print, their own experiences, their own carefully written stories. These things which, not too long ago, had to be used by the whole class from a large chart, or a single copy of their class-made book, now can be easily duplicated or dittoed and individual copies made available for every child's own use. Dittoing makes it possible for the teacher to provide well-planned choices in materials, through which individual children can show their needs and perfect their skills of communication as children have never been able to do before. In other words, it makes individualized teaching and individualized learning more potentially effective than has ever been possible. It enables the teacher, furthermore, to provide practice on a particular skill in a way and at the time when it can be of most value to children, individually or as a group. It makes it possible for children to understand through their own reading and writing experiences, the processes of printing, of mass communication.

Teachers discover very quickly some of the rules and the shortcuts for making good ditto sheets and for making them rapidly. To use pencils that are not too sharp, for example, or ball-point pens that will make a strong even line. To develop a good clear style of manuscript writing, which practice helps them to do quickly. To learn to estimate distances rather than having to measure, realizing that ample spacing, even margins, attractive clean-cut, readable arrangements are more important than exact measuring. When they want to make light lines as a guide to their own or the children's writing, to use a large card or blotter, holding one end parallel to the side of the ditto carbon, with two dots marked on the blotter to indicate margins, and drawing across it quickly as they move the blotter down the page. To quickly trace around different-sized cards, even round-cornered tickets, for making the shapes they want for framing certain words, say, as the "budget," weather, or special bulletin. Even to use round metal lids for making circles, twisting them a time or two to make the good clear imprint rather than tracing around them. Teachers and children too are on the alert for different usable shapes such as these, and other effective time-saving devices in their use of the ditto sheets.

Dittoing then is a simple process, simple enough to be used by teacher and children, without special office help. It is comparatively inexpensive, too, when one thinks of the extensive and continued cost to the schools of the usual commercial workbooks. A ditto machine in the primary wing of the building, as Mrs. Golden is about to suggest to her principal, and perhaps a second one on the upper floor, can pay their way very soon through the increased effectiveness of the school's reading program. They can pay their way time and again in the hands of alert, resourceful teachers who know their children individually, and can help all of them to become increasingly and satisfyingly competent in the skills of written communication.

7

The teacher's role: setting up the classroom to invite whole learning

Children in the preceding chapter are learning to read. They are learning and using the skills of reading and writing every single day in real communication with one another. They are learning these important skills in situations deliberately devised by their teachers to call for the use of the skills as a natural thing in the achievement of the children's purposes, as a natural thing in the successful management of their everyday affairs. The teachers in these pages are becoming increasingly adept at thoughtfully preparing, with a minimum of time and ado, appropriate materials to facilitate children's use of written communication as a tool for successful group living in the classroom.

And they are doing this in such a way that individual responses to the materials can give them increasing insight into their children's individual resources and problems and needs, which the teachers then use as cues for determining the kind of specific next steps or offerings to make available. Thus teachers deliberately provide for choices geared toward learning to read. And, to repeat, the children do learn to read. In their own individual ways, thoughtfully responding to those offerings that have meaning for them, the children are learning to read. Needless to say, it is a very pleasant, very satisfying, very exciting, very reassuring process for all of them to be in on, however gradual or however rapid their individual progress may be.

The picture in the preceding pages, however, as anyone knows, is only a partial though highly important one. Just as in all of the preceding chapters the exciting pictures of children learning to read through the wide use of the books they select are also partial ones. Put them all together they spell READING, a name that's very dear to teachers and parents and boards of education our culture over. Even this is a partial picture, in a good wholesome program of learning—or of democracy generally.

For reading to have real meaning it must be in context. It must be an integral part of a program sufficiently rich to give children something to read and write about. It must provide for experiences that are real because they are whole—not divided up into tight little compartments or periods of day which, in the case of human learning, when added together do not make the whole. As we have seen, the way in which the teacher sets up the classroom can considerably help or hinder children's progress in learning to read. The sensitive planning and arranging of a classroom that *invites* children to read, that is so full of challenging, usable materials and situations that reading in school, just as outside it, is a very natural and useful thing to do, is a major continuing part of a good teacher's teaching.

A classroom effectively geared to the learning of reading skills is not a classroom set up for reading alone. Ideally, reading of one kind or another runs through every aspect of the total program, sometimes more and sometimes less significantly. The richer the offerings generally, the more effective the reading program. In an important sense the total program *is* the reading program. Building meanings and drawing generalizations through varied, challenging firsthand experiences make up a basic part of the reading process. The more varied and profitable the activities in which a child selects to engage, and the more wholeheartedly he enters into them, the more meanings he develops. Hence the more equipment he has for use in his own interpreting of an author's message, for his own resourceful participating in the written communication of the classroom. In other words, the better he reads.

Nor is it pampering children to make it comfortable and conducive for them to work hard at a worthwhile task. An adult, attempting a creative job, gives himself every bit of help he can for letting the ideas or the processes come well and aptly. He may loosen his clothes, take off his shoes, spread out his materials in rough but, to him, organized fashion for no one else to touch. He may insist on having a supply of well-sharpened pencils handy or a choice of pens, at having his typewriter at just the right height, on having a cushion under him and another behind his back as he works. He may want to drop the sheets or scraps of writing he has finished with on the floor as he goes, stooping to pick them up only after the good hard creative working hours are over. He may prefer to work for a while at his desk or typewriter, then get up and stroll back and forth across the room or stretch out on the sofa as he thinks. He may prefer to have two places for work—two "nests," as it were—finding it helpful to shift from one place to the other as he comes to a plateau or a rough spot in his work. He may prefer at times to stop work entirely for a while—to give his mind to something else and let his subconscious take over, so to speak. Or he may be the kind who, once putting his mind to the task, wants nothing and nobody to come between him and his thinking until the job is completed, thank you! This is a highly individual affair. People find the ways and the particular conditions most conducive to creative work *for them*, conditions under which they can do their best and most productive thinking.

To allow children something of the same privilege we are always glad to grant the creative adults—indeed to set up conditions that will make it easier for children to work well—can hardly be labeled as unfair or soft. To help them find ways in which, without encroaching on the same right for others, they can work most comfortably and effectively—be it reading a book, writing a story or newspaper, preparing a report, composing a poem or an operetta or whatever else—is not an indulgence but a sensible inducement. Knowing children and knowing her particular children, a teacher can set up the materials, provide the time, the atmosphere, and the friendly help to invite the children's creative efforts. Their behavior and choices can show her what seems to work best for individual children.

Individualized teaching is based on the recognition that it is the individual who must do his own learning, in his own unique ways—that no one can do this learning for him. It does not assume, however, that he does his learning apart from others. Indeed this he cannot do. He develops as a self, as a responsible, healthy human being, only in relation to others. Individualized learning is at once a condition and an outcome of good social living, the kind of group living that enhances, rather than levels off, the individuality of its members.

Deliberately structuring for individualized learning in the classroom, then, as previous pages have shown, implies the continuous maintenance by the teacher of several conditions quite unlike those which we, the children's teachers and parents, ourselves experienced as school children. These combinations are:

1. The working out of time schedules to *insure,* not interrupt every twenty or thirty minutes, the continuity and wholeness of children's learning.

2. A thoughtfully planned variety of materials from which children can select those best suited to their particular

purposes, rather than sets of the same carefully-graded, standard materials which the entire class, or ability groups within the class, are required to use.

3. The organization of space in the classroom to *provide for,* not discourage, genuine face-to-face communication among the children.

4. The provision of the kind of friendly help that individual children need.

Some possibilities which teachers are finding useful, related to each of these conditions, are spelled out in succeeding pages of this chapter.

Working out Time Schedules that Insure Continuity of Learning

LARGE BLOCKS OF TIME.   It is quite obvious that the usual, regularly broken-up kind of daily time schedule with which we adults grew up through elementary schools will not serve the program of individual learning and self-propulsion that good materials carefully set up can invite. For years now teachers have been moving toward longer and longer blocks of time in the school day to allow for flexibility in this regard. Longer blocks of time, with opportunities for children's choice within the period, is the common and necessary trend. A required work time, perhaps an arithmetic period or word study time, when children go to the Work Table and select one or two, or more if they desire, of the worksheets set out for them to do, the teacher helping wherever she feels she is needed or the children ask for her help. A social studies or study club time, when individuals, pairs, or small groups of friends pursue the variety of studies or projects they have chosen to take on. This may include dictating or making books at one's own desk, work at the Writing Table or Letter-Writing Desk, the Make-It Table, the Reading Table, work with the science materials, posting a request or list of plans on the bulletin board, previewing filmstrips with the projector, or perhaps making some use of the recorder—any or all of these things going on concurrently in the hour labeled on the schedule or plan for the day as Committee Work, Study Clubs, Social Studies Time, or whatever.

Even regular Gym Time may be extended to involve constructive choice. Perhaps the first ten or fifteen minutes can take care of the total-group requirements through a running game in which all participate, the child leader whose turn it is having signed his choice of game on the dated sign-up sheet so the others will know. After this, individual and small group choices are in order, with materials and equipment signed up for ahead of time, as earlier pages indicate.

MORNING WORK TIME OR CHOICE PERIOD.   Teachers the country over are coming to look upon the Early Morning Work Time—when individually or in small groups of friends, the children come in from outside, perhaps chatting merrily for a time as they write their names on the sign-up sheets, get their needed materials together, and go right to work without ado— as the almost indispensable hour of the school day. Teachers cherish this opportunity to come to know their children as individuals, visiting with them one by one or a few at a time as they settle down to the business of the morning. For this is the time when children can really be self-propelling, the time when they come bursting in full of enthusiasm and ideas for a new venture they've been putting their minds to since yesterday or another good session on some project already under way. Here is where the wide-awake teacher can look and see, can listen and hear, as children show, through their unpressured behavior in a situation resourcefully set up for choice, their keenest enthusiasms, their most creative ideas, their most disciplined selves. Here too is the essence of their relations with other children—the warm, outgoing helpfulness so sure to be repaid, the shy, hesitant overtures or the flambuoyant cockiness of the child who is worried and insecure. Here is where the competence and the confidence, the problems and the needs really show. And the teacher, interpreting the signals, will know just when and where her help can be of most value. Taking Judy Wray's dictation, meeting Mark's request that she hear him read, working with a little group in the corner on their newspaper, the teacher, although still able to take in the group as a whole, is able to learn from the widely differing individuals within the group, that which she most needs to know for helping them further.

Mrs. Barnes, who knows her individual children so well, helps the student teachers working in her classroom to learn resourceful ways for working with the children during this kind of period. She frequently writes and posts in some agreed-upon place for them, "so we won't be constantly having to talk about it," such carefully thought-out but quickly typed-up suggestions as the two examples following:

Dictating stories. One of the best sources of good reading material is a child's own story or book. We should have a table now where we keep our own books since so many children have written them. Often children need to be asked if they'd like to dictate as they don't think of it.

Games. Zoo Lotto, Winnie the Pooh, and all such have good reading and arithmetic in them. Usually the children need a grown-up to play a game or two first as this is a hard age for understanding winning and losing.

Science. There are always science activities, although the children may not label them as such. It would be fun to make blueprints on the roof, rig up a doorbell for the house, plant sweet potatoes, make an artificial fireplace for the house, go to Morningside or Riverside Park to collect rocks, worms, bugs, etc.

Plays. Children can act out ideas in a corner of the room, the library, or even out-of-doors in clear view of the classroom.

Some reading possibilities:

Anne, Barbara, Becky, Michele, and Patsy could read together very nicely—each with her own different book. Patsy might well prefer not to be with a group. All of these children enjoy writing stories and reading them to other children.

Ben wants to learn to read so he can use his chemistry set. He needs to read alone right now and we need to write materials for him which deal with chemistry.

Billy is very pleased with his own dictated stories. Whenever we can we should print these large (the primer typewriter in the office is available) and use them for some of his reading material. He prefers reading alone or with Tuck when Tuck is in a listening mood.

Carlos could dictate some things about Puerto Rico. Cindy and Sandy especially are interested in everything about his different language. Perhaps there are some possibilities for these children to work on some ideas together. Carlos illustrates very easily and would be very proud to read his own book to our group or perhaps to other interested groups in the school.

Cheryl is reading with an older child after school every day. We'll have to find out what effect this is having on her feelings about reading during school. The new plan is Cheryl's idea according to her father. Yesterday she checked out *The Curious Kitten* for her special reading.

Danny and Jerry like to read together. And they like reading the same story over and over. It would be good to read often with them now as they are enjoying the first success of independent reading. They can choose any of the books from the top shelf of the corner bookcase.

David needs help finding adventure stories. He tends to think that comics contain the best adventure stories. *Nature Detective* might be worth trying with him—especially since he is interested in the out-of-doors.

Hugh wants to start a weather station. He listens to the weather report each morning, so he could print that (short). He could make a weather flag to fly too (half blue and half white—white half on top means fair weather, blue means rain). I have two or three good weather books. He might like to make a barometer,—go to the weather station at the airport with a couple of others, etc.

Johnny could well read a dictated book about Indians and go on from there to other fact books. He has an amazing amount of information. A trip to the museum as part of it would be good. He likes making scrap books.

Tuck writes wonderful imaginative stories which he reads, and which are very revealing and helpful. He might also like to dictate a book about his trip during the holidays. He has some photographs he could put in it . . .

Nor are these well-equipped and carefully set up work periods in the schools confined to the lower grades, as has tended to be true unfortunately through the years. As children grow older, as they gain more maturity and insights and big ideas, the more not the less opportunity they need to exercise their initiative, to work out the problems they set for themselves, to deepen and extend their self-styled investigations. This is the time when, with adequate facilities at hand for writing or typing and dittoing, Benji and Richie and Jan and Joan and Barbara can put out their independent newspapers. This is the time when informal groups of interested children can bring in those self-teaching records and books now available and teach themselves a second language, can work at their various projects such as composing an operetta for the class to put on, writing a book about aluminum or the Renaissance or the World Health Organization, perfecting a choral rendition of a favorite poem, making anthologies of their favorite poetry, as Miss Bosner helps the children to do in an earlier chapter (page 50). This is the time when the children can work with clay and lumber and leather and paint, can experiment with materials of all kinds, in art, science, music, can work on their club or committee activities, can design their own stationery or cards, can write needed letters or invitations, can make needed tickets, posters, announcements. Can make or try out their games and puzzles and comics. Can read their favorite stories or travel or biography or history books, here by themselves or with one another, always with friendly help close by.

Not that this is the only time of day that a good variety of sincere, interesting projects can be busily under way. But the point of the Morning Work Time is that teachers can feel secure with this kind of period, for which they and the children plan and prepare, whether as a starter in a program where to date there has been but little real choice for children, or as part of the kind of program which is typified by such choice. This is the kind of real situation, stressed over and over again in the previous chapter, in which both children and teacher are helped to develop the skills most important to them. Indeed, there are some teachers who extend this more or less free way of working, with materials under supervision, to most of the school day, only bringing the children together as a total group when there is a real need for checking or sharing or working together as a class.

READING TIME.   Reading periods are scheduled to fit into this pattern of longer blocks with more choice also. Mr. Carlson's plan for beginning the day with the one-and-a-half to two-hour period, within which his sixth-grade children follow their own selected order of participation in three specified kinds of activities, organized through use of sign-up sheets, is a case in point. Other teachers' designation of a particular forty-five minutes or hour a day for Reading Time, when everybody engages in some kind of reading activity, individually or with friends and sometimes with teacher, is also in line with the pattern. There is Mrs. Callen's "Friendly Reading Time" every afternoon, when her first- or second-grade children delight in just this kind of arrangement. Teachers of every age of children find such informal supervised times with books mutually profitable. Many teachers are increasing the once-a-week library reading period in the classroom to a daily library period, whatever other reading activities they are *required* to carry out with their children.

A common characteristic of these plans is that children are encouraged to assume an increasingly large share of the responsibility for deciding the nature of their reading during this time, the choices of course being closely related to possibilities which teacher and children have already explored together. Most children will use the time for reading individually and uninterruptedly from some self-chosen book they have under way. The teacher, the student teacher if there is one, or particular children, will be seated where they can respond to requests for needed help at any time. As already stressed, this usually takes the form of telling words quickly and casually when asked by the occasional child who needs this kind of help. Or it may be "hearing a child read," if that is the request of either teacher or child. It may be helping a youngster to select a new book that he has in mind or is looking for. With young children, it may be helping him jot down his own reading record, as planned and provided for by the teacher (pp. 144–148).

Some children may prefer at times to read in pairs or small groups of friends from the same favorite book, working out their own plans for taking turns, and probably settling somewhere off to themselves in some private spot—sitting on the floor in a corner with backs to the wall, fitting their chairs into the unused spot behind the piano or the teacher's desk, maybe even moving out into the hall or the cloakroom if the situation warrants. As Mr. Carlson stressed earlier, the more reasonably free the children are to set up their own plans and arrangements, the more apt they are, with a minimum of suggestion, to make reasonable use of them. This may be the time when the teacher will meet with a different group of children each day to give some help she may feel they need or just to keep in touch with their reading. On the other hand, she may want to keep herself uncommitted as a usual thing during this hour, to be in a better position to look and listen and work with individual children in a closer, more functional way. Undoubtedly she will want to vary her role from time to time, depending in part upon other help or other resources available, and particular problems that may arise.

Such a Reading Time may be scheduled as a regular occurrence for any hour of the day's plans. Many teachers prefer to schedule it right after midmorning break or first thing in the afternoon, to enable children coming back a few at a time to select their books or set up their plans and get started without waiting for the whole group to return. In case the specified period proves too long for some children, the teacher will plan with them accordingly, with other materials and centers in the classroom set up for responsible use. There will no doubt be other times in the school day also when individual children can select to read—perhaps the Morning Work Time or Choice Period just discussed, the scheduled hour and other visits to the school Library, a kind of Club Time which some schools provide, and other such possibilities.

Some teachers prefer to alternate, but increasingly more prefer to supplement, these more informal reading periods with some kind of reading in groups as described in the earlier chapters. Whether it is to comply with school requirements or because they feel more comfortable working in this way, a number of teachers prefer to have three special times set aside for giving help to reading groups, with individual children reading along in different books as earlier described, their prescribed readers mixed right in with the other choices. Under this plan, of course, there is no reason for the children to be arranged according to ability. Various ways for voluntary arrangement are tried by Miss Floyd, you remember, throughout Chapter One. Mrs. Rogers suggests still another variation, using the sign-up idea. She writes on the board early in the day:

```
I can help with reading at these
times today. Please sign under the
time you prefer:

10:15-11:00  11:00-11:45  1:45-2:30
```

In this way the children have a choice of time and of particular friends with whom they enjoy reading. Friends can sign up together if they wish, without regard to who reads better than whom. Again, because children have a chance to choose, they are more apt to assume responsibility for the consequences of the choice, gearing their planned use of other equipment and materials to fit in with this signed-for time.

There are other possibilities for scheduling time for reading, to be sure. Every teacher will seek and develop the ways that make most sense to her, that seem best suited to her particular classroom, that give time for every child to read—in his own way and at his own rate, without holding up the progress of some of his classmates or making others feel inferior to him because he must wait for them. The important consideration here is that for maximum growth in reading, children need *time* to read— unharried, unpressured, uninterrupted time to enjoy the books and materials they select from those provided. This is all part of setting up the classroom for individualized learning.

STUDY CLUBS.   Occasional reference has been made through these chapters to the Space Club, the Bird Club, and several others in connection with the children's experiences in informal work groups. Many teachers are finding these study clubs a profitable way of organizing children's choice and good hard work at almost any level. Knowing that children want and respect reasonable limits within which to work, Mr. Arnaldo and his fifth-grade children together structure their system of study clubs for the year's work in social studies. Their plans run something like this: everyone will participate in at least four different study clubs during the year, the topics selected to be related to the science or social studies syllabus requirements. Other clubs can be organized around any areas the members choose. There will be from four to eight study clubs to choose from each time. The duration of the study club will be about six weeks, after which, or if they are through earlier, individuals or smaller groups can pursue any further activities in this field they may want. The people will sign for new clubs the Monday following the sixth week. There will be no more than twelve members in any club. Study clubs will meet daily from 11:00 A.M. to 12:00 noon. Each club will be responsible for keeping a directory of its members, with telephone numbers included.

The sky is the limit so far as sources of information are concerned—trips, interviews, invited lecturers, any materials in classroom or library or home. Mr. Arnaldo will provide a good selection of reference books for the clubs to use and to which they will add their own. They will be expected to keep a complete bibliography or record of sources used, and some record of the discoveries they make or information they find—fact cards organized in card files, notebooks, or whatever they select. The clubs can also get information from one another. They can ditto information or information tests as they like. Sometimes Mr. Arnaldo will want to help provide worksheets, guide questions, or tests for them also. The study clubs are free to set up discussion forums, quiz programs, television shows, pertinent movies, study club exhibits—whatever they choose for sharing with the total class. They can write and ditto club newspapers or plan and write a book on their topic if it seems advisable. Mr. Arnaldo will be glad to advise or to give help in whatever way he is needed. These are the plans. If later they need to be modified for some good reason, the class will make the decision at the time. The children are "raring to go" as they explore possibilities for their first choices. Mr. Arnaldo is in good spirits too. He has used study clubs before, but this is the first time a class of his has set them up in this particular way.

Organizing Materials and Equipment that *Teach*

Individualized learning at its best calls for organizing materials and equipment so thoughtfully and so resourcefully that these things themselves help to do the teaching. So thoughtfully and responsibly that they *invite* the children to reach out, to respond to motivation which they initiate within themselves, to tackle important jobs and to see them through, individually, in pairs, or in small groups of friends. It is not enough that the classroom be an attractive place to look at, with bulletin boards, exhibits, charts, pictures, photographs, perhaps an interestingly arranged science table. The classroom must be set up primarily as a place for active learning, with the focus on "doing centers, not just looking centers," in the words of college student Edith a couple of chapters hence.

Some of these doing centers and the materials involved, which teachers and their children are successfully working out in their classrooms at different times through the year are: bulletin boards that truly communicate, the Work Table, painting and clay centers, the Make-It Table, toys and gadgets, science materials, radio and television, the Writers' Table, the puppet theater, the house, the cooking center, the victrola, filmstrips and films, and of course first, last, and always the

Library Corner or Reading Center. Some of the useful ways teachers are finding for organizing each of the above will be discussed below.

BULLETIN BOARDS THAT COMMUNICATE.   The large, easy-to-reach bulletin board which the teacher deliberately sets up as a clearing house for genuine written communication in the classroom, has been referred to in previous pages. Here children or teacher at any time post sign-up sheets, important notices, requests, checklists, ideas they want to share, most of which call for individual or group response of one kind or another. Along with a recently dittoed copy of somebody's newspaper, the newest chapter of Mary Ann's continued story, David's sketch of the latest guided missile, say, and a copy of the teacher's notice to the parents about polio shots, with a class list close by for children to check if they have delivered the notice to their parents, may appear any of the communication examples included in preceding pages. Especially helpful may be those sign-up sheets enumerated on pages 131–132.

The bulletin board is a place to which children continually and eagerly go for careful reading. They don't want to miss anything that may have significance especially for them. Then too, this is a contagious affair. One person's or one group's idea leads to another, which is just what the teacher has in mind as she provides and uses such a bulletin board.

THE WORK TABLE.   Elsewhere in the classroom a long narrow table set aside for the purpose, or maybe the low counter running along under the windows, becomes known as the Work Table. Teachers find it helpful to have a definite place where the children always go to select from the choice of work materials she sets out for them, for the day or the week as the case may be. Several at a time of such worksheets as those suggested in the preceding chapter, for example, designed to give practice or help teach a specific skill which the teacher may have in mind —but contributing at the same time to the children's own purposes—will be arranged neatly on the table or counter designated for this purpose.

From the teacher's standpoint, as earlier indicated, there are several points to keep in mind about these worksheets. They will of course be interesting, challenging, fun to do. They will be closely related to, frequently grow out of, children's own particular experiences and concerns. The worksheets will be of such type that a youngster can respond in his own way without feeling inferior or superior to friends with whom he works, without feeling unduly pressed or held back to a group standard or tempo.

There will not be too many worksheets out at a time. Sometimes the favorites will be brought out again and again through the year, indicating children's changes and growth in attitudes or skills. Here is the place also where appropriate pages, selected and cut out of commercially prepared workbooks, can also be used. Indeed the value of commercial materials is enhanced through this kind of set-up, where children diagnose their own needs and choose pages from those set out on the Work Table the ones they specifically need. There will be times when the worksheets will be geared more especially to a particular science study, mathematics or social studies experience, sometimes to preparations for a trip. This may or may not be the place, too, where the more or less constant supply of forms for recording individual reading records will be kept, with now and then a new possibility being included in the choices.

Again, the specific arrangement of the materials and of the Work Table itself, in relation to the rest of the program and changing room arrangement, will be deliberately varied from time to time. Teacher and children work out their own routines for going about this, perhaps with some of the work and some of the times stipulated as "required," and other materials and times left more to the children's initiative and discretion. The important thing is that the children come to think of and accept the Work Table as the place to go to choose the work they will do for the day or for the week or whatever, thus making total class discussion and teacher explanation of such matters quite unnecessary. Whatever the specifics, teachers and children in many classrooms are finding the Work Table an efficient means of organizing materials and individual choices offered.

Perhaps the point should be stressed that it is the child's choice rather than the teacher's estimate that determines which of the worksheets provided the particular child will take. If there is genuine choice, a child can let his teacher know which of the possibilities she has set up are right for him and which are not. In this way the teacher learns, rather than prejudges, the children's individual abilities and needs and ways of working. For children can know when the teacher cannot know without their help. For her to say, in her concern with meeting individual differences, "This book or this assignment or this worksheet will be for Group I, because it is the hardest. This is the material I have picked out for you, Group II. And Group III, these are for you," has no place in an individualized program. For thus judging and labeling children ahead of time, the teacher gives them no chance to show which of the materials *are* best suited to them as individuals, no chance to show what they could do, or even what they would try to do, if they were free to select. Here is where lack of challenge or interest can be confused with lack of ability. Here the teacher cuts off her own chance to learn from individual children's behavior, since they are not free to behave in such a way that the cues are there. Children following directions, or choosing what the teacher asks them to choose, cannot give these insights to a teacher. They can only tell her what they are like while trying to follow her directions.

On occasion, this may be precisely what the teacher wants the children to do. She wants them to tell her what they are like under certain prescribed conditions. And when this is her intention, she will mark a particular worksheet *required*— perhaps using a rubber stamp which she has specially prepared for just such purpose, and the official nature of which the children respect. Important to realize here is the fact that the children are not confused about what is and what is not the choice. If something is required the teacher clearly states this fact. She does not lead the children into thinking that they have chosen it. Also, the teacher is aware of the limited value of this kind of experience for children. It gives her certain diagnostic information, yes, and gives children the opportunity to diagnose their own responses in the kinds of situations where they are doing what someone else has required them to do. But more and more teachers welcome the use of the Work Table where genuine choice is possible, where children can help them know which of their offerings are suitable for certain individuals and which are not. This kind of organization enables teachers to *see* the children's reactions, and to change or introduce new materials and plans accordingly.

PAINTING, CLAY AND WOODWORKING CENTERS. Certain designated centers for painting and other creative work are also important if children are to express and create meanings which matter to them. Not that these centers need be used only for the specified purpose all day—which would be very inefficient and impractical in most crowded classrooms—but for certain times of day when the situation warrants. One or two large tables, or several tables or flat desks pushed together, a large table-sized piece of plywood or wallboard laid across several desks, or some other arrangement where children can stand and paint freely, can serve the purpose well in many classrooms. Even painting on the unused floor space under the window, in the back of the room, or in the hall just outside the door, has its advantages. Easels are unnecessary. Indeed they are thought by many teachers to be far too space-consuming and restrictive to be of maximum use in the classroom. Designed for the use of oil paints, not for paint that drips and runs and makes life difficult especially for young children and their teachers, easels are giving way in many classrooms to other arrangements less space-consuming and more conducive to free, unrestricted painting.

Having good strong, clear-colored paint materials available in quantity, already mixed and set up conveniently and sturdily for young children in particular, is essential of course to the encouragement of good use of paint. So also is the chance to select and use from a variety of other media from time to time —different kinds of paint, pastels, crayons, different sizes and kinds of paper too, perhaps organized through sign-up sheets— thus appealing to more children and giving opportunity for wider experiences. A special table for working with clay, or several desks so designated in one part of the room, with oil cloth or newspapers, a container of water and supply of towels, a good fat supply of clay, and whatever other materials are needed (access in the school to a good kiln, for example) can invite creativity from children of any age. If there is room for only six children at the clay table, then six blanks on the sign-up sheet can take care of this matter with little ado. Children need a good specified place for wood construction too, with tools nearby, and with wood and materials easily moved away when time for working with wood is over and space must be put to other uses.

THE MAKE-IT TABLE.   By whatever name it is called, this is usually a designated place—a large table or counter—where children can always find a selection of materials for making and creating. These materials, provided by the school, by the teacher herself, and by individual children, are available for use by anyone who has a need for them. Materials which might be found on the Make-It Table, and on shelves or in boxes close by, at some time during the year, are: scrap pieces of lumber (the shapes of which themselves often suggest uses), interesting boxes and cans, buttons, cloth pieces of various kinds, plastic material, foil, white and colored paper tissues, scraps of bright-colored leather or simulated leather, hat braiding, lacing, cord, pipe cleaners and other malleable wire, straight clothespins, reed for making baskets, spools, plastic cosmetic bottles and jars, stiff cardboard, large cartons, foam rubber pieces, colored plastic straws, yarn, tongue depressors—the list could go on and on. Unless the piece of material has on it the name of the person who brought it in, indicating that he plans to use it himself, any child is welcome to make use of whatever is there.

Before long, teachers and children have their eyes open wherever they go for what might be thus put to use—shells, post cards, gift-wrapping paper, popsicle sticks, colored twine, and other materials which might earlier have been discarded. Neighborhood grocers, druggists, dry cleaners, liquor store operators, and of course parents and grandparents are encouraged not to discard anything that might possibly have use in this way. Individual children and teachers make regular calls to pick up whatever might be put aside for them.

The particular selection (or collection) of materials on the Make-It Table, and the way the Make-It Table fits into the general room arrangement, will change from time to time in accordance with the season or the current interests or the deliberate introduction of specific materials which the teacher feels will give new challenge needed. The tools required, and the help needed, will be close at hand. And whether the actual construction is done at the table or at some more adequate or private place elsewhere in the room will depend upon the particular classroom facilities. Again, whatever the specifics, a Make-It Table of some sort, set up with imaginative materials to invite children's ingenious making of things, together with the required time, space, and accepting atmosphere for putting it to maximum use, is helping to provide whole learnings for children in many classrooms. Another of Mrs. Barnes' brief notes to parents may be helpful to teachers here:

"DEAR PARENTS,
This will be the hurried note of Suggestions for Children's Gifts which I promised to send you.
Certain materials which we use in the room are popular enough that they would be welcome holiday gifts for these children. Any of them would love a box of interesting foods for exploring in cooking. A few marshmallows, some tooth picks, cranberries, pudding, Bisquick, cinnamon and sugar mix, gum drops, are only a few suggestions. If you prefer that they not cook, the kind of pudding that can be made with an egg beater is popular with them.

A kit of building supplies would be fun too. Different sized locks (with keys!), hinges, pulleys, odd shaped nails and cup-hooks and similar treasures from a dime store counter are all fun.

The girls are wild over flowers and jewelry, and would be excited with a kit containing odds and ends of paper flowers, glamorous-looking beads and buttons which could be strung or put on chains, bits of lace and ribbon.

American Handicrafts on Forty-First Street at Fifth Avenue has every kind of craft possible. Popular with these children have been basket weaving, leather, felt, shell jewelry, painting of all kinds. Leather and felt can be bought in scraps and generally speaking are more satisfactory this way than in already prepared kits, as children can plan their own creations. There is one set of permanent paints which can be used right from the tube without a brush. They dry immediately, do not wash off, and cause a minimum of mess because of the manner in which they are used. The paint will adhere to glass, leather, paper, cloth.

Industrial Arts Cooperative has many useful educational toys. One which seems to lend itself most to apartment living is a $2.50 set of pulleys which could be used in many ways.

Books which they have loved enough to have read over and over are *Mary Poppins, The King's Stilts, The Secret of the Ancient Oak, If I Ran the Zoo, Friendship Valley, The Forbidden Forest, Curious George, The Dead Bird, What Do You Say, Dear?* A science book which would be very useful for work we'll be doing after Christmas, and which also has many good experiments for doing around home, is *Let's Find Out* by Herman and Nina Schneider.

I have several catalogues from educational toy firms which have boxing gloves, clocks to assemble, telephones with switchboards, and all such. I also have a few favorite "haunts" where I go when I need to buy the kinds of equipment that don't come in a catalogue, —the Salvation Army store on 125th Street, the leather stores under the Brooklyn Bridge (an interesting excursion for a vacation day), stores in the hat district which sell feathers and other kinds of glamorous trim. I'd be glad to give more complete information about any of these.

Again, I appreciate so much your helpful observations and suggestions. The last part of the year promises to be stimulating and profitable. Perhaps some of you would like to come in soon after the holidays to talk over plans. My best holiday wishes to all of you!"

Toys and gadgets.   With toys and gadgets, children play out and pick up the vocabulary for ideas which they read about in books. At one time children were prohibited from bringing any such things into the classroom. "The good potential learning materials were checked at the door," one teacher laughingly puts it. Or at best they were consigned to the kindergarten and maybe first grades, where the fact of children at play for at least part of the day was not so damaging to school and community concepts of good education. Now teachers and other grownups with eyes and ears open are aware that toys available for children today, particularly those that work, are in themselves *teaching* children a great deal, both at home and at school. They are sometimes teaching children more than the well-trained teacher herself can know—until she makes it a point to catch up—about principles of traction, magnetism, sound, air pressure, static and dry-cell electricity, and other information about which even young children these days are surprisingly literate. To have such toys in the classroom, for children to use and discuss with one another, to repair, at times to take apart to see how they work, is an important way for them to see principles of science in action, to have learnings reenforced and misconceptions cleared up, and to ground their science reading in impressive firsthand experience.

Some teachers of older children, as a way of approaching the requirements of a science syllabus, are saying to children: "See what toys or other apparatus you can find that work on the principle of air pressure [or whatever the current focus]. Borrow some toys from your brothers and sisters or neighbors and bring them in," the only stipulation being that they be able to tell, in good scientific terms, how the items work. After this rather than before it, or perhaps accompanying the experience, comes the reading of various references provided by teacher *and* children, come the self-initiated experiments on air pressure, otherwise frequently so *overtaught* as to waste the time of many children and bring forth little real learning. A lesson on watching the egg being sucked into the milk bottle, to which everyone in the class has to give close attention, can be conceived of as an insult to even a second-grader who already knows, through actual experience, varied observation, and help from a number of out-of-school sources, much more complicated applications of the principle the lesson is designed to help him learn. Better that teachers help children to deepen their insights into those principles already in action in the materials of their everyday world. Intelligently selected toys and gadgets in the classroom can help to do this. They can reenforce meanings gained through other experiences as well, through the trips the children take to see construction projects, say, or roads under repair, through the science programs they see on television, through their extensive thoughtful reading from the wide variety of attractively written and illustrated science books. All of these, related and interrelated, can help today's children to understand better the complicated, exciting, scientific, technological world in which they live. Toys of the type mentioned here should be available for the realistic dramatic play of even the youngest children today, if their own background of social as well as mechanical information is to form a useful basis of interpretation for the reading they need to do as active, informed citizens of their society.

Other kinds of toys, too, representing other values, are important if children are to read and think intelligently about the world they live in. Dolls of different types and sizes and color of skin, and the real or improvised equipment required for use in the "house." Carriages, wagons, building blocks, balls and bats, puzzles, games of numberless variety. Nor need these toys be expensive to be valued by or suggestive of ideas to children.

OTHER SCIENCE MATERIALS.   Science materials and science conversations permeate the good modern classroom. Instead of being confined to one particular table labeled the "science table," the materials may well be deliberately placed in various spots in the classroom, where children can manipulate them, try them out, or put them to practical use. In this way magnets, bells, light bulbs, wire, dry cells, a tuning fork can become part of a person's real as well as his verbalized world. A table or bookcase top may be temporarily used by a group of children for making a telephone, say, concocting a signal system of bells for the teacher to use for calling them in from the playground, setting up an aquarium, or whatever is the problem at hand. Then when the job is finished, the materials are put away or moved to the side-by-side desks of a couple of interested children, as the case may be, and the table or space used for other things. Informal use of toys and gadgets in this connection has just been discussed.

Some of the materials brought in for the Make-It Table will no doubt be put in the science category from time to time— the plastic bottles for experimenting with air pressure, for example, the small magnet ingeniously used by a pair of children as the arms of a puppet, the willows that Louie brings in on a Spring day, just right for making whistles. A few children reading from one of the Herman and Nina Schneider science books, a Herbert Zim book, or even Blough and Huggett's *Elementary School Science and How to Teach It,* may ask for or bring in the special materials required for certain experiments suggested, and go to work with them wherever in the classroom seems to be the most sensible place. When children are free to select from choices made available to them, *they* become the discoverers, the sensible arrangers, the curious seekers and findouters. They are the ones whose skills are being put to use and learned.

RADIO AND TELEVISION.   Children need to learn to weigh or "read" critically radio and television shows just as they need to learn this skill when dealing with books or other printed material. They need to realize that persons involved in the organizing and carrying out of such shows are in effect "authors" as they plan and execute what the children see and hear. That these people utilize certain language skills and techniques, both logical and psychological, for making their messages persuasive. That any mass-communication author (used in this broad sense of the word) has a purpose in mind—be it entertainment, education or other information-giving, selling, or whatever. And they need to know just where they the viewers and listeners stand in relation to this purpose. Planning and presenting their own "television and radio programs" in the classroom can spell out this realization to the children, as well as give the teacher an opportunity to guide them in their own critical evaluation and judgments. And, of course, radio and television facilities in the classroom or school are no longer uncommon. For teachers and children alert to what is available over these media, they can serve as valuable, powerful sources of good, up-to-date information. Study clubs or committees frequently include joint viewing of selected related programs, whether this be at school or in one of the children's homes, as an important part of their study activity. Communication skills of the children today— reading, writing, listening, and much else—are integrally related to, and can be further developed by, intelligent use of these great instruments of human communication unique to our age.

THE WRITERS' TABLE.   The Writers' Table in the classroom is another means of inviting children, without teacher direction, to put their skills of reading and writing to work in healthy, creative ways. We have read of the Writers' Corner in Miss Bosner's school library (page 48), where children from kindergarten on up are free to write or to dictate their stories. Teachers are working out their own versions of the Writers' Table or Writers' Corner, depending upon the age of their children and other factors. Miss Kenyon arranges for a particular time of day, place in the classroom, and children from other classrooms to take dictation, for those who want to use these facilities for writing stories (pp. 201–203). In another classroom the table used for a writing desk, with post cards, stationery, and stamps provided, and lists of words the children might need for writing letters, serves as a similar businesslike way for making the skills functional. The important features of the Writers' Table, whatever the name, would include: a specially designated quiet place with an air of privacy about it, perhaps a label which gives it respectability and special significance, the needed materials close at hand, maybe some lined ditto sheets and other pages ready for use, arranged in suggestive, inviting ways, with provision for self-help and for friendly help from others as needed.

THE PUPPET THEATER.   Miss Rose's father builds a puppet theater for her classroom. The day it arrives the children are beside themselves with excitement. They have known for some time that "Grandpa" Rose is making it for them, so they have all the puppets ready for the occasion. "It's like a grand opening!" one of the youngsters calls out. And the others agree. "Grand opening of Grandpa Rose's Theater!" And that's the beginning—the beginning of several happy months of frequent puppet shows, variously organized and presented by small groups of children. Favorite stories acted out, plays about their families and friends, special holiday shows with exciting decorations, scenery, and clothes for the puppets, exciting westerns and other programs adapted from television. Miss Rose is interested to note how spontaneously some of the quieter children respond, once the talking is done through the puppets in their hands or on the simple strings they learn to manipulate.

Miss Rose takes down in writing some of the improvised plays as they move along. She puts them into book form for the children to illustrate, read, and enjoy. Some of the children write their own individual plays, along with stories and poems and other forms of expression which, in this kind of situation, young children are so full of. Some of these they send to Mr. Rose, having long since dispatched to him their thank-you notes and cards, invited him to one of their shows, climbed upon his lap and treated him like the kind, warm-hearted grandfather he really is.

Long after this, when the interest in puppets has waned, the beloved theater, its trimmings and labels changed a bit, serves variously as Supermarket, Service Station and Garage, bunk bed for the house. Each of them fits into and serves as incentive to developing language patterns and skills appropriate to the role it plays in the culture and age in which these children live.

THE HOUSE.   They come in various styles, these houses in which children play. Some are very elaborate with good siding walls, real doors and windows, with curtains fluttering and maybe plants abloom. But those that seem to best serve the purpose in many classrooms are put together by teacher and children without as much as a roof over their heads. A low bookcase jutting out to give privacy to the corner kitchen, and to serve as a place for small-sized but real pots and pans and dishes and "silverware" conveniently organized for use. The other two corner walls, one including a large window, say, give space for a very sturdy table for holding the electric hot plate, a two-shelved, improvised "refrigerator" made from a cereal display rack the neighborhood grocer had planned to throw out, a sink made from two upright orange crates with an oval dishpan between them, reaching from one top to the other and secured with wood cross-pieces front and back connecting the crates. The tops of the crates, covered with linoleum or oil cloth make good sideboard space, and the crates, facing front, provide shelfspace for supplies. The bottom space may be used for the bucket, brush and dust pan and other cleaning materials. The table is in the center of the kitchen where it can be most conveniently used. The fourth wall is really the game and puzzles cupboard, also jutting out, but leaving room for children to move easily to the adjoining center, where victrola, records, some books, an easy chair, the doll bed, and dolls also make an inviting place for imaginative carrying-on. The hot plate is real, the food is real, and the children respect this reality.

THE COOKING CENTER.   There may be two or three children cooking in the classroom kitchen at almost any time during the day. Soup, pudding mixes, juice, raw carrots, raisins, crackers, fruit, make good snacks for children who prepare their own meals, setting the table and carrying on their household conversations with enjoyment and growing skill. In a number of classrooms, including those of older children, electric hot plates or cooking facilities of some kind, are not uncommon. A few children cooking at a time, now and then for themselves, but usually as a treat for the whole class, perhaps refreshments for a planned party, are obviously in on whole learnings. This is quite unlike the class cooking we used to know where each one of us in the class had his half-minute turn. Mine might be peeling an apple, pouring the water in the kettle, helping to put the peeled apple quarters in the water, making two or three stirs with the big spoon, or whatever little piece of the class-wide undertaking I was fortunate enough to be assigned. Here, there is opportunity throughout the year for any child who chooses, to have the satisfying experience of actual cooking. Gathering and exchanging recipes, reading and following them, increasing or decreasing the proportions as needed, printing the most successful recipes for others to use, or as the worthy project of a small interested group, making a book of good hot-plate recipes for classroom use or for gifts to the cooks in the family—these are among the children's choices for putting their skills to work which the teacher has in mind when she makes the provision or sets up the facilities for cooking.

FILMSTRIPS AND FILMS.   It is always a help if teachers can have ready access to films they know and would like their children to see in the classroom, in intimate enough surroundings that they can comment on the film as it goes, see it again if they like, maybe parts of it without sound to enable them to discuss certain points or to improvise their own script. There is so much to learn from and about children in this kind of situation, and the skills of communication have a much freer flow. Although it is difficult as yet for many schools to provide this kind of classroom experience with films, it is quite within the range of practicality to have filmstrips available to classrooms, together with the filmstrip projector. Where this is the case, especially where children can select the filmstrips, study clubs or other small groups can assume responsibility for selection, operation of the projector, and any explanations or discussions their planned presentation may require. Even young children are able, with very little help—sometimes with less than their teachers require—to operate this handy device. The variety of good available filmstrips is increasing right along, in science, travel, history, literature, art, and many other fields.

THE TAPE RECORDER AND RECORD PLAYER.   Recognizing that *listening* is the first and basic skill used by children as they learn to accommodate themselves to other people's language patterns, many teachers are now providing special listening centers in their classrooms. Children love to work long and hard to make their own tape recordings of original stories, poetry reading, live discussions, singing, their own plays and programs, Manuel's and Marita's "lessons" to help other children in the class learn Spanish, and Enrico's to help them learn Italian. They also become adept at making tapes of "outside" voices—for example, resource people from their neighborhood who come in to talk with them about interesting firsthand experiences relating to history in their own community. And as the children play these tapes and listen, they are not only taking in interesting information, they are also learning to read. They are learning what it means to learn from other people's language patterns. And they are learning the specialized vocabulary from a host of fields which they also encounter in their reading.

This is also true when children listen to a record player. Whether they are listening to favorite folk tunes or to moving descriptions like Folkways' story of "The Rain Forest," the children are taking in messages which other people have organized for them. They are materially extending their orientation to reading. In many schools now the same careful effort is given to collecting a good library of recordings as is devoted to the collecting of books. These improved communication facilities provide children today with opportunities for learning which their parents and teachers knew nothing about.

THE LIBRARY CORNER OR READING CENTER.   Among the most exciting products of our technology today are the children's books, magazines, maps and globes, and other printed materials which help make the world's information and pleasure available to children. Teachers and children in various classrooms find their own best and most convenient ways for organizing these attractive products for use. Some teachers prefer a Reading Center set off with the privacy that a bookcase or low game cupboards set at right angles to the wall can give it, with perhaps a large table and a number of chairs to complete the set-up. Others prefer that the books not be confined to one particular place. They arrange a library corner of some kind for the large quantity of reading materials, but plan also for books a few at a time to be in other places about the room, handy for children to pick up and read.

The teachers in earlier chapters of the book, like teachers throughout the land, are faced with the problem of what sources to turn to for providing the wide and varied collection of books they realize is essential if children are going to develop the needed skills—all of the skills of good reading, for example, listed by those thoughtful enthusiastic teachers in the Reading Workshop described in Chapter Four (pp. 83–84). The important thing is that they do find answers to their problem, answers most of which are being exploited by resourceful teachers everywhere. They use the public libraries for limitless armloads of books, using the cards and the carting facilities of children and teachers alike. They generously contribute their own books on loan, and encourage the children to do the same. They help parents and children to know the value of giving and asking for books for birthdays, Hanukkah, Christmas, and other occasions. They exchange books and certain collections of books with other classes in the school or in the system, maybe outside. They work with parents to put on book fairs, Hallowe'en carnivals and other enjoyable functions for the purpose of raising money for books. They help children to write stories and make books for use.

Nor do the teachers discard any of these ways as they turn

foremost and always to their own schools and administrators for help. Submitting their carefully thought through book orders to the administration regularly, invited or not. Suggesting increased use of the school budget for a *variety* of books to meet the children's individual needs and to extend their reading possibilities. This seems to teachers so much more sensible than allocating the same amount for several sets of identical books which are bound, for a large number of children, "to be too hard or too soft or to break it all down," as the good bear story goes. In this case, more seriously, to break down the self-respect or the interest or the eagerness to read of children who cannot find books suited to them. To break down too, the possibility for children to read widely and hungrily and skillfully, in search of particular information they are seeking.

These teachers are making maximum use of their own school libraries. Cooperating with the sixth-grade teachers and their children who are working so hard to operate the libraries on at least a part-time basis, until their boards of education can answer the urgent request for the more extensive and skilled services of a trained, full-time librarian. Once they have these services, making the widest use of them possible for helping individual children—all of the children—to read, to know and love reading as related to all of the human relationships so richly experienced in the libraries of Miss Bosner and Miss Menlove in Chapter Three above. Organizing and working hard to set up a school library if they do not have one. Giving more and more active support to the gradually spreading kind of school administration, such as described previously in Chapter Four, in their very earnest attempts to set up school libraries and bookmobiles, purchase increasing numbers of books for good classroom collections, and in countless other ways to help teachers better to meet the needs of children in learning to read.

Realizing that so many of the important reading skills can be learned only or best when children have responsible access to a wide and varied selection of books, teachers are labeling

Number One in their plans for setting up the classroom with materials that *teach*, the provision for good book collections.

Arranging Space to Invite Self-initiated Learning

THE PROBLEM IN CROWDED CLASSROOMS.   Just finding adequate space for the inviting arrangements of materials and equipment just discussed, is not an easy matter. Particularly is this true in these days of overcrowded classrooms, bus-transported children, newly constructed buildings filled to overflowing almost before they are completed, everywhere school facilities just bursting at the seams! Frequently, in the all too common classrooms where screwed-down desks are still the order of the day, there seems to be room for little else than the rows of seats, the aisles, and the teacher's desk. Even the new movable furniture, teachers are finding, especially the one-chair-and-one-table-per-child variety of furniture, is altogether too space-consuming for most purposes.

The space problem is twofold in the setting up of these classrooms. Where and how to house the varied materials and centers in the classroom so they will invite whole learning, and how to arrange a crowded room so that children, thus invited, can use the provided materials freely and creatively, can work out projects with a best friend or with several of them, can look for and comfortably receive from the materials, from one another, or from the teacher the kind of help they need? How can a teacher make friendly help available to individual children and to small groups making use of her carefully set up centers, if they have to climb through desks or walk around rows of other children on the way?

Smaller classes and more ample classrooms are the solution, of course. But smaller classes in our time of rapidly expanding enrollments are more the rare and courageous exception than the rule. In the meantime resourceful teachers are making out. Not as well as if the classes were smaller and the classrooms larger and better equipped, but they are making out. Concurrently, as they work with their colleagues and supportive groups in their communities to secure better facilities for children, teachers in new schools and old are seeking ways to rearrange their classrooms, to make possible the face-to-face communication necessary to responsible, cooperative living for their children, whose one and only childhood is now. They realize that the larger their classes and the more crowded their classrooms, the more important it is to arrange a variety of choices so children can take on more, not less, responsibility for self-initiated, self-propelled activities, individual and small-group.

ARRANGING AND REARRANGING THE CLASSROOMS.   Teachers in different sections of the country, whatever the size of their classes, are seeking ways to set up their classrooms to facilitate face-to-face communication. To encourage communication among the children, not to discourage it, as in the days when we were seated in school, one behind the other in each row, boys and girls alternating, with an aisle on either side—all of this by deliberate design to keep us from communicating with one another. We were punished if we talked. We were punished if we wrote notes. Oral or written communication among children as a usual thing was strictly forbidden—and this in a school set up by the public to teach the children the skills of reading and writing and speaking. In these same classrooms, where the same rows of screwed-down desks still persist and would otherwise fill up the rooms, many teachers and principals are having their custodians mount the desks and seats on individual pairs of runners so they become movable and can be grouped together as needed—grouped together to make sensible, responsible, face-to-face communication possible. Where this arrangement is not practical, they have the entire *rows* of desks put on these long wooden runners so the "movable" rows can be pushed together. In this way, only half the aisle space is required, freeing the other space for more flexible and profitable purpose. Some teachers are able to secure, from one source or another as does Miss Floyd in Chapter One, large group tables and enough chairs for part of the class, eliminating first one row and gradually more rows of the fixed seats. They find this half-and-half arrangement allows for much more flexibility.

In classrooms with furniture already movable, teachers are arranging it to provide for more varied uses. So children can more comfortably plan and work with friends in small groups, so they can sense the feeling of independence that semiprivacy engenders, teachers try to break the room up, as it were, by arranging the furniture to suggest "rooms" or interest centers just described. This is possible by using a bookcase jutting out from the wall as a kind of partition, between the book corner and the adjoining center where the quiet games are kept, let us say, and where the desks of four or six of the youngsters who enjoy being together are grouped like a large table. Because the partition is low, these children can still be part of the larger group as needed. They can still be seen by the teacher from any part of the room. They can have the feeling of a group when working at something private. And yet their tables can be used by other children during a Choice or Work Period, when children select to pursue various activities in different parts of the room.

As many as five or six of the centers suggested can be easily arranged by putting other bookcases or cabinets or tables at right angles with the wall, including the piano or teacher's desk or even the large supply cabinet at the back of the room. This does not *add* furniture. It merely rearranges for more possible uses, by individuals or by different-sized groups, the equipment already in the room. A Library Corner, a Make-It Table, a letter-writing center, Work Table, painting and clay centers, puppet theater—any of these arrangements can be worked out in this way. And as has already been suggested, the materials needed for such activities can well be kept in convenient cabinets or shelves or in cartons close by, rather than all together in one big cupboard or closet, or off in one section of the room.

Other groups of the children's tables are elsewhere in the room, of course, probably of different sizes and arranged in the central or front part of the room, wherever and however con-

venient to the program planned. Most teachers like to have one
clear place in the room too, or one easily and quickly clearable,
where children especially in the younger classes can gather
together to listen to a story, read in a group with the teacher,
sing songs, discuss plans, learn a new step in arithmetic. The
older children, *because* they are older and larger, are able to
function as a total group when necessary from wherever they
happen to be working in the room, merely by turning their
chairs.

This kind of flexible arrangement, teachers are finding,
makes possible privacy as well as face-to-face communication
among the children. It facilitates the self-initiated projects of
the children, individual and small group, which a carefully set
up classroom can invite, allowing for the children to move about
as needed, with a minimum of getting in one another's way.
Continuous improvement of whatever arrangement is worked
out, with a change here and another change there to meet particular needs, with occasional total reorganization as new activities are undertaken and new materials brought in, goes on
throughout the year.

This kind of total reorganization, with the required planning and rearrangement of classroom facilities, to invite children's whole and self-selected action appropriate to a favorite
season in their culture, is described by college junior Doris.
Doris writes of her own participation in Mrs. Barnes' classroom,
where preparations for gift-making are begun in early December:

When I came to Mrs. Barnes' room on Thursday morning I
was really amazed at how well she had succeeded in turning the
classroom into (as you had so aptly put it in class) a real "children's
workshop." Plenty of work space was provided by rearranging the
tables and covering them with brown paper so as to form three
separate work tables and one display table. Each work table had
different materials on it and a sign indicating for what correspond-
ing activity it was intended. Thus, on one table, with "self-harden-
ing" paint that could be applied to objects fired in the oven, the
sign indicated it was for "Painting clay, dishes, and glass;" on another table, containing tempera paint, the sign showed one could
use the table and materials for "Painting cards, wood, leather, and

reed;" while on the third table, with reeds soaking in water and other basket-making materials, a sign indicated it could be used for weaving.

The classroom store also had been "renovated" to a certain extent. All kinds of material were made available for the children to buy with the money they had set aside for their special gift budget account, so they could all make the presents they wanted to for the people on their Christmas lists. The gift budget sheet had the money that could be spent, 75¢ for each child, arranged in columns of pennies—the first column being a single row of pennies, the second a double row, etc., so that the children, when crossing off the amounts they spent, were thus able to get practice in counting and adding by ones, twos, threes, fours, and fives, and in this way could review the arithmetic skills they had learned during the year.

Budget Sheet

0	00	000	0000	00000
0	00	000	0000	00000
0	00	000	0000	00000
0	00	000	0000	00000
0	00	000	0000	00000

Some of the materials that I saw available in the store for making presents were:

1. Foam rubber—for making dolls, etc.
2. Plastic material—sold instead of leather—for making wallets, etc.
3. Tiles—to paint
4. Dishes, glasses, salt and pepper shakers—to decorate
5. Reed—for basket weaving
6. Curtain rings—for making coasters and for decorations
7. Hat trimming and ribbons—for costumes and to use in decorations
8. Upholstery fabric (stiff)—for place mats
9. Wool yarn—for stitching
10. Wood pieces—for making trains and other toys
11. Paint brushes—for painting cards, etc.
12. Pin and earring backings—for making jewelry
13. Shells—for making pins and earrings

Each article sold was listed on one of a number of price lists posted on the bulletin board in back of the store. I was able to pick up copies of two of the price lists available on Thursday, and I am attaching them to this report [see Figs. 7.1 and 7.2].

```
        P R I C E    L I S T  -  1


Leather . . . . . . .4 square inches for . . . .   1¢

Snaps . . . . . . . . . . . . . . . . . . . . .   2¢

Key hooks . . . . . . . . . . . . . . . . . . .   3¢

Paint brushes . . . . . . . . . . . . . . . . o   3¢

Baskets . . . . . . . . . . . . . . . . . . . .   7¢

Pin Backs . . . . . . . . . . . . . . . . . . .   2¢

Barrettes. . . . . . . . . . . . . . . . . . o    6¢

Cups . . . . . . . . . . . . . . 2 for . . . . .   7¢

Foam Rubber. . . . . . . . . . an ounce for. .    3¢

Wire . . . . . . . . . . . . . 4 inches for. .    1¢

Trimming . . . . . . . . . . . 4 inches for. .    1¢

Bowls. . . . . . . . . . . . . . . . . . . . .    8¢

Sprinklers . . . . . . . . . . . . . . . . . .    2¢

Salt and pepper shakers. . . . . . . . . .each    4¢

Cups . . . . . . . . . . . . . . . . . . . . .    5¢

Saucers. . . . . . . . . . . . . . . . . . . .    6¢

Earrings . . . . . . . . . . . . . . . . . . .    3¢

Shells . . . . . . . . . . . . . . . 20 for   1¢
```

Fig. 7–1

```
P R I C E   L I S T  -  2


Glasses . . . . . . . . . . . . . . . . . . . . 6¢

Flower pots . . . . . . . . . . . . . . . . . . 4¢

Mustard jars . . . . . . . . . . . . . . . . . 9¢

Baking dish . . . . . . . . . . . . . . . . . 11¢

Vase . . . . . . . . . . . . . . . . . . . . 11¢

Salad fork and spoon . . . . . . . . . . .each 4¢

                        Bargain . . . . . 2 for 7¢

Wool. . . . . . . . . . . . . . . . . . . . . 5¢

Small ash trays . . . . . . . . . . . . . . . . 2¢

Mops. . . . . . . . . . . . . . . . . . . . . 3¢

Wash cloths . . . . . . . . . . . . . . . . . 2¢

Mirrors . . . . . . . . . . . . . . . . . . . 7¢

Tiles . . . . . . . . . . . . . . . . . . . . 8¢

Small baskets . . . . . . . . . . . . . . . . 4¢

Velvet material . . . . . . . . per square foot 5¢
```

Fig. 7–2

As I worked in the classroom with the children during the day, watching them buy things in the store and helping them in their work when they needed assistance, I saw that this was really a wonderful opportunity for the children to do creative work for a worthwhile purpose. In making the presents for their relatives and friends out of the available materials, they had to use their ingenuity to a much greater extent than if they merely went out and bought the presents in a store. Thus, while the children were relieved of a great part of the commercial pressures that the Christmas season brings, they were, at the same time, experiencing the joy and satisfaction of making things for other people with their own hands. Often working in small groups and helping each other to complete various gifts, the children were getting valuable experiences in social relations. While watching the class work, I had the general feeling that each child was able to enter wholeheartedly into the spirit of doing things together with other people *for* others. (This incidentally also meant giving much thought to and becoming aware of the particular wants and needs of others who would be the recipients of the gifts.) In this "communal" classroom atmosphere which existed, the children could feel accepted in the group, no matter what their religious beliefs or individual philosophy about Christmas was at this time.

As I worked with the children, I was amazed at the many skills they were able to learn and to use in a natural and practical way while they were purchasing materials and making gifts in their classroom workshop. For instance, in buying plastic material that was being sold by square inches in their classroom store (the square inches marked off with pencil on the back of the material), and ribbon and lacing that were being sold in running inches and feet, as well as foam rubber which was sold by the ounce, the children had to make practical use of various arithmetic skills, such as counting, adding and multiplying. At the same time they were acquiring a good understanding of various basic measurements, as well as getting an accurate general conception of area in relation to size. The children were also able to get much practice in reading, writing and spelling skills, as well as getting the opportunity to enlarge their written and oral vocabulary, by doing such things as writing gift notes and Hanukkah and Christmas cards, reading price lists and labels on paint bottles, reading signs on the different activity tables. The class had to use its science knowledge in many practical ways too—such as when they made, for their younger brothers and sisters, "magic balloons" that stick to the wall because of static electricity, and when they figured out, with the help of an oven thermometer, how hot to make the kiln so the paint on their clay pottery would glaze properly. Working with many different materials gave the children a great deal of opportunity to learn many new and useful scientific facts in a natural way—such as discovering what some of the properties of plastic are, after noticing that their plastic paint boxes melted when they were exposed to too much heat near the oven, and were also dissolved by the acid in the paint remover when that was left in the paint box overnight!

Thus, the children's use and practice of skills and knowledge evolved in a natural way from their own activities and experiences. I felt that learning in this classroom situation was really much more meaningful and spontaneous than if the children had been forced to go through the regimented Christmas preparations I had so often seen take place in more "traditional" classrooms, where carrying out the "spirit of Christmas" means mainly copying figures for stilted Christmas cards and making uniform presents, while the children are told that they must, at the same time, keep up with the unrelated drilling on various skills.

On Thursday of this week I was assured by Mrs. Barnes that the children on the history committee, that I have been working with the past few Thursdays, were still very much interested in continuing their research and planning activities, along with all their holiday preparations. So I arranged with Mr. Jackson to show three very good films about the pioneer days that the history committee had chosen with Mrs. Barnes during the past week in my absence. The committee had agreed during our previous discussions together that presenting the films about pioneer life in America to the whole class would give everyone a better idea of what this "period" of our history was really like and would make the work of the committee clearer to all.

The three films were presented in two showings, because they were quite long (about one-and-a-half hours in all). Mrs. Barnes made a brief intermission in the middle of the eleven o'clock showing of the first film (which dealt with Columbus' discovery of America) in order to discuss and clarify some of the main points presented in the action. From the way the children answered Mrs. Barnes' questions and discussed what the picture was about, I saw that the class was apparently very much interested in the film and understood very well the main trend of the story and the basic ideas presented, despite the fact that the movie was supposedly on a fourth grade level.

Their interest and enthusiasm continued to be evident during the afternoon showing of two films, describing the Western movement and the life of colonial children. I think the relaxed atmosphere which Mrs. Barnes maintained in the visual aids room during the film showings—allowing the children to talk to each other quietly and change their seats if they desired while the pictures were being shown—contributed greatly to the children's continuing interest in the films, and cut down on the "fidgeting" and restlessness so often present when children are made to sit and watch passively for a long period of time. The history committee had previously compiled, together with Mrs. Barnes, a nice program folder which gave a brief summary of the films that would be shown and was correspondingly illustrated by various members of the committee. Each child received a dittoed copy of the program folder before the film showings began, and I think this also helped a great deal in stimulating interest and fostering understanding of the material presented in the films.

I almost forgot to mention—I had a very interesting meeting with the history committee in the morning before the films were shown, upon one of the boys' request, to discuss some of the things the group had been doing in my absence during the week. (I am sorry you weren't sitting close enough to hear it, too, during your visit to our room.) I was really delighted to find that every committee member continued to display a genuine interest in finding out more about the pioneer period of our history, and I saw that the different children had done quite a bit of reading and discussing among themselves since our last meeting. It was interesting to notice that one or two of the children (such as Michele, for instance), who had been quite reluctant about reading things for research purposes when we first formed the history committee, became most enthusiastic readers and talkers once they were more engrossed in the subject matter and interested in finding out added information. In reading many different books in order to obtain the information they desired, the children were acquiring the ability to form their own critical judgments as to which books were rich in resource material and were interesting reading, and which were not as good. In recommending different sources to each other and in talking over information they had gained from their readings, they were learning to work well together for a common purpose.

During our meeting we discussed plans for the puppet show which the committee would present to the class in the near future in order to inform the rest of the children, in an interesting and lively way, what life during the pioneer days was like. (The children had decided, during our previous meetings, that this was a good way of reporting to the class on the work that the history committee had been doing.) The children decided they wanted to have at least one pioneer family and perhaps one or two Indians represented in the puppet play, and since the puppet heads of a man, woman, and child were already left in the classroom from previous shows, the children decided to start making new clothes for what would now become a pioneer family. In order to make the clothes so that they would resemble what the real pioneers wore, two of the children suggested that we look at some pictures of pioneer people, which they had come across in a few books they had read. Using these pictures as our guide, we bought some plastic material from the class store and began making a "leather" jacket for the pioneer man. One of the girls used the old jacket that had previously been on the hand puppet as a pattern for measuring enough material to cut a jacket of the right size. While some of us began sewing the sleeves as well as the back and front of the jacket body, one of the girls who did not feel like sewing decided to make the jacket look really "authentic" by cutting fringes on the bottom of the front and back parts. Although we were able to work only for a little while on the costumes, because of all the Christmas activities and film showings going on during the day, I feel that the history committee at least got a good start on Thursday on the preparations for the puppet play, and will be able to continue their plans and activities with a large degree of independence when they again have the opportunity to work together.

Because I felt that careful planning and setting up of the room for different activities contributed, to a large extent, to the success of Mrs. Barnes' teaching methods, I decided to stay after school in the afternoon and help her get things ready for the next day. Together we changed the work table setup somewhat by converting one of the tables, which had been used for painting different things, into a "sewing table," and leaving all the painted materials to be used on only one table. Mrs. Barnes and I placed around the sewing table some "samples" of gifts that could be made with the materials available in the store, and thus indicated the wide variety of things which the children could make if they used a little ingenuity and had a "creative spirit." These samples included stitched place mats made from upholstery material that could be cut to certain sizes (the children would get practice in measuring and adding when they bought this material in the store by the square inch), coasters made by stitching curtain rings together, and yarn flowers that could be made for decorating presents or making corsages. I got the idea of making a sample of simply constructed yarn flowers, because during the day one of the children had asked me how to make flowers out of paper for the purpose of decorating a package. In setting up the materials on the sewing table, I remembered how I had myself, when I was younger, made attractive flowers out of yarn for decorating packages. I had done this by weaving a circular pattern in and out of vertical "ribbings" of yarn that had first been stretched over a small cardboard "brace," and then removing it from the brace when the flower was completed.

By helping prepare the room for the following day, I was able to get a really good idea of the great amount of planning that is necessary if the teacher wants to be sure that the children have valuable learning experiences in as many areas as possible.

OUT-OF-SCHOOL FACILITIES.   The limitations of this chapter will not permit discussion of all the space facilities available for children's self-initiated learning, beyond emphasizing the fact that teachers are making increasing use of school grounds, too, and of places of educational interest in the community, through trips, interviews, and other procedures planned with the children, already referred to in these pages.

Providing the Friendly Kind of Help that Individual Children Need

For too long we have thought of the teacher as the one who asks the questions, who does most of the talking and telling and giving of directions in the classroom. More basically, we have come to think of the teacher as the person in charge of motivation, with motivation conceived of as something which can be organized outside of the learner and applied *to* him. This kind of thinking has created an active-passive relationship between a child and his teacher—the child being the passive receptor of learning which the teacher actively presents to or pours into him. In such a relationship learning loses its power. The reaching out—an action so important in learning—is done by the teacher, when in reality it is the learner who needs to seek, who needs to reach out. It is as if we falsely separated learning into two parts—the seeking, which is to be done by the teacher, and the taking in, which is to be done by the child.

When we care about the learning of *individual* children, we see a new relationship between teacher and learner. This new relationship is not just a reversal of the old. That is to say, in the new relationship we do not simply place the child in the role of reaching out and the teacher in the role of supplying needs. Child and teacher are both reaching out when good learning is going on. The child is the one who is setting the pace, however. He is the one who needs to learn. He responds to motivation which he *initiates within himself.* He gives the cue to the teacher, as it were, and her help is offered not prior to but following the original seeking of the child. In other words, the teacher is the one who, in a deeply significant way, speaks when she is spoken to. And the child is the one who has responsibility for organizing and in other ways making sense out of what his teacher says. He is the one who knows what is useful to him and what is not.

When Barry selects his next book to read from the Reading Table, you remember, he rejects one book after another until he finds a book that he knows he can read, not that some test or reading book says he can read. He picks up the book, tries it out here and there, with or without the help of his teacher looking on, and he knows if he can read it or if he can't.

INTERPRETING THE SIGNALS IN CHILDREN'S BEHAVIOR. Teachers can tell, through their own skillfully developed ways of interpreting the signals, when children are making headway with their learning, with their individual selecting and figuring out, and when and how they need help. Teachers can tell these things, at whatever age-level they teach, when the children are engaged in real live learning situations. In reading situations, for example, where the purpose or the research is theirs, the children's, where the children are focusing on content. A child reading the recipe for making Jello for the first time, by way of illustration. A young child signing up for a piece of playground equipment on a class sign-up sheet. Chucky and his friends trying to figure out if they have enough money to send, prepaid, for the roller skates they are ordering through the school supply catalogue. Bonnie and Elisabeth reading a story to see if it will make a good class play for Book Week. Several children at the Reading Table enjoying their own selections.

First-grader Rachel making her book, *The Story of the Garden,* for her classmates. Fifth-grader Herbert trying to reorganize his Table of Contents for the extensive book he is writing for the school library on *The Making of Aluminum,* his periodical and newspaper references laid out close at hand. Three children planning and organizing a treasure hunt for their class party. Two girls trying to figure out from the directions how to use the new can of plastic spray on their carefully made gift coasters. A trio of friends reading an article about the Echo I balloon satellite. Another group reading about the latest Discoverer and other news in the two papers to which their class subscribes. David and Timmy going after their plans for a book on *What Young Historians Should Know About the Renaissance.* Billy, Laura, and Kaye at work writing their individual newspapers. Charles and Franklin getting out the latest issue of *The Space Club News.* Jan and Barbara making a United Nations Crossword Puzzle. Suzanne and Curtis searching for information about the new dam which their class will be visiting next week, which they will need for their trip booklet.

And so it goes. Resourceful teachers provide for and recognize the comprehension skills in action. They learn to know what these skills look like in the behavior of individual children at work—at work by themselves or in purposeful cooperation with others. They become increasingly competent in recognizing the cues as to when to stay out of the picture, when to proffer direct help, when to work along with the child—or a group, or the whole class. When to offer a child a book with the comment, "I wonder if this would help," or, "Have you seen this map of Africa? It's right up to date, you know—if one can be these days." It is in these real situations that teachers learn to interpret behavior that signals to them: "Am understanding— am making out all right," or "Am *not* making out—need help of some kind—now."

GIVING HELP AT THE POINT OF NEED.   Being able to sense this point of need for help is most important to both teacher and child. It is at just this point that help can be of greatest

worth. It is at just this point, in just this situation, where motivation and need are most sincere, that a child can incorporate
the new learning with maximum meaning. "Ooooh, so *that's*
it!" he may respond, thoughtfully nodding his head. Or "Hmm-
mm now, that makes sense, doesn't it?" Or "Yes-sir, here it
is right here. Say, this is just the book I needed." Or he may
say nothing at all—just give a quick nod of recognition or a
smile of triumph or whatever is his signal to show that he has
it! Just this bit of help at the time it is most needed—from
teacher, from neighbor, from some new piece of material—can
help him over the rough spot, can open the gate, as it were.

This kind of help, as already emphasized, is worth more
than any amount of systematic, repetitive drill, apart from the
point of real need. Once a child comprehends—by himself or
with the needed help—once he gets the hang, discovers the
pattern, he is competent to move ahead under his own steam.
It is then that the follow-up activities which his teacher provides, such as those in the previous chapter, for him individually
or for the group, will also be full of meaning. Practice will be
based on insight and understanding rather than on repetitive
drill or memorized rule. For rules or patterns make most sense
to children when they can be *discovered* by them—be they
rules of language, mathematics, science, whatever.

The teacher provides the conditions, and gives direct help
as needed, to enable children to move ahead comfortably in
their learning. She provides lined ditto sheets—a variety from
which to choose—so children can write neatly and evenly within the margins without having to think about it; so they will
be accustomed to writing, and reading, neat, attractively spaced
pages instead of messy, crowded ones. She has the paints already
set out for mixing, particularly for the younger children, the
clay ready for use, the newspapers or towels close by, so the
youngsters can get to work at once, having signed up for the
job, perhaps with plans ready. As these children grow older,
knowing the importance of having their tools ready for work,
they will no doubt plan and set them up accordingly.

The teacher tells the children the new words they need as

they read, to teach them the habit of focusing on the whole word and letting the context help move them along. She spells or writes for them words they cannot spell as they write letters or stories or newspapers, so they will be accustomed to using properly spelled words and will not be spending their time writing words incorrectly. She provides a writing table or desk with all the materials handy for choice and use. Not to make life easier for the children but to make it easier for them to write good letters or good stories, and thus to better develop the skills of writing and reading.

THE CHILD WHO CAN'T READ.   But where is the child who can't read? Where is the child who, multiplied by several in almost every classroom in the land, has difficulty getting started, can't read the words in his reader, seems not to know the sounds, is reading several years below grade. Where is he?

He is here. He is sitting close to his teacher or a friend who can help him with words in this wonderful book he has selected from the Library Table. He is here, pencil in hand, carefully pondering his choices on the worksheet about people he would take to the moon, or filling out the check list his teacher has read through with the group and with which she is helping him now as he reads it. He is here, skillfully drawing, perhaps by request, the letterhead for the Reptile Club's stationery, or finding the pattern in one of the exciting arithmetic worksheets that his teacher has put out on the Work Table for the children to choose from. He is here, using his own unique language patterns in the book he is writing—spelling out language patterns which he can read, thereby improving his own reading skill. He is here, tongue out in concentration, and with the slip of paper close by on which he has asked his teacher to write the words he needs, energetically making the sign he plans to put on the bulletin board, saying: *If you want copies of this comic sheet please see me,* and his name signed below.

The child who "can't read" is here, helping to wire the playhouse for the kindergarten, agreeing to make the very technical illustrations for Herbert's book on Aluminum, which he

himself comes to read with a fair degree of independence before the cooperative project is completed. He is here, selecting
gradually more complicated, interesting books from the Library
Table, or helping to draw up the week's schedule for the film
projector in the school, which he and a couple of other children
are responsible for operating. He is here, all right, reading along
as he sings with the others, from the words to *The Marine
Hymn,* which the teacher has quickly typed and dittoed for all
of the children to use, or helping his new friends to make a
Spanish-English dictionary for use by the other Puerto Rican
children in the school. He is here, all right, working hard,
playing hard, *reading hard,* assuming his respected role in the
day-to-day business and exciting group living for which his
teacher has so carefully and resourcefully planned, partly with
him in mind. He is here all right . . . no doubt about that.

THE "GIFTED" CHILD.   And where is the so-called "gifted"
child, the one whom so many fear these days is forgotten, and
well may be in the lock-step, unchallenging, everyone-move-at-
a-time kind of classrooms. Where is the gifted child, whom
people are trying to identify early so that he and those like him
can be separated off from the other children and given the best
that a school system's hard-come-by money can buy? Where is
he, the talented, the gifted?

Well, we see him also in these pages, quite obviously. We
see him working as hard as he can with his hard-working group,
doing many of the same kinds of things that the others are doing,
and doing them with the others—some not as well, and some
very much better, of course. There is ample room here for children's individual differences. Yes, we see him, experimenting
with intricate language patterns. We see him hard at work with
the little group on the Spanish-English dictionary, or writing a
book of stories in French for the beginning French classes. We
see him and a couple of his pals making a study of the Middle
Ages in European history. Right now we see him reading selected travel books like a house afire, planning himself to write
a "full-length" biography of a recently deceased uncle who trav-

eled widely throughout his life, and whose adventure-packed letters the family has kept through the years.

He is here all right, the academically advanced child, practicing hard to justify his left-field position on the sixth-grade baseball team, spending a good deal of time at the Inventing Corner with a friend, making a transistor radio. We see him studying carefully a chapter on jet propulsion from the physics book his teacher has borrowed for him from a high school brother. We see him helping to make the slides on magnetism for the second-grade class downstairs, working with a group of boys on the choral reading of a favorite poem, working with a trio of friends (one of whom doesn't read very well but this is irrelevant) to put out a weekly newspaper. Helping some of his classmates to stage a puppet show of part of Shakespeare's *The Merchant of Venice,* say, or a few scenes they select from Marjorie Rawlings' *The Yearling.* We see him writing his account for the sixth grade's book about their marvelous trip through the state. Typing up an introduction and table of contents for the Food and Agriculture Committee's illustrated pamphlet. Hunting up information for the proposed United Nations trip booklet, and writing it on the ditto carbons. Helping to wire the playhouse for the Kindergarten. Planning with his classmates who are going to meet with the town officials, with whom they have already been in correspondence, about having some streets on Havelock Hill blocked off for sleigh-riding during these fine winter days . . .

THE SKILL REQUIRED OF THE TEACHER.   In a classroom deliberately and skillfully set up for individualized learning every child in the group is provided for. Every child in the group is challenged to select and reach out, to find his own kinds of "giftedness," resources and growing skills, within a framework of good social living. The teacher sensitively and continuously organizes materials, time, space, friendly help, to invite the healthy kind of group living that enhances—rather than levels off, ranks in order, or segregates—the unique capabilities of individual children. The teacher structures deliberately for her all kinds of children. For all kinds of children is what every teacher's class is made up of.

But what about the all kinds of teachers in the classrooms? This way of working with children requires superior skill on the part of teachers, we hear on every hand. And so of course it does. It does require increasingly, carefully developed skill— but not more than the great majority of earnest, sincere teachers have and, where conditions are right, want to and can give to their work with children. This is true, as chapters of the book indicate, of teachers in city systems or in smaller scattered schools throughout the country. It is the reason they chose to be teachers in the first place.

8

A closer look at children as authors in a planned situation

Back of every book there is an author—a person who organizes ideas into words and writes them for other people to read. Children who read need good authors. They are dependent on the quality of the author's ideas and on his skill in putting them down.

Children Write in Patterns that Other Children Can Read

Encouraged by their supervisor and visiting consultant, the teachers of Harris County believe that children, by virtue of their being children, can qualify uniquely as authors of good reading materials for children. To begin with, they point out, children write in patterns that other children can read—a skill the importance of which cannot be overestimated. When a person reads a book or newspaper or any form of written language, he senses that there is pattern in what he sees. Because language is patterned and because he has been using language all his life, a person looks at a page of printing with a built-in readiness for discovering pattern. And children write in pattern, using words to signal to the child reader just what he needs to know.

"We plow the garden first," writes first-grader Rachel on the first page of her own illustrated book, *The Book About The Garden*. Then comes, "We cultipack the garden next," with its accompanying crayon drawing. On page 3, she writes: "We disc the garden next." On page 4, "We plant the garden next." On page 5 comes the lovely change of mood that is right for growing things: "See, it is up now." (See Fig. 8.1.)

Many children in Rachel's school—children of all ages— are able to read and enjoy her book when they find it on their reading table. Words like *cultipack* and *disc* are not too hard for first-graders in a farming community, when their book is written by an author who uses words as dependably as Rachel does. Notice her careful use of the words *first* and *next*. Rachel's friends know the process of farming well; and with the meaningful use of these two words, her teacher notes that even those who cannot yet read a first-grade reader are able to figure out which farming process each of Rachel's pages is about. When *The Book About The Garden* and others quite as reliably written are among those on the reading table, there is no reason to be concerned about allowing young children to select their own books for reading.

Children Use Pictures to Help Their Words Communicate Ideas

Rachel's classmate, Noah, is also a qualified author. In his *The Book About Frogs* Noah has maintained the same respect for continuity that Rachel shows in her book. But Noah does not use words like *first* and *next* to signal this continuity. Instead, he uses pictures to help his words express the step-by-step development of a frog. "Here are some frog eggs," Noah begins, to caption his carefully drawn pictures. Page 2: "Here are some tadpoles in the eggs." Page 3: "These tadpoles just got out of the eggs." Page 4: "Here are some tadpoles with spots." Page 5: "Here are some tadpoles with hind legs." Page 6: "Here are some tadpoles with front legs." Page 7: "Here is a frog with his little tail." Page 8: "This bull frog is sitting in the sun." A delightfully clear-cut, informative book for children to read and study!

Teachers are always on the alert for books in which a reader's long searching look is rewarded—in which children find something worthy of their concentration. Noah's is just this kind of book. Each detail of the developing frog is drawn with the meticulous detail that will arrest the reader's attention. *The Book About Frogs* is well worth its place in the children's repertoire.

Children Use Language Freshly and Creatively

Another favorite of many children in the county is *My Book About The Sky* by second-grader Milton. The children like the way his water color pictures seem to carry out the mood of the simply but beautifully expressed ideas. Page by page, Milton's book reads:

1. The sky is up above me.
   I see many things in the sky.
2. I can see the stars.
   Many many stars.
3. I can see the moon.
   I can see the man in the moon.
   The moon is pretty.
   It makes the dark light.
4. I can see clouds in the sky.
   Big fluffy white clouds.

5. I can see rain clouds.
   They are black.
6. I can see airplanes in the sky.
   Jet airplanes!
   Zzz Zzz they go through the sky.

Even without the painted sketches here, one can see why children like reading Milton's book over and over.

Children Use Language Skillfully

Like his somewhat younger fellow authors—indeed, like so many of the children in his county, Simon lives close to the soil. Out of his intimate experience, and with his growing skill in patterning language, Simon begins his book titled *Wheat* with the following straightforward Table of Contents:

Simon, as well as his classmates, has had enough experience with books by now to know that a table of contents is a useful way to pattern language for his readers. It gives them a sort of preview of things to come. And as the books are traded from classroom to classroom in the school, even younger children selecting *Wheat* from their reading table take note of this convenient device, learning not only to respect and use it as they read, but also to incorporate a table of contents on occasion in their own writing.

Figure 8.2 is a copy of one of the pages the children find in Simon's book, when they turn to the section listed in the Table of Contents as: "A. Getting Ground Ready."

Children Can Organize Information for Reading

Not all of the books in Harris County are produced individually. There are authors and coauthors. There are also teams— of a voluntary nature, to be sure. An author who knows how to organize information for readers, to use word patterns effectively—phrases, sentences, paragraphs—may or may not want or feel competent to illustrate his own story. Sixth-grader Gary, an expert on the subject of maple syrup production, being one of a family who make their living from the sap of their own maple trees, asks two of his friends to work with him on the substantial project, *The Book About Maple Sugar Products.* (See Figures 8.3 and 8.4.) Eventually dittoed in quantity and proudly used throughout his school—even the county—the book carries on its cover the names of Gary, who wrote the book, Steve, who illustrated, and Judy, who printed it in her almost flawless manuscript letters. It requires the combined, skillful work of all three—the faithfully organized story, the elaborate illustrations, and the good clear writing—to help the reader get the feel of the long hard process of maple sugar production, one step after the other. And the reader does feel as if he has had a share in the making of it by the time he finally reads Steve's label, *Pure Maple Syrup,* on the cans. Child reader or adult, he is quite ready by then to join Gary and his guests in the well-desired change of mood of the final page.

Here then is the young author's story, unfortunately without the helpful pictures, from *The Book About Maple Sugar Products:*

1. Gathering Wood
   The first step is gathering wood. We gather most of it in the fall. Sometimes we run out before the season is over so

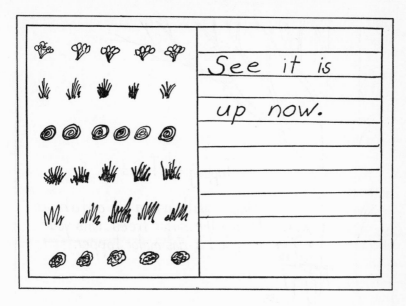

Fig. 8–1

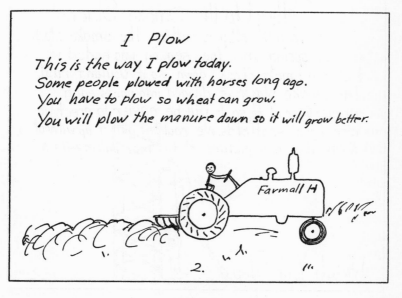

Fig. 8–2

Tapping the Trees

We usually use a bit and a brace to tap the sugar trees. This year we used a *gas motor tapper.*

Fig. 8–3

Setting Up the Smoke Stack

The fourth step is setting the smoke stack up. Last spring when the season was ended we took the smoke stack down so it wouldn't rust. The smoke stack is divided into parts each about 6 or 7 ft. so it will be easier to erect. We also have scaffolds. We couldn't put it up without them. This is a picture of two men putting it up.

Watch Your Step

Fig. 8–4

we have to get more. We use maple, pine and beech. The wood is cut with a power saw. We haul it to the sugar house with a tractor-trailer.

2. Scattering the Buckets

The buckets are scattered at the first sign of a break in the weather.

The buckets are loaded onto wagons pulled by horses. Most of our trees have two buckets. Usually we scatter from 1,300 to 1,500 buckets.

3. Tapping the Trees

We usually use a bit and a brace to tap the sugar trees. This year we used a gas motor tapper.

4. Setting up the Smoke Stack

The fourth step is setting the smoke stack up. Last Spring when the season was ended we took the smoke stack down so it wouldn't rust. The smoke stack is divided into parts each about 6 or 7 feet, so it will be easier to erect. We also have scaffolds. We couldn't put it up without them. This is a picture of two men putting it up.

5. Gathering Sap

The fifth step is gathering sap. Different people use different ways of gathering sap. Some use horses, some tractors, and some use a little caterpillar. We use horses.

We take the horses and hook them to the 300 gal. tank. Then we take it out in the woods and gather the sap all up. Then we put it in the storage tank.

6. Taking the Sap to the Sugar House

The sixth step is taking the sap to the sugar house. Some of our trees are a long way from the sugar house. So we take the tractor with us to the edge of the woods. Then we take the horses into camp and gather the sap. We bring it back to the road. Then we unhook the horses and take the horse tongue off the tank. Next we put the tractor tongue on and hook the tractor to the tank. Then we take it to the sugar house.

7. The gathering tank holds 300 gallons of sap.

8. Sap going from the gathering tank to the sugar house.

9. Emptying the Gathering Tank

The sap is poured out of the gathering tank into the receiving bin. Then it is piped under ground to the maple sugar house to be made into syrup.

10. Sometimes to make the work easier the receiving bin is ¼ of a mile from the sugar house.

11. Boiling the Sap

The seventh step is boiling the sap. After the sap is brought to the sugar house it is poured into a big storage tank. It is piped under ground into the sugar house. Then it goes into the evaporator. The sap is controlled by a float.

There are thermometers to tell when it is heavy enough. After the sap has boiled enough we strain it off on the side.

12. Draining off the Syrup

We drain the syrup off in a five gallon bucket. Then it is strained into a filter tank.

13. Filter Tank

The three felt strainers are so thick they catch the lime and all the dirt.

14. Some people think that $5.00 is a lot for a gallon of syrup. But you work for every penny of it. It takes about 50 gallons of sap to make one gallon of syrup.

The syrup is put in gallon cans, one-half gallon cans, quart and pint cans. (Across the center of the page, Steve has drawn diagrams to scale of these cans, each labeled Pure Maple Syrup, with prices below.) We also sell it in 32 gallon drums. Sometimes we make maple taffy and sugar cakes.

We charge $5.00 a gallon retail and $4.60 a gallon whole-sale for our syrup.

15. Where our Syrup Is Sold

Our syrup has been sold in Vermont, California, Pennsylvania, Virginia and Maryland. Surrey, England is the longest distance we have shipped syrup. I scaled the map. It was more than 6,400 miles.

16. The white settlers who came to our county in 1765 found the Indians making sugar of the sap of the maple tree.

17. Sugar on Snow

Maple sugar time is a good time for our friends to visit us. We all enjoy talking, working, and watching the syrup boil. Best of all is the wonderful smell that fills the air. The smell makes you hungry. Sugar on Snow is a favorite of guests at our camp. All the visitors ask for this. The syrup is heated to a temperature of soft boil on the thermometer. As soon as it reaches this temperature it is poured without stirring on snow or ice. It forms a thin glassy taffy-like sheet.

This also makes good Sea Foam or cake icing.

Warning—don't eat too much or you might get the stomach ache. Everybody asks for seconds or more.

Children Have Worthwhile Messages for One Another

What a good feeling comes with Billy's message that there are friends in the world! Both words and pictures speak so clearly the language of reassuring friendship that Billy's readers identify at once with *The Book About My Friend.* This is how it goes, page by page (see Figs. 8.5–8.8).

1. This is my friend.
   This is Johnny.
2. Johnny was my friend when I was in the first grade. I am in the second grade now and he is still my friend.
3. Johnny and I have fun together. Sometimes we play with my pet rabbits.
4. Sometimes we play ball together.
5. Sometimes we ride our bikes.
6. Sometimes Johnny stays all night with me. We sleep together. We have fun in bed. We get out of bed and go downstairs when Mother isn't looking.
7. Sometimes we read to each other.
8. And sometimes we fight.
   Not real fights though.

This genuine appreciation for people seems deep in Billy's nature. In another of his books, written and illustrated with feeling—*The Book About Things*—is a page each about Spring, trees, birds, his teacher, and then:

> Friends help you.
> They share frozen custard with you.
> They fly airplanes with you.
> Georgie does this with me.

Fig. 8–5

Fig. 8–6

Johnny

Fuzzy

Fluffy

me

Johnny and I have fun together.
Sometimes we play with my pet
rabbits.

Fig. 8–7

And sometimes we fight.
Not real fights though.

Fig. 8–8

Children Write Stories that Are Exciting

Children are so adept at bringing the excitement of their own experience to their communication with other children that they make good listeners and tellers alike, whenever the situation is real. With something unusual in the subject he selects for his readers, Leon has their attention from first to last in *My Book About Cheetah:*

1.   Our Pet
   We have a pet monkey.
   His name is Cheetah.
   Most of the time he eats with his hand.
   He eats what we eat at the table.
   He eats everything.

2. My uncle got Cheetah down in Florida.
   He rode in a truck.
   He was little when we got him.

3. He does lots of tricks.
   He turns around.
   He can hang by his tail.

4. He sleeps on a big box every night.
   He curls up his tail when he sleeps.
   He can sit on the box.

5. He gets loose sometimes.
   He likes to run loose.
   He runs loose too.

6. Mother can wash him.
   He does not like to wash.
   Mother gives Cheetah a bath once a week.

The charming book by Paul, *My Book About The Lioness,* carries a different kind of excitement, relying on the interest and vitality of his pictures to help maintain the mood. Paul's story reads:

1. Here is a mother lioness and her three cubs.
2. They are going for a Deer to eat.
3. Mother Lioness plays with the Deer
   before she kills him.
4. They are eating a Deer.
5. They eat birds, goats, and other animals.
6.   The End

The Teacher Sets up the Classroom for Authors to Go to Work

The number of authors producing books in the schools of Harris County is steadily increasing. Especially has this been true since the very impressive county-wide exhibit of such books held at the public library last Spring. It leads one to ask: Just how does it come about, this remarkable interest and skill of the children in writing books for other children to read? How do the very young children, for example, know to organize their books so invitingly? How do they know to put so few poignant words to a page, instead of crowding all of the story on one page, as children, for whatever reason, are wont to do? Do the teachers instruct them to do it in this way?

No, *not in words*, they don't. But these teachers do structure the situation in advance. They do set up their classrooms and provide a range of possible choices for children in particular ways to achieve their purpose. Harking back to the previous chapter, the materials, time, space, atmosphere, available help, are all so planned and so provided as to invite children to become serious and skillful authors. To invite them, furthermore, to *choose* to be serious authors, to reach out and take the initiative in the process and work hard at it in their own individual ways, as their varied books show. This is their way of teaching.

In the beginning, to suggest some possible choices for her first-grade children, one of the teachers, Mrs. Bartok, uses the ditto machine to run off several stacks of sheets all ready for use. There are white or colored book-cover forms framed with a double-lined margin, and in large print THE BOOK ABOUT—with ample space for the child to complete the title —and the word *By* down below for the author's name. There are several stacks of sheets for book pages—some with the dittoed lines for writing on the top half, some on the lower half and some at the side, with the rest of the simply margined page to be used for illustration. (See Figs. 8.9–8.11.) On some of these pages, Mrs. Bartok has printed in a few words to suggest a beginning, such as "This mother is . . ." In addition to these, there is a choice of pages with no lines, only a frame for the

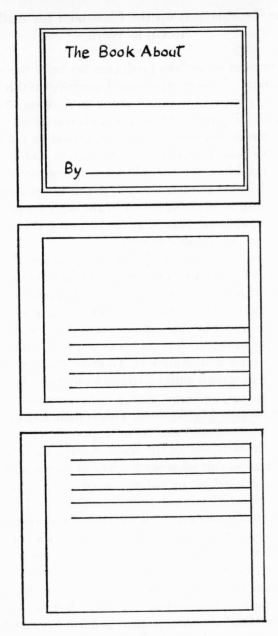

Figs. 8–9—8–11

margins. Also a supply of perfectly blank sheets. All of these are arranged in convenient piles on a table or counter for the children to choose and use.

"I like to give the children a number of choices," Mrs. Bartok explains, "and let the materials rather than my own talking do the trick. Some teachers use only the cover-forms and leave the paper blank, reminding the children from time to time to put only a few lines to a page. That is all right too. But I prefer to indicate, through the materials, a choice of several possibilities, and watch the individual responses."

With their work materials thus at hand, and a brief explanation of what they are for, the children go to the stacks on the table, matter-of-factly selecting the cover and the pages they want for making a book. Sandy takes a cover and writes the word *Mothers,* making his title THE BOOK ABOUT MOTHERS. Then he picks up several sheets beginning *This mother is,* and straight off goes about making his book about the different things that different mothers do. "This mother is spanking her child," one of his pages says, to explain his accompanying picture in the space above. Other pages follow, as: "This mother is combing her child's hair." "This mother is buying big ice cream cones." "This mother is out in her garden."

Some children do their own writing. Others dictate their stories to the teacher. While one child is dictating several children may stand around and listen with rapt interest, eagerly asking to read it as soon as the book is finished. Others, while waiting their turns for the teacher to help them, may leave a space for the word they need and go on, perhaps draw their pictures on the pages ahead and come back later to fill in the words when they can have help. Some read one another's stories while they wait, or just sit back and relax, enjoying the anticipation of what their book—and maybe their neighbors'—will be like when completed.

The children's other choices are interesting, too, Mrs. Bartok observes. Some children so strongly prefer the ditto-lined paper that when the supply runs out, they take their rulers and laboriously line the sheets themselves, until the teacher has time to run off a fresh supply. A few children, from the beginning, choose pages with nothing on them at all. They enjoy being free to decide for themselves just where they will put both the words and the pictures of their stories. Some prefer to design their own covers, too.

It should be remembered that these books, as the purpose is defined in the first place, are written *to be read,* to be added to the school's supply of good books available for children's reading. As the children finish their books Mrs. Bartok gives whatever help is needed. If the book is to be for the class's own reading table, as are Rachel's and Noah's, Mrs. Bartok helps the author to staple and put it together. If he has had trouble with his writing, she may quickly type it for him on the primer typewriter. Sometimes, for the sake of durability, she carefully covers the pages and cover of the book with clear contact paper. Better still, once the idea strikes, she helps the author to paste his own pages one by one right over those in an old discarded music or library book—"any old book we can lay our hands on!" (As a matter of fact, this proves to be so practical and satisfying a feat that the school's shelf of old discarded books, still waiting to be hauled away by the administration, is straightaway reclaimed to be put into profitable use through the year.)

If a child's book is to be duplicated, for use by many children in this and other classrooms, Mrs. Bartok helps him to write his story and make his pictures on ditto carbons. (In this connection, she points out, it is important for the teacher to sense when a child's story is the personal kind of thing that need not be made available to other children—as when in his book *Mad Mike,* Michael writes, "I wish I could kill my mother.")

The Enthusiasm and Skill for Writing Books Are Contagious

In these schools the children's books are lent from one room to another at different times, and copies of the dittoed ones are sent to all the classrooms. The idea and the enthusiasm for making books in this way spread throughout the school—and indeed throughout the county. Classes soon have one another's books on their reading tables. This adds to the contagion for making books, as well as to the introduction of new ideas and variations. And the teachers, with something of surprise, make a very significant observation: The children who are still pretty much nonreaders of books are *not* the nonwriters. Neither are they the nonreaders when it comes to reading their own and the books of other children.

Each day, during the early morning Work Periods, as well as other times during the day, children of all ages seem to be going on with their never-ending job of bookmaking. In some classes, as mentioned, teachers provide the cover form but do not bother to line the page sheets. Nevertheless, the idea catches on that a limited number of lines to a page makes a better page, for younger children at least . . . Even the teachers catch the spirit of authorship and begin making books themselves—beautiful books, in good clear-cut language. They know now what kind of books seem to speak best to children. They have noted in what kind of written language patterns genuine communication takes places. These teachers too can qualify as good authors of children's books.

The books produced by the children cover a wide range of titles. We have had a look in one way or another at only a few. Sandy's *The Book About Mothers*. Rachel's *The Book About The Garden*. Noah's *The Book About Frogs*. Milton's *My Book About The Sky*. Simon's *Wheat*. Gary's, Steve's, and Judy's *The Book About Maple Sugar Products*. Billy's *My Friend*. Leon's *My Book About Cheetah*. Paul's *The Story of the Mother Lioness*. Jean's *The Book About Band*. Deanna's *The Book About Dancing* (see Fig. 8.12). There are also Diane's *My Book About Stars and Planets*, Leslie's *The Book About Skiing*, Daniel's *My Story Of An Apple Tree*, Richard's *The Book About My Rabbit*, Karen's *My Book About Night*, also Diane's *My Book About Night*, another Leslie's *The Crooked House*, Billy's *The Book About Things*, Judy's *My Book About Spring*, Swanton's *How To Make Money??*, Larry's very personal *My*

Fig. 8–12

Fig. 8–13

Book About the Big Woods, Milton's *My Book About The Circus,* and of course many many more, adding importantly day by day to the already wide and varied collection which the children in their classrooms, school and county are reading. (See Figures 8.13–8.15.) Books about their own neighborhoods and communities, about farming, animals, birds, food, children, families, travel, science, history, current affairs, people from other countries, the United Nations. The titles, the contents, the organization, the patterning of language, the pictures that help to convey the messages to the reader—all of these cover as wide and diverse a range as do the many personalities and experiences of their individual authors.

Children's Competence, Too Often Underrated, Commands Respect

When children come at writing in this way, they write because they have something to say. Not safe little dwarfed ideas to be spelled out in four-letter words for young children to read out. These children, as we have seen, write big important substantial messages about their world that other children, including the younger ones, both need and like to read. Nor does the class have to discuss the ideas first in order to motivate the children to write. They write because they have something to say. The materials, time, friendly help are there to *invite* the children to write. And most of them do, with enthusiasm. But no one is forced to put something down on paper, to do creative writing in a forty-minute period, say. Therefore, when Noah makes his book about the development of a frog, it is his idea. It is not something everyone else has discussed or is writing about.

Children qualify as authors then because they have something to say that is worth saying, that is worth other children's reading. They qualify, too, because somehow they know how to write what they have to say in language that communicates to other children. They have the knack for using words that "trig-

The Crooked House

This is a house --
a crooked house

It will be a lovely house

when it is finished.

Fig. 8-14-2

LESLIE

Fig. 8-14-1

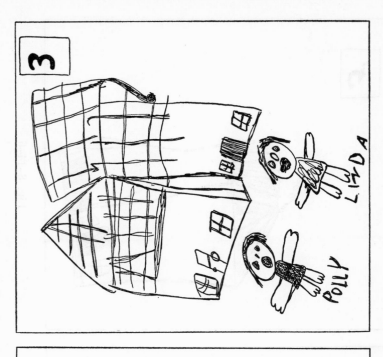

2

Two little girls come
to see the wonderful house

One is named Polly and
one is named Linda

One is six
The other is seven.

Fig. 8–14–3

3

POLLY

LINDA

Fig. 8–14–4

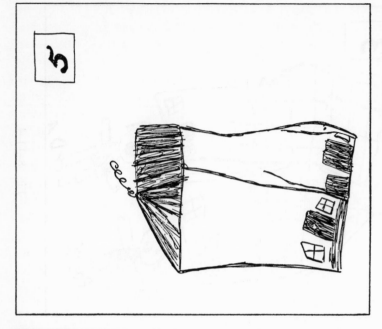

Fig. 8-14-6

They are sweet.
They just went out for a walk
when they saw
the crooked house.

Fig. 8-14-5

ger off responses," as one teacher expresses it. They do not write—any more than they speak—in strings of disconnected little four-letter words that so many young children everywhere are having to be *taught*. (Because they don't come naturally, these little words, and they bear so little resemblance to children's ways of thinking or speaking or living.) When children talk about anything that importantly cuts across their living today, they have to use words and language patterns that say what they mean, whatever the length of the words or their phonetic make-up. And when children read about these things, they expect to and usually can read the meaningful words and language patterns to which in their everyday world they are more or less accustomed. Children qualify as authors for children because they know how to write in this straightforward, unafraid kind of spoken language pattern. They come at the business new, so to speak, and are quite unaware of the limitations which certain adults, misjudging their natural compe-

I like to sit on a log
and just listen.
I can hear birds singing.
I can see squirrels in trees.
Once I saw a big snake.

Fig. 8–15

tencies as children, are so carefully imposing on their first-, second-, fifth-, eighth-, any-grade reading vocabularies.

The Harris County teachers' lengthening list of qualifications which, they maintain, enable children to be good authors for children, takes on more significant meaning in this context:

> Children write in patterns that other children can read.
>
> Children use pictures to help their words express the message.
>
> Children use language freshly and creatively.
>
> Children use language skillfully.
>
> Children know how to organize information for reading.
>
> Children have worthwhile messages for one another.
>
> Children write stories that are exciting.
>
> Children write "spoken" English.
>
> Children invite their readers to think, to imagine, to wonder, to know, to learn, to feel, to explore.

Nor do these teachers stand alone in this understanding view of children, as every chapter in this book will attest. They are giving expression to the working philosophy of the thousands of teachers the country over who work with children sensitively, creatively, and with eyes and ears wide open.

Children Learn to Read as They Write Books

It is clear by now that the content of this chapter belongs in the earlier Chapter Five, *How The Reading Skills Look In Individualized Learning*. The skills of orientation are in continuous development here, every one of them, with individual authors from the very youngest up. The skills involved in sensing reading as two-way communication, in moving from left to right across the page, in starting at the front of the book and moving on, page by page, in putting one's self in the mood for different kinds of reading (and writing), in seeing reading in a broader context, in sensing the author's purpose, in keeping the reader in mind . . . all of these we see in progress as Rachel, Milton, Simon, and Gary respond in their own individual ways to the very real purpose of making a book for their classmates to read.

And what of other basic skills? How is it that in this thoughtfully structured situation even those children hardly yet able to read, are among those to bring their ideas and experiences and competencies to the rewarding business of making books for others to read? How is it that these children can read the books they write, and the books their classmates write, quite without the difficulties they experience with their vocabulary-controlled readers?

Children, being newcomers to the world, write with respect to the newcomers, because they know intimately the living of the newcomers. When adults write books for children, theirs is the perspective of the outsider looking in. And it is important to realize that many of the mistakes which adults make are due to the difficulty of simply being the outsiders looking in on the child's world. The outsiders, for example, look in on children's reading and decide that little words are more easily learned than big words. Everyone who has worked closely with children, however, and particularly anyone who has encouraged children to write their own stories, will attest to the fact that the children themselves prefer the exciting, exact, colorful, complicated words of their new world. That is why a first- or second-grader will use the word *twinkle* in its appropriate context, and why children of the same age will successfully read the word *twinkle* in an appropriately written book. The outsider adult, unfortunately, writing the same book, will search and search for easy words to use which, because they are so general, are actually more difficult for the children to read.

Children naturally write good books for children because they live in a child's world. Grownups try to write about friendship in pared-down words for children, while Billy, immersed in friendship, writes about friendship from deep in the friend-

ship. The fact that children have their own individual ways
for knowing and figuring out new words they meet in a story,
whole words which the context calls for, is perhaps nowhere
more convincingly demonstrated then in this kind of situation.
A situation so planned that children can write books *for* and
read books *by* other children, in good clear language patterns
which all of them understand. And this reassuring and sometimes startling revelation of insight is not limited, these teachers
tell us, to the children just beginning to read books. All along
the way the reading and writing competencies seem to develop
hand in hand. It is the teachers of older children, perhaps more
especially, who find children's interest and power in reading
remarkably heightened in this suddenly new and exciting context—where the possibilities for depth and pattern and content
and purpose, on the children's own initiative, can be so resourcefully and increasingly extended.

We have already spelled out, through the whole of this
chapter on writing and reading books, including the paragraphs
immediately above, how comprehension skills are being learned
by these children from first to last. Children comprehend the
world they live in. Therefore they write comprehendible materials. Through writing their own books they learn to be critical
of the authors and aware of the devices authors use for organizing their messages. This becomes part of the children's growing
comprehension skills which they put to use as they read the
books of other authors. Here for a certainty, the reading and
writing skills are all at play, in what student teacher Bobbe no
doubt would call the "realest" kind of reading.

9

Student teachers react to individualized teaching

Education students, too, respond to this type of work with children. Experience over the years has shown that in classrooms where opportunities for self-selection have been provided for children, participating students and student teachers too, have been more free to learn. In such instances the planning has been generously extended to include these students and their resources. Wherever this happens, wherever education students have the chance actually to partake of and to reach out, themselves, to help with the continuous setting up of such a program, their own insights are deepened and vision sharpened remarkably. This, of course, is not surprising. Certainly, conditions that make for maximum growth in learning to be a teacher must necessarily involve the principles of identification and self-selection which underlie effective human learning generally.

It may add a realistic, practical note, then, to view more outstanding examples of individualized teaching through the eyes of those who are eagerly and thoughtfully studying to be teachers. These students, by and large, consider themselves very fortunate to find that what they are learning in class or reading in books really works. They vie for the chance to share their experiences and insights with wide-eyed, almost unbelieving classmates or fellow student teachers who may themselves be telling of the science, reading, or arithmetic "lesson" they had a chance to prepare and give before the class this week. What at first may have been disappointment that "I've never had the chance yet to teach something to the whole class," usually develops before long into a proud: "No, there is seldom a time when all the children in our class are working on the same thing. Even Mr. Carlson is working with individual children or small informal groups most of the time. That's what I do too, mostly, and it gives me a good opportunity to observe and get acquainted with the children as I work with them on different things and in different ways."

The excerpts that follow were written by students during their late junior or early senior year; that is, a semester or two *before* their full-time student teaching begins. *Participation,* a supervised part of these students' general course in Guiding Children's Learning, is largely confined to one morning a week, for eight weeks, which the student spends in a selected classroom of one of the elementary schools in the area.

Learning the Individual and Cooperative Power of Children

These few paragraphs taken from college student June's participation log reflect her growing insights as she works with a sixth grade group:

... We then went outside for physical education. Most of the children started a kickball form of baseball. Since they were completely free to choose their own activities, I noticed the class interest (sixth grade) and the group game interests. A few of the girls were playing catch and pottsey. They asked me to play pottsey with them and they were so sweet in making allowance for my high heels. I noticed during all of the games the sense of fair play and good-natured cooperation that went on. The children (my class) had no teacher supervision and they didn't need it. I became just one of the children, playing with them. I loved it. When the half-hour was up, I asked them to go back to their room. The baseball people begged me for five minutes more—which I gave. I was surprised that at the end of the five minutes they cooperated beautifully in breaking up the game and I had no trouble in getting them back to their room. (I don't know whether I was right or wrong in allowing them the five extra minutes, but I couldn't break up the game with a man on first and third and someone up to bat!)

Then, a couple of Thursdays later:

Back in the room (from the art room), the class carried on a discussion about finishing their block prints. Each child is making a block print (to go with an article about a certain explorer) and dittoing a whole set of them, one for each member of the class. They will use their own covers for their books. A few of the children had already finished up their prints, and while the discussion was going on, I noticed something very interesting. Miss Horne did not demand their rapt attention, and so the youngsters each took out something to keep them busy—all on their own. Several were working on arithmetic, several reading magazines and books, some were coloring, some feeding the hamsters, some just talking, and one or two making some mats by weaving some strips of paper we had left over from earlier work. There was no confusion, no loud noise—just complete activity. I felt a sense of satisfaction and hope that I can stimulate my own class to show some initiative. Not one child looked bored. They then had a discussion about selling tickets for the presentation of their play on May 29th. How I wish I could attend! The children were very much disappointed when I told them I couldn't make it.

While a few of the children were finishing some things, I took most of the class down for recess. They organized themselves quickly and efficiently for a softball game. Carson, who is doing about "third year" work academically, is clearly superior in ball, and he has the complete acceptance of the other children. Here on the field he has a chance to gain prestige which he cannot do in arithmetic and reading. . . .

The girls are just about as proficient as the boys in playing ball, in hitting and pitching as well as in fielding. However, there are signs that the boys are beginning to show their strength a little more.

While I watched the game a few of the youngsters kept coming over to talk a little, teasing me, asking questions, and we had several friendly little chats. I cannot relate how much I've learned about the abilities, backgrounds, and personalities of the children. One quiet girl who used to stay out of our informal discussion, on the field or in the classroom or art room, has now for the last three weeks joined us readily and contributes often to the discussion. This pleases me.

About the fifth morning of June's participation, she writes:

At eleven, I left a few of the children down in the art room and took the rest to assembly for a puppet show given by one of the men student teachers. It was a professional job and everyone loved it. The youngsters relaxed and enjoyed themselves. During the show there was much spontaneous, enthusiastic applauding and laughter. The children had "enjoyment" written all over their faces. I have never seen such enthusiasm in my life. They gave the puppeteer such a rousing cheer at the end that it felt as if the building shook.

I noticed during the morning that the youngsters have free use of the library, art room, science room, auditorium, etc., at any time. All morning different small groups were scattered all over the school, finishing up various projects. This seems to be successful.

Still a later entry:

When I went into the room this morning, the children greeted me warmly. Some of them said they had something to try out on me. As mentioned before, they have been studying about explorers and making books about them, using their block prints as covers and illustrations. They have also made slides—and this is where I come in. They are having the parents come in some time in June, and they are going to show them this project, have a quiz (for the parents) and serve refreshments. They wanted to try the quiz out on me. One youngster put in the slide (of an explorer or scene) done by the children. The child whose explorer it was gave me hints about him. The other children would also give me hints. I was then to guess who the explorer was. I was amazed at how much factual information the children had and what interesting things they could tell about each explorer. Out of fifteen explorers,

I could only get eight, but I certainly learned a lot. We all had a wonderful time, and the integration of all the explorers was aptly handled.

While this was going on, other children were either writing their reports or dittoing them for the books. All were busy and interested. I cannot emphasize this point too much. Every time I have been in that class, the children have been busy at different things—and with much enthusiasm and interest. Miss Horne told me later that she believes in giving them the freedom to choose from many available activities. . . . We have had other talks about various things, and I learned a great deal from her about the progress of individual children, about flexibility, and the long and hard work of the teacher. As I was walking out today, another teacher came in and the three of us chatted for a while. The other teacher was impressed with Miss Horne and told how good a teacher she was, then gave her a great big kiss on the forehead. The teachers seem to be warm and friendly here and have a wonderful relationship with the staff as well as the children. It is a wonderful place to be in.

Observing Children's Interaction within a Carefully Set Up Classroom

Marilyn, observing and participating once a week with lively seven-year-olds, shows enthusiasm for her own learning about the children as she writes:

Miss Franklin participated with the children freely. She gave suggestions when asked and was called upon often for her services, such as one little boy telling her that if she would hold the wood for him, he could drive the nail through much better. This was just one example of the freedom of communication that seemed to exist in the classroom. . . .

As I mentioned in my first report, the movable furniture was so arranged as to promote speaking or intercommunication among the children, which is good. While the teacher was busy with one thing or another, especially when working with a smaller group of children, I noticed how freely the children walked about the classroom or stayed at their seats, working or playing at various things. Some would write stories, some would take books to read, some were drawing or painting, and still others just sat around and talked casually of things that were of interest to them. Everybody had the opportunity to express himself, to exchange ideas and experiences with others.

I saw many ways in which the classroom environment developed the need for reading and writing—such as sign-up slips, committee charts, books, games, library and science corners, materials of all kinds, through which each child could pursue his individual interests, or work in groups if the need be such. What is important, is that there was a variety of things for children to look at, work with, and choose from.

After a three-page description of the science materials and possibilities in the classroom for investigation, exploration, and discovery, comes this observation:

The classroom is full of resources for helping children with everyday scientific explorations and discoveries—such as keeping clay in tin cans to protect it from drying out and then hardening; when paints thicken, so that they are difficult to use, adding water or turpentine (depending on the paint). Even handling simple machines such as scissors, hammers, staplers, etc., gives children an idea of how machines do work. All of these things—investigating and taking care of the plants, checking temperatures and weather, etc., are all part of our daily living—and taking part in all of these activities helps to make what the books say real. . . .

After describing in her log their holiday activities—toy store, purchasing and decorating a Christmas tree, reading Hanukkah stories and planning a Christmas play, Marilyn continues:

The freedom which these children (second grade) used in making decisions and the ways they carried them out, stem from the free and permissive attitude that has been incorporated into the classroom (full of attractive varied materials). It isn't something that has happened overnight, but something on which Miss Franklin has worked.

What was most enjoyable to me and to the children was hearing their voices played back to them on a recorder. The children had learned some Christmas carols and had recorded them. They reacted in the very manner in which I would expect them to, upon hearing their own singing. Some giggled, others listened attentively, singing softly along with the recorder. Still others would wave their arms in the air, pretending to be conducting. It was the first experience of such a kind for many of them.

In this connection, but in another situation, Bobbe (whose longer report appears later) finds the same understanding and appreciation of the ways of young children. Her perceptive observation seems worth insertion here:

Many teachers have set up in their minds a list of actions on the part of children that they consider "naughty." Many of the items on this list are really not naughty but only a part of the child's maturation. Mrs. Barnes takes this situation into account and doesn't punish children when they spill things, fight, have difficulty working in a group, sharing, etc. She realizes that her adult standards of behavior are not necessarily those that a child could attain. She knows that most sixes are at the "I" stage. They do not act or think in terms of "we." She expects them to be egocentric. Therefore, she does not punish children when they are.

In still another classroom, and with a satisfying sense of participation, Florence notes the effects on children of an accepting, thoughtfully structured learning environment:

Knowing children as well as she does, Miss Shell is able to capitalize on their insatiable curiosity by providing exciting experiences for them. Two weeks ago she and the class fixed up an aquarium of guppies, which are a species of tropical fish. This apparently stimulated the children's wish to know more, for several of them, on their next trip to the library, spontaneously took out some books on the habits and care of tropical fish. I was able to carry this still further myself through the good fortune of having a younger brother whose specialty happens to be the breeding and raising of tropical fish, and who generously offered to give the class several species unknown to them. The youngsters have discussed the fish they had, as well as the fish they found in the books, and as a result have become quite sophisticated in their knowledge of tropical fish. One youngster, on learning that a mother fish often will eat her newborn young if not separated from them, asked if the newborn were put into another mother's tank (not into that of their real mother), would they be eaten by this strange female, or would they only be acceptable food for their natural mother. (This will probably be followed through as soon as productivity is high enough for the sacrifice.) Quite a deep question for a second-grader!

Another activity which Miss Shell has set up for the youngsters to use by themselves is the puppet stage, a simple painted cardboard affair with a curtain. The youngsters made puppets several weeks ago, and spontaneous dramatization is a favorite activity. Here the children are able to and do create on their own, without needing Miss Shell's close supervision. There is a Xylophone on the window ledge from which often emanate simple and sometimes original tunes.

I was in school earlier than Miss Shell last Thursday. Most of the youngsters were already there. There was no confusion, no wild running. Several of the youngsters were reading. Some helped themselves to drawing paper which Miss Shell had provided and busied themselves with that. Others clustered about the science table. Still others talked to one another, particularly about Richard's coral and St. Patrick's Day.

Miss Shell has done a fine job of providing a large variety of stimulating activities which the children can engage in without her close supervision. During the day, the children are free to use the many, many books on the shelf when they have finished a piece of work. They can draw or paint, make up stories, stage a puppet show, use the science corner. Materials are abundantly provided in the room, so that children are offered the greatest freedom and encouragement in manipulating and discovering, in growing intellectually and creatively.

Sensing How Classroom Organization Affects Relationships

Thoughtful Edith, still a college junior, gives serious consideration to much the same problem. How can a teacher best organize a crowded classroom for maximum knowledge on the part of all of the children? She brings to the problem her participation experiences in two different schools, the first in a four-year-old nursery-school group, the second in this larger first-grade class.

Edith writes:

Although I can see that it is indeed possible to work with an entire class, I would prefer not to. Even reading a story to over thirty children at once provided me with a contrast to the many story situations I was in last semester. Thursday I felt rather as though I were an actor performing for the benefit of an unindividualized audience. I found it almost impossible to note individual reactions and found it necessary, because of the size of the group, to insist on attention and quiet more than I should have liked. Reading a story to a group of seven to ten children, I used to find it quite possible to elicit individual reactions from the children. Frequently, the story would start us off on some other interesting topic and, when it did, I felt that the discussion was group initiated and directed; I was not forced to be the moderator or chairman of a large group. The drawbacks then of working with a large group seem to be the difficulty of recognizing the individuals rather than a more impersonal group reaction, and a certain formality and rigidity that a large group must have, to some extent, for workability.

I do think that if I were teaching this large first grade class, I would try to set up the classroom so that it would be more possible for the school day to have an informal fluidity. I think the physical set-up is important in achieving this; especially must the physical space be carefully organized where it is at a premium. I would organize the crowded room into activity centers even more carefully than the uncrowded room.

Everything that did not have a definite purposeful function would have to go. In Mrs. R's classroom, for instance, there is a large heavy table that looks as though it might have been meant for woodworking, but which at the moment is simply a sloppy catch-all for various papers, drawings, etc. I would either use that for a woodworking center, or throw it out for more space. The large teacher's desk also seems to me to be dispensable—that is, in a room where space is at a premium. So does a large number of the tables and chairs. Mrs. R. used part of the wall space for a museum table (table against the wall). The idea, of course, is admirable; but where there are so many children, if the teacher wants the children to work in informal groups, I believe she should use wall space for doing-centers, not just looking-centers.

If the teacher is to work in a small room with a large group, I believe her planning must be proportionately more careful. She must be prepared, for instance, to vary the set-up and centers as the needs of the children change; and, although she may herself be working with a small group of children within the larger class, she will still find ways to be alert to the interests and attention span of all the children so as to be able to introduce new and stimulating activities gradually into the program. In order to make this type of program at all feasible, the teacher must constantly encourage a great deal of self-direction.

In conclusion, then, I believe that a teacher can work successfully and be able to focus on the children's needs both with the whole group and with smaller groups working simultaneously. I feel, however, that as I have stated, there are advantages in working with smaller groups that, for me, far outweigh the extra effort and alertness that are necessarily involved.

Learning to Define Teaching as Helping Children Learn

College junior Rita seems happily aware of her own professional growth, as she comes to see effective teaching and learning in a new light:

Another activity which the children participated in was outdoor play. Here the children could choose to play whatever they wanted —jump-rope, slides, see-saw, ball, jungle gym. They seemed very eager to enter into this activity, for they ran out with gusto and made many sounds of joy. They suddenly seemed to gain a new physical energy which they had not shown before. They could play with whomever they chose, and frequently they changed playmates.

The children seemed to need little help in managing themselves. One of the boys, Pat, got a bloody nose. He didn't worry or cry about it—he simply came up to me and said, "I have a bloody nose. I'm going in to see the nurse." The same was true of Ellen who skinned her knee . . .

The children had gone to the homes of some of the other children to bake cookies and brownies. They had written their own thank-you notes to the mothers involved, and some of them read them to the class. The notes were so varied and individual, as indeed was the reading of them varied . . . The pictures drawn and colored, the folding of the paper, the color of the paper used, and the ideas expressed were all very individual. I especially enjoyed Bruce's comment to one of the mothers— "I should like to crown you Queen of Cookie Land."

I have not yet participated for long, but a few of Miss Shirer's underlying principles of teaching have made themsleves evident to me:

1. Miss Shirer has many materials available for the children's use. This she does for two main reasons, I believe: (a) she believes that children learn more meaningfully through direct experience, and so she has a family of mice in the classroom, sea shells, a pumpkin, a turtle, goldfish; (b) she believes that having materials available will both inspire the children to work hard and help them give vent to their ideas. Near the Mouse Corner she has several books which deal with mice. In the art room, the paints are generally in large jars from which the children help themselves. Miss Shirer asked me if I would get the paints out from the jars and have the paints all ready for the children. This is to make it easier for

them to express themselves. Miss Shirer has a large jar of pencils in the front of the room for all to use.

2. Miss Shirer makes use of current happenings to help the children learn. She used my wedding to help the children learn some reading and writing. She used the pumpkin to help the children use numbers and reading. She used their baking cookies to help them write thank-you notes. She made use of the mother mouse having babies to teach of life, mother care, and need for milk.

3. Miss Shirer believes in giving the children freedom to make decisions, in helping them gain independence. On the playground, a child asked Miss Shirer if she could take off her coat. Miss Shirer answered, "If you think you will be comfortable without it. Decide what you think best." When the children hurt themselves, they do not ask, "What should I do?" Rather, they say, "I'm going to the nurse."

4. Miss Shirer speaks in a relaxed, soft voice all the time. This, I believe, has a calming effect on the children. They are relaxed, at peace, and feel capable.

5. Miss Shirer believes in helping each child to feel worthwhile. She never fails to admire a child's work when a child has put his heart into it . . .

Miss Shirer told the class that I was going to be married on Hallowe'en. The children seemed interested, and she suggested that they might want to write cards to me. When she asked them what words they would want, they said words such as bride, groom, cake, wishes, sweet, wedding, happy. Miss Shirer wrote them on the blackboard, but not without the children's help. She would slowly pronounce each word, and the children would call out the letters for her to write on the board. After getting the spelling of "bride" from the children, Miss Shirer also asked them how they would spell "slide," "wide," "hide." The children's getting the spelling from Miss Shirer's careful pronunciation indicates that they were learning the sounds of the words.

A brief (rather modest) excerpt from the final entry in Inge's log reflects an appreciation for the way in which a well-set-up classroom and creative, helpful atmosphere can challenge older children also to learn. Inge writes:

In this sixth-grade classroom there was always opportunity for children's choice. The equipment in the room was of enough variety that every child was able to find something to meet his needs. One small group of friends became interested in writing a class newspaper and, because they were encouraged, it was in its final stages when I left. The people who liked to write did so. Some wrote news reports, others original stories, and one child wrote a poem. The art was taken care of by a boy who was clever at caricatures, while another who enjoyed making maps was able to include a beautiful map of the world as part of the cover. They used stencils, learned to organize materials, worked cooperatively and were able to use their individual abilities in work that interested and challenged them. As a final triumph, they were going to be able to do their own mimeographing the day I left, and that to them just made the experience complete. Originally only one boy had the idea for the paper, and through his enthusiasm at least eight or ten children became interested and learned a great deal. The product indicated that the children had considered it something worth doing well.

Gaining Competence in Teaching Skills through Real Situations

A classroom program designed to make the most of individualized teaching, as each of the above references so clearly implies, is built on a very sensitive understanding of children and learning. In this rather remarkable summary and evaluation of her eight mornings of participation in a combined first-and-second-grade classroom (plus the few extra half-days she herself managed to sqeeze in!) college junior Bobbe reflects her own growing insights and sensitivities. She seems to be aware that her learnings, too, have grown out of carefully-structured opportunities for self-selection, in an accepting atmosphere, with friendly help available as needed. This is the way Bobbe expresses her learnings:

I feel that I have gained a great deal from my participation in Mrs. Barnes' classroom. The very class atmosphere is conducive to the learning of the youngsters. The children are given an opportunity to explore their environment. There is a wealth of materials about the room that invites learning. The children, in this free situation, can use these materials as they see fit. Many of the classroom materials invite experimentation. They have a walkie-talkie that the youngsters can use and can take apart, for example.

They make various foods in their kitchen. They work with clay, paints and other arts and crafts materials.

INDIVIDUALITY is and should always be the key note of any classroom situation. The teacher realizes that youngsters have indi-vidual differences and their personal needs can only be met and satisfied by considering each child as a person and not only as part of a group.

The children are encouraged to solve their own problems, social and otherwise. When one of the youngsters is in the "kitchen" making something good to eat, she may disregard the recipe, use her own judgment and learn from experience how much flour, shortening, etc., to use. She feels free to experiment without fear of punishment if the results are not good. She learns from this experimentation the amount of each ingredient necessary to make a cake, etc., which tastes good. She gets the "realest" kind of arith-metic (arithmetic with meaning) using exact measurements as well as better group relationships, since a few of the children usually cook together and learn from this experience how to cooperate in their endeavors.

This individuality in activities is practically unlimited. The youngsters feel free to ask the teacher if they may go to the store to buy something, (if they are building and need a certain kind of nail, etc.) go for a walk, go on a short trip. If there is some adult around to accompany them, they are free to leave the building. Because of this atmosphere there is little jealousy and competition in the class. Since there is none of this pressure on them they are able to concentrate on things that are of interest to them and which satisfy their needs instead of worrying about the activities of the other youngsters.

Most of the youngsters feel no scholastic pressure unless it is instigated by the home. Each child feels free to work on his own achievement level without fear of the teacher making an unfavor-able comparison between his ability and that of another child. The teacher knows that all the children are not on the same level in the so-called basic skills. Therefore, she provides materials that are suited for many levels of ability. The classroom is just full of books, ranging from the beginning stage of reading to what would be considered third and fourth year level. The children feel free to read any of the books; their choice of books is not ridiculed. Read-ing is therefore a pleasant occupation that has no unpleasant stigma attached to it.

In this classroom, the youngsters do not learn any of the skills just because they are required. The teacher structures the situation so that they learn the skill because they have to use it in a "real" problem. The youngsters didn't learn to add and subtract money for no reason at all. They had a class store and in order to buy the things they wanted they had to consider the amount they had and the cost of the objects. When they went to the Zoo they had a real money problem. The use of real situations makes arithmetic have meaning to the youngsters. When they go shopping for nails, etc., they are aware of the amount of money they have, how much it will buy and how much they will have left over for a treat.

Arithmetic is fun to them. It isn't disconnected from their life. Once they comprehend addition and subtraction in real situations they enjoy learning it in the abstract, as long as it is not forced on them. When work sheets of problems are stenciled and placed around the room the children pick them up willingly and do them; it is a game to them. They have fun making their own problems and having their classmates do them. Here the youngsters are free to work at their own ability level with no pressure on them. Some of the problems are harder than others and the children who are more advanced choose to do them. The youngsters move along at their own level of achievement. This is as it should be. Each child is an entity in himself and should be treated as such.

Reading was also introduced into the classroom in a functional way. The children learned to read because they wanted to know what the words on the board said, what the names of the toys were, so that they would be sure to sign up for the doll or toy they wanted to take home. In this field as well as in arithmetic, the skill was never learned for the sake of knowing it, but for the sake of using it in some real situation.

One of the most important jobs of the teacher is to know each child's needs physiologically, emotionally, socially and intellectually. You must help the child overcome any difficulties that he is having. The teacher must structure the situation to the best advantage of each child as well as for the group. Mrs. Barnes seldom had the whole group engaging in one activity. She called the group together occasionally. If they were going on a trip they got together and made plans. When she felt that there was a need for doing abstract arithmetic she called the group together. If the behavior of some of the children was definitely upsetting the group, she would have a discussion with the youngsters about it.

Most of the time there were several activities going on at the same time. Patsy took charge of the "kitchen" and cooked by herself for a long while. Later on she was able to include other children in her activities; this was a big step for her. David sat off in a corner and read to himself most of the day. After a while in this free situation he was able to persuade Ben, his idol, to become his friend through the inducement of reading comic books to him. In a traditional system, these children would have been outcasts. Patsy, who needs to prove herself, would be looked upon as a disciplinary problem, and David, who needs encouragement, would crawl further into his shell and never participate. But Mrs. Barnes is well aware of the problems of these youngsters and attempts to help them instead of just making them conform to the regulations when they are unable to do so because of emotional difficulties.

The attitude of the teacher is of prime importance. Children are very sensitive about their activities. If they feel that the teacher disapproves of them, their whole pattern of behavior will change. They will either attempt to do the things she approves of or they will purposely do things that she disapproves. If the teacher is accepting, they will feel freer and will learn more.

Mrs. Barnes has a fine relationship with the youngsters. They feel free to go about their activities without worrying about what she will think. She shows no favoritism, encouraging and guiding the activities of all the children. Her understanding and love of the youngsters make her classroom a wonderful place to be in (even for me).

I feel that the situation itself has been of great value. Because of the policy of the school and the beliefs of Mrs. Barnes, I have had the opportunity of participating in the situation physically as well as mentally. I felt free to work with the children and to get to know them intimately. Through Mrs. Barnes' explanations of why she did various things, I got a clearer idea of what she was trying to accomplish and how she went about it. She freely explained her ideals and the value of them.

My participation in Mrs. Barnes' class has been an invaluable experience for me. Aside from getting a clearer insight into effective methods of conducting a class, I feel that I have learned a great deal about children, how they learn best, how they think and how they act in many varied and different situations.

Through my contact with the children and the various problems I have encountered (Danny's escapade on the window ledge, etc.) I have gained confidence in myself. At the very beginning of the participation I was always fearful that my judgments were wrong. After seeing that I did the right thing in many instances, I began to structure situations that I would have hesitated to do in the beginning without fear of failure. Now I feel that I will enter my first teaching experience with confidence and will be able to help the children solve their problems instead of concentrating on my own.

My attitude toward children has changed also. Instead of viewing them only as a group, I have become aware of them as individuals. I have learned how to handle types of children (Hugh, David, Ben, Patsy, etc.). I clearly see their individual differences and how their environment has helped or hindered their development. Mrs. Barnes' help in this field was invaluable. I got to know individual children better because of her explanation of their background and what she saw in their activities in the classroom. This combined with my own observations gave me an all-round picture of each child and his specific needs. I worked from this, trying to help each child as much as I could.

In conclusion, I should like to reiterate three of the most important requirements of good teaching that I have already noted in this evaluation.

1. The teaching of skills through use of real experiences.
2. Sensitivity to needs of children and active attempt to satisfy these needs.
3. Constant consideration of the individuality of each child.

Perhaps then, with Bobbe's appropriate conclusion, the chapter can end.

10

Reporting individualized learning to parents

Because they realize that children are learning from their out-of-school living quite as much as from the living for which they so carefully provide in the classroom, teachers genuinely concerned with individualizing teaching are usually seeking ways to help the parents of their children to understand their purposes and ways of working. The teachers in earlier chapters, through conferences, meetings, school functions, classroom visits, correspondence of one kind or another, are continuously attempting, in whatever kind of community their school is located, to keep parents informed of the kinds of opportunities they are providing for the children. Convinced that whole learning at its best requires continuity, consistency, sympathetic understanding and acceptance of children, these teachers are trying to help parents know their children as competent, hardworking individuals, too.

We have read several of the letters Mrs. Barnes sent home to her parents during the two successive years their children were in her classroom, highlighting particular experiences and learnings of the children. We have read her suggestions for helping them at home. We have noted the careful way she planned with college students working in her classroom, to help them understand the individual children and ways of recognizing and trying to meet their needs. And we can visualize the children themselves carrying home their varied enthusiasms and interpretations of what went on at school.

Now this, the last chapter of the book, is to be given over to the two much longer yearly reports which Mrs. Barnes sent home, one each spring. Knowing her parents well, she geared her writing accordingly. The accounts represent an exciting restatement of what has been stressed in the foregoing chapters, highlighting the fact that in an individualized setting the reading skills shine through the total school program.

This first account, a delightfully detailed summary of the year's activities, was sent home with each child's individual report:

When we went to the Book Fair last fall, each child carried in his pocket a small handbook. Not very much was written in this handbook.

My name is_____.

My school is _____.

The phone number is UN 4-7000.

Ask for Mary or Bill.

My phone number is _____.

Anne was separated from the rest of the group. Crowds of strangers were on all sides but in typical Anne fashion she showed her handbook to a museum attendant and he was able to help her. WORDS were important! Instead of being in a predicament with no way out, she had enough *power* in that little book to solve her difficult problem.

Skills give people power if they have learned to use them for solving their problems. The people who buy certain brands of soap on the vague promise that they will be as attractive as movie stars do not use reading to solve their problems. Reading gets them into a trap because they accept the surface meaning of a particular arrangement of words. The people who rush to a "Half-price Sale" do not use arithmetic to solve their problem if they spend money not in their budget. Arithmetic gets them into a trap because the "correct answer" of *saving* twelve dollars and fifty cents on a twenty-five dollar dress makes them forget that they do not own money they are *saving*.

These are days when people need power to solve the difficult problems they face. It is the responsibility of the school to so teach the skills that children will make the habit of using these skills for solving important problems.

Some of our activities this year which have required the use of important skills are:

1. *TRIPS*

Skills used: Reading   Arithmetic
              Writing   Map reading
              Listening   Following plans
              Planning   Observing
              Speaking,
                    especially inquiring

We have prepared a handbook for each trip. Each one emphasized a different skill along with the reading involved. For example, the zoo had pictures of clocks to tell the different times at which we planned to do certain things; the Ford Factory handbook had a map showing the different directions in relation to the Hudson River. The Long Island handbook was, of course, the most complete of all. Among other things it included short biographical sketches of the people we would meet and eight pages each emphasizing the importance of a different "question word," as: "WHEN do we go?" "HOW do we go?" The question mark was intentionally omitted from one page heading and the children quickly saw the relationship between the word which started the sentence and the punctuation at the end. Where it was appropriate, the handbook also had a banking section where a picture of each penny of a child's money was made so that he might keep track of his budget and do sensible planning.

A letter of permission was also a part of each trip. At the beginning of the year the children wrote only a small part of each letter. Toward the end of the year they were writing the letters independently. An adult always wrote the information the children could not write, again in the belief that the importance of the written word in a message was what mattered most.

Planning was a part of each trip,—not "what do you want to do" planning, but the organizing of a framework within which individuals were to operate. Following group plans is a mighty important though difficult task for six and seven year olds who are still strongly individualistic in their actions. At first the adults took major responsibility for making the over-all plan, encouraging the children to see their contributions as deciding individually how to use the freedom within the framework. "How shall I spend my time or my money?" was a legitimate contribution from a child early in the year. Gradually they assumed more and more responsibility for the actual working out of the over-all framework. This made planning more difficult, as it had been easier to follow a clearly-defined "teacher plan." It also made learning more important.

Other specialized skills for particular trips were making fishing poles, fishing, cooking out of doors, rowing a boat, reading certain weather predictions in the cloud formations.

Living is real on a trip. When on the Long Island visit, Jerry swept the Duke's back stairs at nine o'clock at night before going to sleep, no one had asked him to do it. It was a spontaneous expression of his feeling of responsibility toward the man who made part of our fun possible.

A part of all trips was the skill of human relations. It reached an all-time high on the Long Island trip when people everywhere did nice things for the children just because they were so very nice to be with!

Our important trips were:
>   Bronx Zoo
>   Book Fair
>   Museum of Natural History
>   Planetarium
>   Ford Assembly Plant
>   A.S.P.C.A. Shelter
>   "Navajo"
>   Fishing in Prospect Park
>   Over-night trip on Long Island

2. *BANK AND STORE*
>   *Skills used:*   Adding
>   Multiplying

Subtracting
Dividing
Estimating
Writing
Spelling
Critical thinking
Reading

Most of the school supplies which we would ordinarily give to the children were "sold" to them in our store. In addition, we sold some of the popular gadgets of the day which the stores, television, and other advertising persuade children to buy. Most of the children learned to read and spell the days of the week by writing checks to buy things in the store. Each time they bought something they learned subtraction in a practical way by crossing out pennies to see how many were left in their bank accounts. Their "allowance" was always a bank deposit in the form of pictures of pennies deposited. The pennies were arranged differently each time, so the children were introduced to practical multiplication by counting the number of two's, three's, ten's, or whatever the particular deposit happened to be. When children were ready to understand multiplication and division in terms of "groups of things," we sold raisins, peanuts, and other small objects which could be grouped. When they were ready to understand parts of things we sold in halves and fourths. On "Store Day" there were signs in the room as:

Today the store has 5 telescopes. Do you want one?
They cost 3¢. (Sign here)
1. _____ 2. _____
3. _____ 4. _____
5. _____

Many children began to realize that the feeling of "wanting a gadget" was not connected with the gadget itself, as buying the gadget did not bring satisfaction. They also began to make a list of gadgets which wasted children's money because they broke so easily.

3. *COOKING*

Skills used: Reading
Following directions
Measuring
Counting
Understanding safety precautions
Timing

When a child read "one *cup* of water" instead of "one *can* of water" on the chicken noodle soup can, and when the cup he used was a two-cup measure he learned the importance of the written word and measuring in cooking. The children were free to cook any time in the morning before eleven o'clock. In addition to the recipes on boxes and cans they used, we posted their discoveries on the bulletin board so others might try them. One of the most popular discoveries was Bisquick and cinnamon.

4. MAKING THINGS

Skills used:		
	Measuring	Reading
	Sawing	Designing
	Hammering	Working with leather
	Sewing	Working with clay
	Painting	Cutting
	Planning	Creating

When Billy made his father "a table really as high as his chair" for Christmas, he measured, nailed, painted, and kept with a job until it was finished. Hand-eye coordination were in constant demand, and were improved through constant use.

When David made his work folder, he planned a most intricate system of pockets and envelopes for holding his various kinds of work for the year. He then made a guide telling in which "jungle" (his name for the pockets) these could be found. When Patsy and Becky were "best friends," they invented a novel way of painting twin pictures. Children love to make things. And because interest in what they are doing is so high, so is the learning value in whatever skills are brought into use. A sensitive person watching a child at work on something he wants to make can learn a great deal about the child's way of working and his needs. It seems there was never a time this year when construction of some kind was not under way in the room. We used clay, countless jars of paint, lumber, leather, shells and plastic for jewelry, cardboard boxes, reed, copper and aluminum, cloth, Kleenex, every description of paper, and other materials too numerous to list here. Among the most exciting materials were our treasures from neighborhood junk piles,—old airplane parts, display cases, braided straw, bottle tops, etc. On a few happy occasions, "Mil" was free to help the children in Art.

5. EXPERIMENTING

Skills used:	Observing
	Critical thinking and generalizing
	Problem-solving
	Following directions
	Measuring

Tuck wanted more than anything else to make smoke rings come out of himself like the man on television. When cigarettes were ruled out, he tried using the round covers on the colored chalk. This was not too successful because of worries about chalk dust in his mouth. After trying various other schemes, he finally invented a gadget with a soft plastic bottle, a piece of plastic tubing, and a good supply of talcum powder. He had achieved his goal. Without knowing the verbal explanations, he was able to make a practical application of air pressure do the job. Experimenting was carried on by individual children in much this same manner, and also by the group under adult direction. Among the most important group experiments were those exploring the properties of air, water, and fire. Safety practices were not only a required part of the experimenting, but were also a part of the verbal generalizations made by the children after becoming really acquainted with, for example, fire. "Of course, you wouldn't run if your clothes were on fire. Fire needs air to burn, and you'd only be helping it," was a typical remark.

6. *MOVIES*

Wherever possible, learnings in science, arithmetic, social studies, were reenforced with carefully selected educational films, which were shown two or three times a week, beginning in December. Among such films were those related to weather, animals, safety, addition and subtraction, map-making, water-power, food production, children of other lands. As a special treat, we enjoyed a thirty-minute film version of "Heidi" toward the end of the year, and as a special challenge, saw an experimental farm film highlighting the importance of agriculture in a hungry world.

7. *WORK TIME*

No distinction was ever made between work time and play time in the room. Children worked hard when they were swimming, when they were making things, when they were learning to climb a rope in the gym, when they were writing a letter of permission home. And they knew it. Two distinctions in planning time were made. There was one difference between *work* time and *free* time. Even if it was a matter of a child's choice during work time, he did choose work, that is, something which required effort on his part. There was also a very important distinction made between work time and *required* work time. At work time the children chose their own work. At required work time their only responsibility was to do the particular job assigned by a grownup. This required work might be learning a new game in the gym, doing a science experiment, watching a movie, or doing arithmetic. It was during required work time that I could introduce new skills to the children,—a way to multiply, a way to work with clay, a game requiring higher social organization than that to which they were accustomed; and it was at free time or work time (not required) that I could tell which of the skills the children had really taken on as their own. One example of the real growth of these children demonstrated in this way was in the area of games. Early in the year it was necessary to teach group games at a required work time because the children were still too highly individualistic to want to use their free time in an enterprise requiring the discipline of group games. From March on, group games have been a part of every free time. Another example might be drawn from their writing. Early in the year, letters of permission for trips were required work. Lately note writing to one another, cards to mail, greeting cards to parents, and writing stories and poems have been consistent free time choices.

8. *TESTS*

It was not necessary to give these children standardized tests in order to know their achievement. They lived their achievement and it was evident every minute of the day. However, since many of the children will go to schools which use testing as an important part of evaluation, it seemed fair to introduce the procedure to the children. We used readiness and diagnostic tests at different times throughout the year. In April we used the Metropolitan Achievement Test. This test should be given at four different times so the children have their best chance for high scores. Since we were not primarily concerned with scores, it seemed silly to drag it out over four days. The children sat from ten to twelve one morning doing one section after another. Even given under such strenuous circumstances the majority of the children scored comfortably in third grade. (If our children had been in a graded school, about half would have been in first grade this year, half in second.) In many cases the test did not even measure the children as they went as far as it went and could have gone further. This was particularly true of arithmetic, since the problems on the test did not go beyond simple subtraction. The very *meagre* expectation of accomplishments for children this age as set by the tests emphasized dramatically both the inadequacy of such tests as true measures of a child's use of skills and the rich varied understanding of living which these children would bring to any classroom.

(Then came the specific discussion of the particular child whose parents were receiving the report.)

The next report, a dramatic but thoughtfully organized review, highlighted the children's *second* year of wonderful living and learning together, with Mrs. Barnes. The pictures on each page (sketched by a friend) held very special meaning for these children as well as for their parents. All together, the pages served as a pleasant, deeply appreciated backdrop to the skillfully written report on the individual child. (See Figs. 10.1–10.6.)

Indeed, Mrs. Barnes found that using these narrative, total-group descriptions—such as the one above and those that follow—as a kind of introduction to the children's individual reports, served a three-fold purpose:

1. They gave parents an intimate look at the whole classroom. This seemed to satisfy their ever-present question, "Yes, but how does my child's work fit in with that of the group? What is the class as a whole accomplishing?"

2. Such reports afforded Mrs. Barnes an opportunity to interpret to the parents the learning significance of certain activities which they might otherwise have viewed as only an incidental, rather than as a planned, part of the program.

3. These descriptive group reports set the tone for and encouraged the teacher to use concrete, specific descriptions of an individual child's behavior, too, rather than the judgmental abstractions so often characteristic of a child's school report. Instead of *labeling* his reading ability—which actually defied labeling—Mrs. Barnes described the particular books he read, the kinds of reports he made, the kind of language patterns, say, which were or were not posing difficulties for him.

Both the class account and the child's individual report were sent to his parents in an attractively decorated folder.

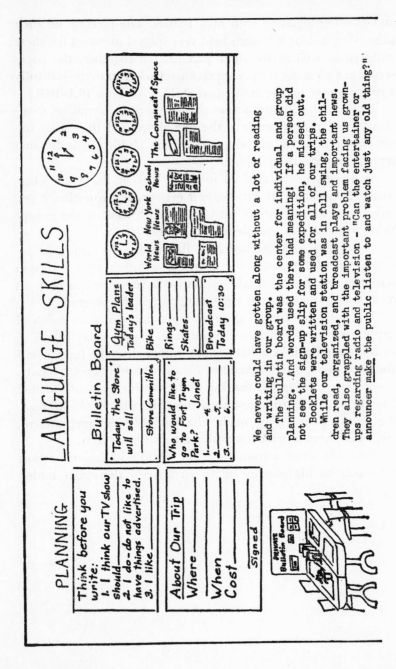

LANGUAGE SKILLS

PLANNING

Think before you write:
1. I think our TV show should
2. I do - do not like to have things advertised.
3. I like

About Our Trip
Where
When
Cost

Signed

Bulletin Board

Today the Store will sell
Store Committee

Who would like to go to Fort Tryon Park? Janet
1. ___ 4. ___
2. ___ 5. ___
3. ___ 6. ___

Gym Plans
Today's leader
Bike
Rings
Skates

Broadcast
Today 10:30

World News   New York News   School News   The Conquest of Space

PRIVATE Bulletin Board

We never could have gotten along without a lot of reading and writing in our group.

The bulletin board was the center for individual and group planning. And words used there had meaning! If a person did not see the sign-up slip for some expedition, he missed out.

Booklets were written and used for all of our trips.

While our television station was in full swing, the children read, organized, and broadcast plays and important news. They also grappled with the important problem facing us grown-ups regarding radio and television - "Can the entertainer or announcer make the public listen to and watch just any old thing?"

Fact and fiction books relating to the children's study clubs and individual interests were read and also written.

News stands were watched for magazines and newspapers containing important information. When the two new children's newspapers were published in New York, the children answered the editors' requests for suggestions regarding features. The children also wrote newspapers of their own.

Private and club stationery was designed and used for writing of all kinds.

And as could be expected, reading test scores at the end of the year showed the results of the children's constant attention to the important words in their world.

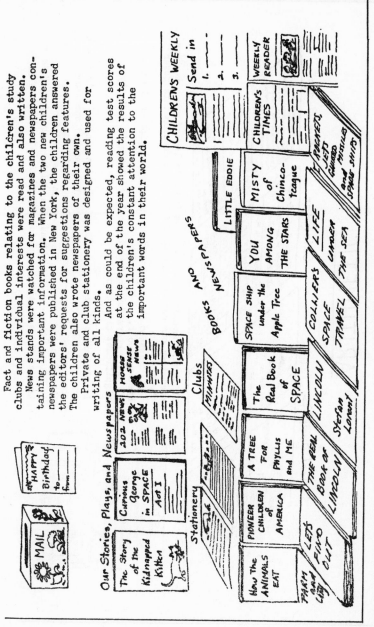

Fig. 10-1

ARITHMETIC

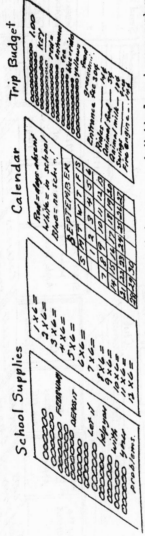

School Supplies

Calendar

Trip Budget

STORE
Marbles   Fish
6 for 1¢

Children increase their power as individuals and group members when they can use numbers skillfully. To develop this power they must:

Understand the construction and relationships of the number system itself.

Use numbers for important problem solving in socially significant situations.

In our bank and store, on all of our trips, and in their attendance and other record keeping, the children had opportunities for consistent experiences in solving their important problems through using numbers. The materials prepared for their use in solving these real problems were deliberately planned to give them, at the same time, repeated experiences in discovering with help the various patterns of our number system. They were not told the meanings of ten's and one's, but budget materials were arranged in such a way that the children's use of them caused them to discuss and learn this important part of our number system. They were not told to learn the multiplication tables.

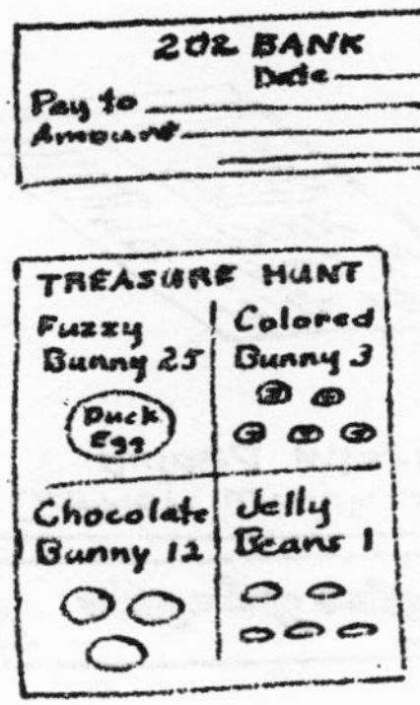

Their banking materials were deliberately arranged so that a part of their spending and keeping track of supply and trip money helped them to organize and learn the multiplication tables through seven's. Similarly they learned to use with understanding, addition, subtraction, multiplication, and division; to borrow and carry; to generalize regarding the "doubles and near-doubles"; to measure with inches, feet, cups, quarts. Scores on the standardized tests at the end of the year gave evidence of the children's fine achievement in using arithmetic fundamentals and reasoning.

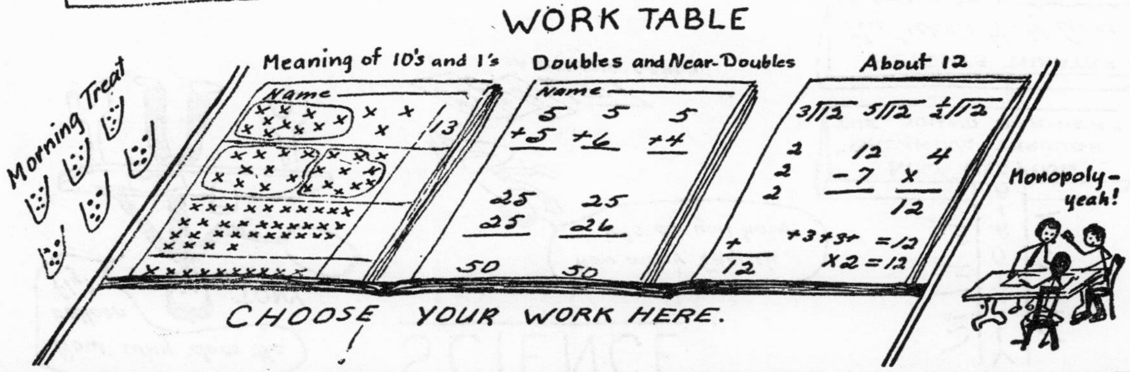

Fig. 10-2

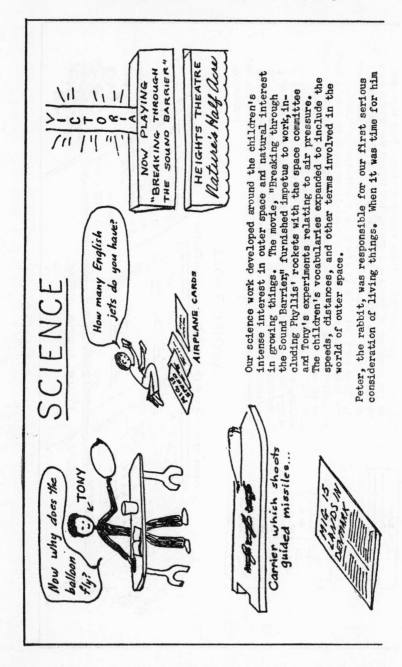

Our science work developed around the children's intense interest in outer space and natural interest in growing things. The movie, "Breaking through the Sound Barrier," furnished impetus to work, including Phyllis' rockets with the space committee and Tony's experiments relating to air pressure. The children's vocabularies expanded to include the speeds, distances, and other terms involved in the world of outer space.

Peter, the rabbit, was responsible for our first serious consideration of living things. When it was time for him to go to another room to live, our two white rats, Gary and Chrissy came to take Peter's place. And wasn't it fortunate that while we fed Chrissy carelessly, she had two such unhealthy babies! How pleased we were when we found that a healthy diet for Chrissy was followed by a litter of nine healthy babies. This was an important way for children in an age of unprecedented technological advance to know that living creatures still require certain conditions if they are to live healthfully.

Our avocado seeds grew too - as did the discarded plants we rescued. In fact, we more or less had the feeling that living things (including people!) prospered in our room.

Study clubs flourished - most of them revealing the children's sincere interest in the scientific facts and wonders of the world in which they live.

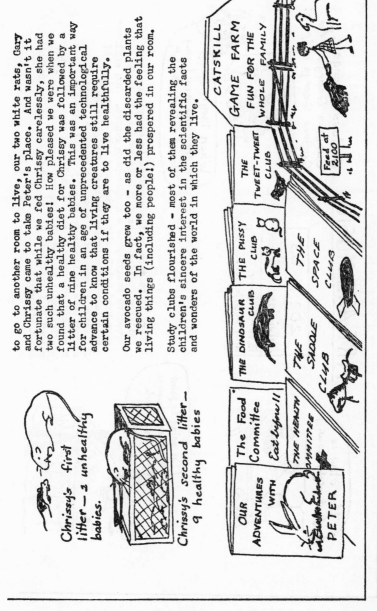

Fig. 10-3

ART AND MUSIC

Curious George ♪♪♪
Curious George ♪♪♪
Curious George in Space!

When they're through I'll show you how I play "Here Comes the Bride!"

202 NEWS

Musicians at School

Peter, Harry, Dike and Walter....

The clay is just right now.

I'm going to paint cups and saucers for our whole family.

There is so much of the creative in everything these children do that it is difficult to confine their creative activity to a single-page report. The children have used paint, clay, wood, and many other kinds of materials and appropriate tools for creating And while it may not have seemed so to the outside observer, the child who creatively organized color and space and movement to make a galloping horse or mountain or fire as it seemed to him, was a child who was being helped to investigate and to understand and do something about his world.

Learning to play the piano and creating original tunes were regular Work Time activities. Somebody was always signing up for use of the piano, for practicing, performing, or composing. Especially exciting were the ways children found for helping one another take on new music skills. The highlight of the year of course was the original music which they created for our play, <u>Curious George in Space.</u> And every day throughout the year there was singing.

Trips to museums and symphony concerts, as well as the lovely children's concert we had at the school, helped the children to extend their appreciation for artistic endeavor well done.

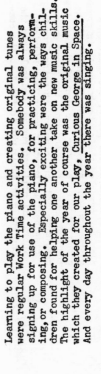

"Workbench Plans"
Susan — book shelf

Ian, Ben, and
Johnny — Carrier
Tisha — coffee table

Michele — table

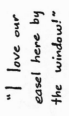

"I love our
easel here by
the window!"

"Here, I've invented
a way to make a
doll out of Kleenex."

Fig. 10-4

PHYSICAL EDUCATION

Horses
Panthers
Dogs

Cowboys and Spacemen

Three Feet
Off...
Jupiter!

Eleven
o'clock
Midnight!

In the gym and at the parks, the children's play has revealed their steady growth in group awareness and interests. At the start of the year, group games were never a matter of choice, toward the end they were. And even the games chosen grew more and more complex, changing from the single-line formation games like Midnight, where all children run at a signal from the one child or adult who is "it," to the com—

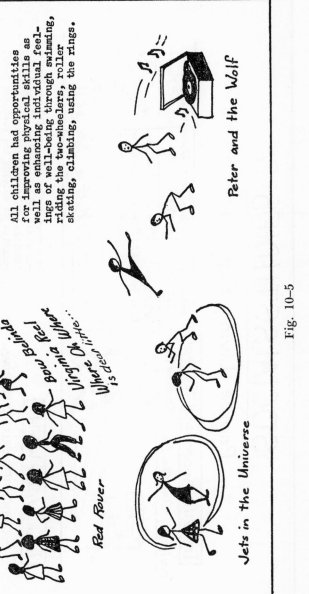

plicated double-line games and dances where children identify with one of two groups and have to play a certain part.

An interesting variation of the more complicated activities, were the dances they created to tell original as well as familiar stories.

All children had opportunities for improving physical skills as well as enhancing individual feel-ings of well-being through swimming, riding the two-wheelers, roller skating, climbing, using the rings.

Bow Belinda

Virginia Wheel

Where Oh Where...
Where dear little
is dear little

Red Rover

Jets in the Universe

Peter and the Wolf

Fig. 10-5

SOCIAL STUDIES

People Living Together

In Our Room and School

Helping One Another	Sharing Work	Sharing Resources	Using Time and Space and Weather Wisely	Learning About People
		Who wants a turn to cook? 1. 2. 3. 4.	"We should go to the Park today while the good ole sun is shin-ing!"	"How big is your baby, Buffy?"

In a Wider World

GEOGRAPHICALLY SPEAKING

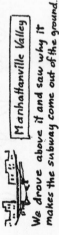

Manhattanville Valley

We drove above it and saw why it makes the subway come out of the ground.

In a very real sense, social studies is our whole school program. In social studies, children learn and use skills in relation to solving the problems people face when they live together. This means: They need to know good living together from experiencing it. They need to know what human beings are like in relation to people living together.

They need to know how the physical facts of the earth affect people's living together. They need to know the skills of communication necessary for living together. They need to learn increasingly how to learn from other people's ways of living together in different times and places.

Our trips and classroom procedures were especially planned to help the children with these important learnings. Coming to know intimately the facts of a few people, historical events, geographical features, and our own group planning and living together should provide them with a background for interpreting future experiences.

HISTORICALLY SPEAKING

Hudson River

We saw it on a map.
We played beside it.

N E W S NEW YORK

We drove up and down it and crossed it on two bridges:
The George Washington
The Rip Van Winkle

Catskill Mountains

We saw them on a map and drove through them.

Let's see now, its 600 miles from Poland to Denmark.

Today I will help the History Committee at 9 o'clock.
Lois M.

ADVENTURES IN HISTORY

Our first film will be Christopher Columbus.

Pinta Nina Santa Maria

LINCOLN'S 7th Birthday
(1816)
Menu
Beans
Corn Bread
Apples

HALF MOON

When Henry Hudson sailed up the Hudson River in 1609...

Fig. 10-6

11

Conclusion

By way of concluding this little book, we should like to use these paragraphs from a report written for her colleagues by a teacher of long experience and real insight, while attending a national conference not long ago. She writes:

Throughout the conference it has seemed to me that the day of the closely organized reading system is on its way out. Each time a teacher lets herself go and watches and listens to the responses of her children in a classroom where provision is made for self-selection (adequate provision of good materials and teacher helps), she experiences a qualitatively different pattern of teacher-learner communication. When teaching is based on teacher-and-textbook-selection of what is to be learned, the teacher and textbook are constantly trying to get the children to come their way. And whether the method is the direct order which says COME or the under-the-table method of ELICITING a pre-determined response, the basic patterns of movement are the same. The age-old theme of chase-flee-catch is organized into the pedaguese of the classroom. And the captured "learner' 'is motivated to free himself from his capturer just as wholeheartedly as is the prisoner in the playground games which utilize this same pattern in human movement . . .

When children are the ones doing the selecting, the teacher experiences the marvelous feeling of having the learners seek her. She then moves toward them in response to their seeking. And they move toward her because they need this response to their seeking. More and more the teacher finds herself able to set up a classroom where her involvement is more indirect. This is different from the falsely conceived indirectness of "eliciting a response" instead of asking outright . . . of getting the student to pretend he is the one needing and asking, when actually, in this manner, it is the teacher or the workbook that needs him to learn some certain trick of the trade. Within the framework of selective interaction where the learner is encouraged to make his seeking articulate, the teacher can be the provider of materials and other resources. Instead of saying, "What do you want to do next in your learning?" at the start of a period of instruction, the teacher provides the kinds of materials where follow-up activities help the learners to take the next steps without talking about it. Children go to the work table and select materials instead of going to the teacher. They go to one another . . . to books . . . to charts and globes and maps. When they go to the teacher for her help, their heads are clear. They are not all mixed up with what she is needing them to learn. They ask the question (or act it out in behavior) in ways which tell the teacher what she most needs to know for structuring their learning environment to make next steps available.

Teachers can't help feeling the difference. They know that they prefer the learning environment where they are not constantly having to chase the children. They are surprised at first when the children don't "fall apart" or blow up at the end of each division in the day's schedule. It is strange not to pull them all together again and into the next round. It is relaxing not to have to hold all this dynamite in some kind of powder keg—with only one's self to keep down the lid. No one works harder than the individual children themselves when they are on the trail of some real, important learning and next steps keep becoming available . . . Here the children are actively dealing with the problem of organizing their power, and reality enters the classroom.

index